Introduction to the Philosophy of Sport

Elements of Philosophy

The Elements of Philosophy series aims to produce core introductory texts in the major areas of philosophy, among them metaphysics, epistemology, ethics and moral theory, philosophy of religion, philosophy of mind, aesthetics and the philosophy of art, feminist philosophy, and social and political philosophy. Books in the series are written for an undergraduate audience of second- through fourth-year students and serve as the perfect cornerstone for understanding the various elements of philosophy.

Titles in the Series

Introduction to the Philosophy of Sport

Heather L. Reid

ROWMAN & LITTLEFIELD PUBLISHERS, INC.
Lanham • Boulder • New York • Toronto • Plymouth, UK

Published by Rowman & Littlefield Publishers, Inc.
A wholly owned subsidiary of The Rowman & Littlefield Publishing Group, Inc.
4501 Forbes Boulevard, Suite 200, Lanham, Maryland 20706
www.rowman.com

10 Thornbury Road, Plymouth PL6 7PP, United Kingdom

British Library Cataloguing in Publication Information Available

Library of Congress Cataloging-in-Publication Data

Reid, Heather Lynne, 1963-
Introduction to the philosophy of sport / Heather L. Reid.
p. cm. -- (Elements of philosophy)
Includes bibliographical references (p.) and index.
ISBN 978-0-7425-7060-3 (cloth : alk. paper) -- ISBN 978-0-7425-7061-0 (pbk. : alk. paper) -- ISBN 978-0-7425-7062-7 (ebook : alk. paper)
1. Sports--Philosophy. I. Title.
GV706.R4395 2012
796.01--dc23
2012028670

The paper used in this publication meets the minimum requirements of American National Standard for Information Sciences Permanence of Paper for Printed Library Materials, ANSI/NISO Z39.48-1992.

Printed in the United States of America

Contents

Acknowledgments

Morningside College and the Ver Steeg Faculty Development Fund have provided time and support without which this book would not have been possible. I am likewise grateful to my teachers, students, and colleagues for their encouragement and inspiration, especially those who offered specific help with this manuscript: Susan Brownell, Daniel Campos, Christos Evangeliou, Warren Fraleigh, John Gleaves, Drew Hyland, Scott Kretchmar, Bill Morgan, Jim Parry, Graham Priest, and Larry Theobald. I am particularly indebted to Mark Holowchak and Jesús Ilundáin who made detailed comments and suggestions on the entire manuscript that significantly improved its quality and clarity. Thanks also to Sherry Swan for her endless administrative support, even from overseas.

Introduction

Why Study the Philosophy of Sport?

I must confess from the start that I have done some extraordinary things for sport. We can leave aside the hours training in the rain, the nights spent on strangers' couches, the thousands of miles on interstate highways, and the scarred knees and elbows of my cycling career—for these might be explained by the enthusiasm of youth and the intoxicating dream of competing in the Olympic Games. But what about the things I've done as an adult, as a philosophy professor trained in logic and value theory, presumably able to distinguish what is important from what is not? I have curled my toes into a rough, stone starting block and then raced barefoot across the ancient track of Greece's Nemean Games. I have ridden my road bicycle up a steep alpine climb and then waited shivering on the side of the mountain to cheer the exhausted racers of the Giro d'Italia as they struggled past. Crazier than that, I then rode the bike back down the hill, threading my way through the crowd of wobbling spectators, my thin tires skittering on the bumpy dirt road. Where does this come from? Why do I care? Why did I get up at four in the morning to watch an Olympic opening ceremony from Italy? These may seem like crazy things, but I am not crazy, and I am hardly alone in my passion for sport. There are reasons behind these passions, and they are not trivial—neither is sport.

Sport is a significant human activity. Its origins reach back into the depths of history and its contemporary practice reaches across cultures and continents. Sport, furthermore, is a meaningful human activity. Some people devote large portions of their lives to it, many people practice it on a regular basis, and most people at least watch it on television—especially when the Olympic Games come around. It is surprising, given the importance so many people attribute to sport, that philosophers have more or less neglected it as a subject of serious inquiry. Despite sport's metaphysical relationship with art and play, despite its ethical association with virtue and fairness, despite its political connection with education and democracy, and even despite Socrates's comparison of himself to an Olympic athlete,[1] serious philosophical discussion of sport did not take hold until the latter part of the twentieth century. There are probably good—or, at least interesting—explanations for this. But the purpose of this book is not to discover why sport hasn't been studied philosophically in the past. Rather, its purpose is to demonstrate why sport should be studied philosophically now and in the future.

We can learn much from the philosophical study of sport—not just about sport but also about ourselves, about society, and about philosophy. Because sport has important metaphysical, ethical, and sociopolitical dimensions, philosophers of sport must engage with all of these philosophical disciplines in order to study it properly. And because students are often familiar with and curious about sport, the philosophy of sport is an excellent platform from which to launch into the general study of philosophy. Students' experience as athletes, or even simply playing games, provides a foundation for discussion of metaphysical issues such as the relationship between games and play, mind and body, and even sport and art. Sport can also serve as a moral laboratory in which theories like deontology, consequentialism, and virtue ethics can be experienced and tested in a controlled environment. Finally, sport is a social experience through which we encounter political issues such as democratic responsibility, social categorization, and the challenges of globalization.

A good philosophical understanding of sport can also help teachers and scholars to communicate difficult philosophical concepts. Philosophers as varied as Plato, Thomas Hobbes, and Jacques Derrida have used sports metaphors to explain important parts of their philosophy. As a young scholar of ancient philosophy, it was Plato's use of athletic examples and metaphors that connected with my own sports experience and gave me insight into his theory of moral education, the subject of my doctoral dissertation. As a professor, sport philosophy has pushed me beyond the comfort zone of my academic specialty and invited me to interact with scholars and concepts from across the philosophical spectrum—not to mention related disciplines such as archaeology, history, and kinesiology. Just as sport improves athletes by subjecting them to challenges, philosophy of sport improves scholars by challenging them to think seriously about this rich and complex human practice.

In this book I have endeavored to provide an introduction to the philosophical study of sport that not only covers the charted terrain but also looks up to survey the horizon and suggest future paths for this very young discipline. I have tried to create a structure that reflects the traditional division of philosophy into metaphysical, ethical, and sociopolitical issues and, as much as possible, to link them together. For example, chapter 3, which explores sport's metaphysical connection with play, is linked with chapter 8, which uses play as a consequentialist criterion in sport ethics, and also chapter 12, which applies these (and other) discussions to the issue of sport in education. Likewise, chapter 4 links sport and games, chapter 9 relates games deontologically to fairness, and chapter 13 applies the concept of fairness to the use of social categories as classifications in sport.

I have avoided the temptation to organize chapters around particular issues such as cheating, doping, violence, commercialism, college sports, Title IX, and so on. These and many more specific topics—as well as many different sports—are instead sprinkled throughout the text in their appropriate philosophical contexts. Just as a beginning athlete should try several sports and strive for general fitness, a beginning philosopher of sport should study several issues and try for a general understanding of the subject. A good philosophical analysis of something like the amateur regulations in intercollegiate athletics, for example, depends on a political understanding of the purpose of the activity, which demands sensitivity to the ethical issues involved, issues that are based on the metaphysics of the practice. This book begins at the roots of sport philosophy, with its ancient history and Olympic heritage, and then works its way through metaphysics, ethics, and finally politics to arrive, hopefully, at the flower of understanding.

Although I carve up the philosophy of sport according to traditional philosophical divisions, my aim is to achieve a whole much greater than the sum of its parts. What we have in this book is not only an outline of this fledgling academic discipline and a summary of much of its pioneering work but also an invitation to join the conversation by connecting these issues to one's own athletic experience. It will be obvious that some topics have attracted more interest than others; in several cases, I have not been able to provide a full survey of the important literature on that subject. It will be obvious as well that I have my own perspective on the field. I have inevitably left out essays, books, or even entire topics that some of my colleagues might deem essential. I can only reply that I have done my best to provide an organized and readable introduction to the discipline that looks both at its past and toward its future, but most of all inspires the reader to think about sport philosophically here and now. Sport is a significant human activity that, beyond its intrinsic worth, has enormous educational potential. It is only by achieving a deeper understanding of sport that we can help it to function in service of the human good.

Siracusa, Sicily
April 2012

I

History and Heritage

We begin with history and heritage not only because philosophical studies should be informed by the history of their subjects but also because there is an important link between the history of sport and of philosophy. The obvious connection is that the two practices share a common birthplace in ancient Greece, but there is also a sense in which the knowledge-seeking spirit characteristic of philosophy was originally exhibited in Olympic-style sport. Before the Greeks got hold of it, athleticism seems to have functioned primarily as a political tool for demonstrating a leader's divine favor and worthiness to lead. We find this function also in Homer, as when Agamemnon claims victory in the javelin event or Odysseus takes back his kingdom by winning an archery contest and stringing the royal bow. But Homer also describes Olympic-style sport, in which the outcome is uncertain and left to the contest to decide—at the risk of challenging existing social hierarchy.

I call this familiar style of sport "Olympic" because I believe it was competing claims to honor among the diverse tribes present at the Panhellenic sanctuary of ancient Olympia that motivated the use of a fair and impartial mechanism for choosing someone to light the sacrificial flame—the mechanism of a footrace. Just as early Olympic sport sought answers through impartial testing rather than preexisting belief, early philosophy sought answers about the world through the testing of ideas rather than the passive acceptance of mythology or orthodox beliefs. Just as sport is essentially blind to social assumptions and distinctions, philosophy sought to liberate truth from cultural tradition. Sport revealed furthermore that excellence could be trained and was not merely a matter of birth, perhaps inspiring philosophers like Socrates and Plato to find ways of training virtue through competitive debate. From these roots sprang also the phenomenon of democracy, and its values remain embedded in sport. Philosophy, democracy, and the Olympic Games are commonly counted among Greece's gifts to the modern world. The spirit of sport is visible in all of them.

The Olympic Games were revived at the end of the nineteenth century as a deliberate expression of philosophy. This philosophy, called Olympism, was not based on the ideas of Plato and Aristotle, so much as the beliefs of the European Enlightenment. Furthermore, it was the work of not profession- al philosophers but rather a group of idealistic enthusiasts, led by the French pedagogue Pierre de Coubertin. Its lack of analytic rigor and precision raises the question of whether Olympism is really a philosophy, but it may also explain Olympism's success as the guiding principle of such a complex and multicultural organization as the Olympic Movement.

Taking a flexible approach we can discern in Olympism the main branches of philosophy: metaphysics, ethics, and politics. Olympism's meta- physics posit a conception of an ideal human that exalts body as well as mind and emphasizes balance and harmony, but the portrait is not so specific as to exclude any gender or ethnicity. Olympism's ethics refer to universal funda- mental principles without spelling out what they are—a weakness that turns into a strength when facing the challenges of multiculturalism. Sport pro- vides the common culture that unites the diverse individuals in the Olympic Movement, and the structure of sport reflects such moral values as equality of opportunity and the pursuit of excellence. Sport also serves as the founda- tion for Olympism's political goal of peace. By requiring people to put aside their differences, treat one another as equals, and tolerate their differences, the Olympic festival creates a model for peaceful coexistence that depends not on a civilizing authority but rather on cooperation. Olympism, to be sure, is a thin philosophy, but it is one intimately connected to sport that has withstood the test of time.

Chapter One

The Ancient Hellenic Heritage

Imagine yourself at the conclusion of a conference championship game in college basketball. The gymnasium is packed full with euphoric fans, the victorious players writhe on the floor in glee, and the coaches shake hands and exchange solemn words as the ritual of cutting the nets down begins. Now imagine that the microphone is given to a famous sports commentator who has been asked to say a few words about the historic victory. He stands at center court as a hush comes over the stands. He looks up toward the heavens and then begins his speech:

> Creatures of a day!
> What is someone? What is no one?
> A dream of a shadow is man. [1]

These poetic-philosophical lines are part of an ancient Greek athlete's victory hymn, but how out of place would they seem in sports today? The arena may stand on a university campus and the building may be full of students, but philosophers, poets, and other intellectuals are usually sequestered in ivy-covered stone buildings—they don't wander into the gymnasium. If we were in ancient Greece, however, the philosophers would be running the gymnasium and poets would staff the sports information office. Athletics and philosophy were close enough in ancient Greece that the great poet Pindar not only described men as dreams of shadows, he nicknamed Olympia the "Mistress of Truth." [2]

It is not just coincidence that philosophy, democracy, and Olympic-style sport share a common birthplace in ancient Greece. There are important conceptual resemblances between these three things, and it should not be forgotten that the eldest of the family members is, in fact, athletics. The conventional date for the founding of the Olympic Games is 776 bce, although the first running contest there happened much earlier. Philosophy arrived on the scene hundreds of years later, sometime in the sixth century bce, while democracy showed up even later, near the end of that century. The resemblance between these three practices begins with their ability to sort out competing claims to virtue, truth, and governance, without capitulating to existing social hierarchies or resorting to the use of violent force. Indeed, sport seems to have helped the ancient Hellenes to question the validity of natural aristocracy and the truth value of mythology. These seeds of doubt were sown partly by intercultural exchange between the diverse tribes and intellectual ideas present at the Olympic Games, as well as the foreign cultures contacted through overseas trade. The evidence that even lower-class athletes could achieve excellence through training likely inspired the educational activities of Socrates, Plato, and Aristotle. Sport was not the subject of serious philosophical reflection in ancient Greece, but philosophy itself was closely linked with sport.

HEROES AND HIERARCHIES

When looking for the origins of what we now call sport, we arrive inevitably at the epics of Homer. The *Iliad* and *Odyssey* are foundational in many ways, but their often overlooked accounts of athletics offer important clues not only for understanding the nature of sport today but also for providing perspective on how sport has changed since those ancient times. Homer describes athletics more or less as they existed in his own era, around the eighth century bce, though he purports to be recounting events that happened much earlier, around the twelfth century bce. And in fact, Homer's contests have much in common with the athletic practices of earlier civilizations such as the Mesopotamians, Egyptians, Minoans, and Hittites. The most important commonality is the perceived link between athleticism and human virtue, specifically the worthiness to lead.

As early as the third millennium bce, the athletic ability of ancient leaders like Gilgamesh of Uruk was taken as evidence of their divine favor or at least partially divine status. A hero, in ancient parlance, was part deity and part mortal. For instance, the Greek hero Heracles (Latin: Hercules) was the son of the god Zeus and the mortal woman Alcmene. The Mesopotamian king Gilgamesh is likewise described in the epic that bears his name as two-thirds man and one-third god.[3] Egyptian Pharaohs were also thought to be the children of gods. Indeed, the link between divinity and kingship survives right through the Roman emperors (who often had their own cults) to the seventeenth-century notion of the divine right of kings. Belief in a ruler's divinity was no doubt of great comfort to societies that attributed most natural phenomena to the capricious will of gods. But even modern politicians like to associate themselves with the divine; they advertise their religious beliefs and invoke divine names during speeches. The conceptual link between athleticism and divinity also persists in modern-day descriptions of athletes as "heroes," or even euphemistically as "gods."

What is remarkable about ancient leaders is that they used athleticism to prove their divine association and royal desert, or at least they tried to. As one might expect, the reality of a leader's athleticism did not always live up to the propaganda. The kind of live demonstrations we expect of great athletes today were at least carefully controlled and often completely avoided. Indirect evidence for a leader's greatness was preferred, such as the (apparently embellished) story about the Sumerian king Shulgi, who is claimed in a song to have run one hundred miles in a single day with rain and hailstones "lashing at his back."[4] In other cases ancient kings' "athletic feats" turn out to be staged game hunts, fixed boxing matches, or ritual acts of little difficulty. At Egypt's Festival of Sed (circa 2600 bce), the pharaohs ran uncontested around two posts placed a mere fifty-five meters apart—hardly proof of superhuman athleticism.[5] Perhaps this ritual was a reenactment of some ancestral feat like Shulgi's, but it is hard to believe that it could convince skeptical subjects of their leader's divinity. Then again, perhaps there was simply not much doubt—or not much point in doubting—the king's worthiness to lead. By the time of Homer's epics, however, that had definitely changed.

The funeral games dedicated to Patroclos in the twenty-third book of Homer's *Iliad* end with a scene eerily reminiscent of ancient sporting practices. King Agamemnon is named winner of the javelin event and awarded the prize without ever making a throw. As supreme leader, his superior athleticism is presumed and honored without having to be subject to a test. This turn of events contrasts sharply with the overall theme of the poem, however, which revolves around a dispute over Agamemnon's worthiness to lead and his refusal to subject his authority to any kind of challenge. What we have in *Iliad* is a novel situation in which many kings—Achilles, Odysseus, and their peers are all the supreme leaders of their individual tribes—have been removed from their familiar homeland hierarchies and asked to join together as equals to fight for a common cause. The situation provokes competing claims to *aretē* (excellence or virtue), or a "crisis of value," in which each man's claim to social honor must be renegotiated.[6] The athletic games staged in book 23 provide a kind of model for that: a relatively open process for (re)distributing honor according to merit.

In the *Iliad*'s games we recognize many familiar aspects of sport: a (relatively) open call for voluntary participation, a common understanding of the rules, a uniform starting line, responsible referees, the resolution of disputes about fairness, the selection of victors, and the awarding of prizes. There are also important differences: only members of the upper echelon are allowed to compete, prizes are not always awarded according to contest results, and gods and goddesses interfere with the contest to help their favorites and hinder rivals. The competitive spirit is clearly recognizable, however, and as it does today, the competitive nature of Homeric society extends well beyond sport. The Homeric conception of *aretē*, or more precisely, *aristeia*, is inherently competitive: it can be neatly expressed in the oft-quoted phrase "being the best and outdoing all others."[7] What is revolutionary in Homer in contrast with earlier forms of sport, however, is that one's *aretē* is not presumed on the basis of social status or ancestry; rather, it must be publicly demonstrated through action—in war, in government, or even in athletic contests. In this context, sport begins to resemble in some measure a form of inquiry rather than propaganda, and so it begins to acquire what I call its "philosophical" or truth-seeking nature.[8]

ANCIENT OLYMPIC PHILOSOPHY

Like philosophy, sport should begin in wonder and uncertainty.[9] When contestants line up on a starting line in Homer's *Iliad*, there is usually uncertainty—an authentic question about who will prevail. In the *Odyssey*, the Homeric epic that describes Odysseus's decade-long return home after the Trojan War, sport is used to prove *aretē* and worthiness to lead. The journey-worn hero overcomes doubt about his nobility by performing athletic feats on the island of the Phaeacians and wins back his queen and his kingdom in Ithaca by triumphing in an archery contest.[10] So, in the *Odyssey* there is doubt, but sport still affirms the aristocratic status quo in a way not so very far removed from the earlier "feats" of Egyptian and Mesopotamian kings. It was with the advent of the ancient Olympic Games that sport would seriously dissociate itself from man-made hierarchies and exhibit authentic philosophical wonder and uncertainty, by leaving questions about virtue and worthiness up to the contest itself.

The motivation for this change was ultimately religious. Long before athletes began to compete at Olympia, the site was a Panhellenic sanctuary that honored all the gods and served all the tribes of Greece. As in Homer's *Iliad*, the bringing together of diverse tribes for a common cause—even the religious cause of worship—was not without its conflicts. Each tribe brought its own social hierarchy to the officially neutral sanctuary, so when the time came to select someone to light the sacrificial flame, the choice was not as easy as simply pointing at the king. Furthermore, it mattered to everyone that someone pleasing to the god was chosen for this honor because the benefits believed to be provided by the gods—such as successful harvests and recovery from disease—were thought to depend upon divine propitiation through such rituals. The process can be regarded as a kind of gift exchange between humans and gods through the ritual of sacrifice.[11] The first athletic event contested at Olympia seems to have been a footrace from the edge of the sanctuary to the altar, where the winner was given the honor of lighting the sacrificial flame.[12] The athletic victor became a kind of symbolic sacrifice or dedication to the god; the olive wreath, palm branch, and ribbons awarded to Olympic champions were also associated with sacrificial animals and priests.[13]

By using a footrace to select a suitable honoree—or perhaps by staging a footrace to allow the god to select his favorite—Olympia was both preserving the traditional association among athleticism, virtue, and divine favor and introducing the novelty of letting the contest, rather than existing social hierarchies, decide the results. The process reflects, in many ways, the emergence of philosophy in Hellenic Ionia during the sixth century bce. The so-called pre-Socratic philosophers—such as Thales, Xenophanes, and Anaximenes—distinguished themselves from earlier mythological and poetic forms of truth-seeking by insisting on some amount of argument and evidence to support their claims.[14] Philosophy is a process of truth seeking that acknowledges the fallibility of existing beliefs, and structures a relatively rational and impartial process for finding a universally acceptable answer, all under the scrutiny of a watchful public. Indeed, I think that the Olympic Games' association with peace derives less from the so-called truce (*ekecheiria*) that protected athletes and spectators travelling to the festival, and more from the pacifying and unifying effects of bringing diverse people together to engage in a fair and transparent decision-making process.[15]

The unsurpassed prestige and longevity of the ancient Olympic Games (over a thousand years) depended heavily on the perceived accuracy and justice of its results. Olympia never allowed subjectively judged events and carefully policed the integrity of both athletes and officials. In wrestling, boxing, and *pankration* (similar to mixed martial arts), pairings for the "heavy" events (so called because there were no weight classes and so bigger, heavier athletes dominated) were drawn by lot, and care was taken to avoid unfair advantages. The boxing events, for example, were staged near noon, to avoid fighters being blinded by the sun. A starting gate called the *hysplex* was developed to reduce the chance of "jumping the gun" in the sprints. And in the horse races, starts were staggered to compensate for the difference in distance from the various starting gates to the central turning post. Violations of the rules were considered affronts to the gods, and stories of divine retribution levied against cheaters were reinforced by the row of *zanes*—statues of Zeus erected with the money from fines paid by cheaters— that lined the entrance to the stadium and reminded passersby that "Olympic victory is to be won not by money but by swiftness of foot or strength of body."[16]

FROM ARISTOCRACY TO DEMOCRACY

The motivation for all this attention to fairness was at least partly religious—selecting anything less than the most worthy victor might displease the god—but the practical effect seems to have been widespread public confidence in the validity of the results. Eventually this confidence became strong enough to create doubt about the validity of existing social hierarchies, whereas pre-Olympic sport had merely reinforced them. Some claim, in fact, that Olympic-style athletics provided a foundation for the invention of democracy (more on this in chapter 14).[17] Athletics in ancient Greece had originally been embraced by the aristocracy as a way to justify their privileged political position—to demonstrate that *aretē* was a matter of heredity, not hard work. As Nigel Nicholson explains, "If quality was not inherited, there was no reason power should be either."[18] In order for the upper classes to keep dominating the Games, however, they were forced to rely increasingly on the competitive edges that wealth can provide: time to train and travel, private gymnasia, personal coaches, top-flight race horses, and professional charioteers. But even as these advantages helped to win crowns for the wealthy, they inevitably eroded the very idea of genetic *aristeia* that such victories were intended to protect. People knew the difference between a victory earned with sweat and one earned with wealth.

Meanwhile, the relatively equal opportunity and merit-based rewards that athletic games provided, combined with the prestige and divine favor associated with victory, motivated cities to look past their internal class distinctions in search of potential champions. The success of the social underdog seems to have fascinated the ancient world no less than it does today. The first official Olympic champion, from 776 bce, is said to have been a cook.[19] Aristotle remarks that a later Olympic champion was a fishmonger.[20] In reality, it is hard to know the social class of Olympic victors since most of our surviving evidence comes from families wealthy enough to erect memorial statues or commission famous poets such as Pindar to write victory odes. But even if nonaristocratic Olympic champions were few in the ancient world—as gold medalists from poor countries are today—the fact that they existed at all reflects the democratic impetus built into the structure of sport.

Democracy, which emerged in Athens more than two centuries after the Olympic Games began, shares with sport at least two fundamental values: liberty and equality.[21] The Greek word for liberty, *eleutheria*, represented first and foremost the coveted distinction of being a free person rather than a slave. Later, it became more closely associated with freedom from tyranny. Part of *eleutheria*'s association with athletics comes from the athletic duo Harmodius and Aristogeiton, who became a symbol of the democratic spirit in Athens after they killed the tyrant Hipparchus in the Panathenaic Games of 514 bce.[22] The Greek word *dēmokratia* (democracy) suggests government by the many, but the real ruler in a democracy is the law, to which all of the people willingly subject themselves. It is likewise characteristic of sport that competitors willingly subject themselves to the rules of the game. The fact that diverse people managed to subject themselves to a single set of sports rules at Olympia might indeed have inspired the democratic idea that citizens of diverse classes could coexist under the authority of a common law.

Not only did ancient athletes subject themselves to common rules at Olympia, but also they understood that they were considered equal under those rules, no matter what their social rank might have been at home. Stephen Miller argues that this fact about ancient athletics inspired the Greek concept of *isonomia*, equality before the law[23] —a concept so closely linked with democracy that Herodotus actually indicates "rule of the many" by the term *isonomia*.[24] A second democratic concept, *isēgoria*, meaning equal access or opportunity to participate in public debates as a free citizen, is also associated with sport, albeit less clearly. Females, slaves, and foreigners were explicitly excluded from the Olympic Games, and participation was more difficult for the poor than the rich. Likewise, Greek democracy limited full participation to a certain subset of eligible males. Nevertheless, it was revolutionary in its time because it reduced the overwhelming gap between rich and poor, noble and commoner.[25]

ATHLETICS AND PHILOSOPHY IN GREEK EDUCATION

Perhaps the greatest legacy of the social changes inspired by sport in ancient Greece was the focus that even diehard aristocrats like Plato placed on education. Since the *aretē* traditionally associated with athletic success was revealed to be something cultivated through training rather than an entitlement of birth or capricious divine favor, the idea emerged that the *aretē* associated with citizenship could also be gained through effort. Indeed, it is tempting, given the sixth century bce proliferation of gymnasia, to recognize ancient Greece as the originator of physical education.

Of course, the Greeks would never have used that term because their metaphysical understanding of persons was quite different than our own.[26] Most ancient Greeks conceived of the human being as a combination of *sōma* (body) and *psychē*, a word commonly translated as "soul" but also encompassing our modern ideas of life, mind, spirit, and emotion.[27] The *psychē* is conceived as the source not only of human thought and creativity but also of physical movement and indeed of life itself. In Homer, at least, a *sōma* without a *psychē* is nothing more than a corpse.[28] So, intentional movement of the body originates in the *psychē*, and *gymnastikē*, the kind of training and exercises associated with the gymnasium, were understood as education of the whole person and not just the body. In Plato's *Republic*, Socrates goes so far as to say that *gymnastikē* serves the soul even more than the body, concluding that its purpose is to stretch and relax "the spirited and wisdom-loving parts of the soul itself, in order that these may be in harmony with one another."[29]

Socrates himself seems to have adapted the competitive spirit and methods associated with athletics to the explicitly educational purpose of cultivating *aretē*, which he identified with wisdom rather than Olympic victory. His preferred educational milieu was the gymnasium or *palaestra* (wrestling school),[30] probably because it was a good place to find the young men he liked to wrestle with—occasionally in the athletic sense, but more importantly in the intellectual sense. Socrates spent so much time at the gymnasium that when his friend Euthyphro finds him at the court house in Plato's dialogue of the same name, one of the first things he asks is why the philosopher is not at his usual haunt: the Lyceum gymnasium.[31] Philosophers' presence in gymnasia goes back a century before Socrates to Pythagoras who is said to have recruited a young athlete to philosophy, first by paying him to study and then by eventually enticing him to pay for his lessons.[32] But Socrates certainly was not after money; he took it as part of his service to the city of Athens and the god Apollo to win the youth over to philosophy—turning their natural and competitive love of victory (*philonikia*) into the love of wisdom (*philosophia*).[33]

There was in Socrates's time no public higher education for the young men of Athens. Instead, wealthy families would hire "wise men" called sophists to educate their sons privately in the skills they would need to be successful as free men—skills such as rhetoric and effective argument. Competition among the sophists was predictably fierce. They would attract clients by giving erudite lectures, answering questions on any subject, and sometimes debating one other. Eventually a kind of verbal contest called *"eristic"* emerged in which a questioner would try to force his opponents to contradict themselves. Publicly observed victory in *eristic* was no doubt good for a sophist's pedagogical business and, even though Socrates denied being a sophist (or a teacher at all) based on the fact that he never collected fees,[34] Plato depicts him in several dialogues challenging and defeating even famous sophists at their own game.[35]

Such defeats, no doubt, were bad for the sophists' business and were probably at least part of the motivation for putting Socrates on trial in 399 bce. Socrates defends himself by arguing that he is making these wise men and all Athenians better by showing them that they don't know as much as they thought they did.[36] After all, he says, it is better to be as he is and not believe oneself to be wise when one is not.[37] He says that what he deserves from the city as recompense for his service is the reward given to Olympic victors, because "the Olympian victor makes you think yourself happy; I make you happy."[38] This criticism of the civic rewards afforded athletes recalls the earlier philosopher Xenophanes, who said, "It is not right to prefer strength to my good wisdom" because victorious athletes do not "fatten the storerooms of the city."[39] But Socrates's point is not that philosophy will bring the city wealth or even prestige; on the contrary, he exhorts Athenians to be ashamed of caring for such things instead of *aretē*, "the best possible state of one's soul."[40]

So Socrates's competitive defeat and shaming of the sophists are aimed at exposing their ignorance, thereby seducing them and, more importantly, their would-be students to the study of philosophy. A philosophical education with Socrates still involves competitive argument, and even some mild forms of shaming, to reveal false conceit. But Socrates regards this intellectual wrestling as a kind of friendship—a cooperative contest in which one opponent's challenge improves the other opponent's strength. This is the very attitude toward competition espoused by enlightened athletes, who use sport as a means not just to win contests, prestige, or even prizes, but also to make themselves better persons through the experience.[41] As Socrates tells his interlocutor Protarchus, "We are not contending here out of love of victory for my suggestion to win or yours. We ought to act together as allies in support of the truest one."[42]

By improving the participants' mutual understanding of virtues such as piety, courage, or self-control, Socratic conversations help to cultivate *aretē*. Achieving the wisdom characteristic of *aretē* is a struggle (*agōn*), and so gymnasium conversations modeled on athletic contests (*agōnes*) must have seemed like a good way to accomplish it.

THE ACADEMIC GYMNASIUM

When we look back today at what Socrates was doing, we might say he was bringing academics into sport or maybe adapting athletic methods to academic uses, but we would deny that his methods are "physical education." In stating that, however, we would forget that the very word "academics" derives precisely from one of Socrates's favorite gymnasiums: the Academy on the outskirts of Athens where Socrates's student Plato set up his famous school.

It is important when we imagine ancient gymnasia that we don't think of buildings with grandstands and basketball courts. Ancient gymnasia were more like modern parks: open-air spaces with easy access to water and room for running, wrestling, and other sports. Sometimes they included covered colonnades to protect athletes from the sun and rain. There might also have been facilities for undressing and oiling the skin, as well as storage rooms and bathing facilities. Besides the tradition started by Pythagoras and Socrates of philosophers plying their trade in gymnasia, Plato may have set his school up in one because he thought *gymnastikē*—exercises such as running, jumping, and wrestling—were just as important a part of education as philosophical debate. In fact, Plato seems to have embraced the customary gymnasium values of military preparedness, athletic beauty, and even erotic partnerships—but with a twist. Plato tries to redirect these traditions away from the body and world, toward the soul and abstract ideals.[43] In Plato's gymnasium, the educational ideal of *kalokagathia*—being both beautiful and good—gets redefined.

There are scholars who explain the entirety of Greek gymnastics and athletics in terms of military preparedness and simulated battle.[44] This is part of the story, but far too restrictive. As an admirer of the gymnastic education in Sparta—a state almost completely devoted to military excellence—Plato clearly understood that many of the benefits of athletic and gymnastic training were beneficial in war. He recognized the value of not just physical qualities like strength but also moral virtues like courage. In fact, in Plato's dialogue *Laches*, two generals debate appropriate training for soldiers and discover that Socrates's philosophical virtue—as evidenced by his performance in the Peloponnesian War—trumps training in armor or even military experience.[45] Socrates's military valor turns out to be nothing more than a kind of wisdom—as do all of the other virtues explored in Plato's dialogues.[46] So Plato's gymnasium would not eliminate military or physical exercises, but it would look for a way to put them ultimately in the service of wisdom and, therefore, *aretē*.

In Plato's *Republic*, this is precisely the function that sport and athletic training serve. They are used to educate and to select the kind of people who will have the self-discipline, psychological endurance, and civic dedication to serve the community as guardians and eventually philosopher-kings (and queens).[47] Plato thought that the same virtues that lead to success in athletics—for example, courage, endurance, and indifference to wealth and fame—also lead to success in philosophy, because the road toward wisdom and virtue is, as Hesiod said, long and steep. Athletes who train for superficial goals, such as a beautiful appearance, gathering admirers, or even winning fame and riches in the games, are effectively letting their souls go to waste. In Plato's later political dialogue, *Laws*, only education aimed at *aretē* is taken to be worthy of the name. "A training directed to acquiring money or a robust physique, or even to some intellectual facility not guided by reason and justice, we should want to call coarse and illiberal, and say that it had no claim whatever to be called education."[48] It is not the means so much as the ends that distinguish Plato's virtue-based gymnastics from the more superficially aimed activities called "physical education."[49]

Even the conventional athletic beauty so celebrated in Greek sculptures such as Myron's *Discus Thrower* is trumped on Plato's view by the psychic beauty characteristic of *aretē*. In *Symposium*, the physically unattractive Socrates is praised by the astonishingly handsome Alcibiades as having a soul "so bright and beautiful and utterly amazing" that the younger man finds him irresistible.[50] What we have in this scene is an athletic aristocrat (who also won an Olympic crown, albeit as a chariot owner) defying the traditional assumption that *aretē* is a matter of genetic inheritance by falling in love with an aged man from the lower classes who is lampooned for his bulging eyes and pug nose. It is superficially a reversal of the traditional erotic relationships between young men and adolescent boys, institutionalized as early as the seventh century bce as means of education in many parts of ancient Greece.[51] But by excluding physical intercourse—Socrates refuses Alcibiades's advances—and focusing instead on the *aretē* of the soul, the partnership resuscitates the educational purpose of these relationships and gives us the elevated idea of what we now call "Platonic love." Beauty and Eros, then, are preserved in Plato's gymnasium, but are given a more ethereal association with *aretē* that leaves material concerns behind.

Another decidedly nontraditional thing to be found in Plato's gymnasium is the presence of females. In both *Republic* and *Laws*, girls and women take part in gymnastic training and athletic games as well as more robust forms of citizenship than were current at the time. There are also reports that Plato's real-life Academy had at least two female students: Axiothea of Philius and Lasthenia of Mantinea.[52] Sparta had gymnastic education for girls—gymnastic even in the sense that they exercised *gymnai*, nude.[53] It is possible that Plato took his cue from Sparta, but the metaphysical rationale underpinning his inclusion of females in sport is the same for all of his educational innovations: a focus on the soul, which he views as sexually neutral.[54] *Aretē*, as excellence of the soul, was accordingly the same for men and women in Plato's view.

ARISTOTELIAN ATHLETES

Plato's most famous student, Aristotle, did not share those beliefs, however. Aristotle regarded females as little more than mutilated males who were not fit to rule themselves because their rational faculty was naturally inferior to that of males.[55] Although Aristotle's exclusion of women from the gymnasium and the military is not stated explicitly, it is implied by their general exclusion from civic life and attachment to domesticity.

A closer look at the relationship between sport and Aristotle's idea of education for virtue, however, suggests that gymnastic training might be ideal for females. Like Plato, Aristotle divides the soul into rational and nonrational parts. It is the nonrational parts that convert rational commands into actual behavior, and Aristotle therefore assigns them different particular virtues and different types of training than the rational parts. Specifically, he thinks the lower parts of the soul are educated through training: habituation into the proper state by repeated intentional action (*hexis*). As he says in *Nicomachean Ethics*, "Virtue of character (*ēthos*) results from habit (*ethos*); hence its name 'ethical,' slightly varied from 'ethos.'"[56] Aristotle then points to training for athletic contests as an example of ethos,[57] although he doesn't describe *gymnastikē* as a form of moral training as Plato does. Since women, in his view, have a harder time than men acting in accordance with the rational part of their souls, it would seem that gymnastic ethos might do them a world of good. Perhaps it could help them to acquire the capacity for self-government that Aristotle believes they lack.

Aristotle is very explicit that *aretē* must be expressed in activity, specifically activity of the soul.[58] This cuts the last thread holding the aristocratic understanding of *aretē* as a passively inherited state that need not be tested or proven. He uses an athletic example to reinforce his point: "Just as the Olympic prizes are not for the finest and strongest, but for the contestants—since it is only these who win—the same is true in life; among the fine and good people, only those who act correctly win the prize."[59] On the other hand, Aristotle thinks that too much athletic activity is harmful—especially for the youth. He chides "the city-states that are thought to be most concerned with children [but] turn them into athletes, and thus distort the shape and development of their bodies" and accuses Sparta of "brutalizing" their youth by subjecting them to rigorous exertion "without training in what is necessary."[60]

"What is necessary" seems to be mostly an ability to discern noble (*kalon*) ends, and to determine the "golden mean"—the midpoint between excess and deficiency—when aiming to perform a virtuous action.[61] At first glance, and in light of Aristotle's criticisms of those who subject children to excessive training, athletics would not seem to be the kind of activity associated with nobility and moderation.[62] But the lesson of avoiding excess and deficiency is one often learned in sport, where performance suffers both from under- and overtraining. Aristotle uses the athletic examples of proper diet and archery (or perhaps javelin throwing) to illustrate the need for balance and aim.[63] In fact, Aristotle regards athletic training as a particularly well-developed science, which requires the same sort of apprehension of noble ends and deliberation about proper means as medicine and ethics.[64] Although he does not promote it explicitly, athletic training is consistent in many ways with the underlying principles of Aristotle's ethics.

What is likely is that athletics, as practiced in Aristotle's fourth century bce Athens, was characterized more by blind excess and pursuit of ignoble ends, such as wealth and fame, rather than the training for virtue valued by Aristotle, Plato, and their prime inspiration, Socrates. Most modern sport philosophers and physical educators would make the same criticism of sport and its role in education today. But just because sport often fails to live up to its potential as education for virtue does not mean that striving to appreciate that potential is a waste of time. What is more, our contemporary separation of academics and athletics—a result of the segregation of body and mind, discussed in chapter 7—deserves to be revisited considering the close connections between philosophy and athletics in the golden age of Greece. By the same token, the ancient Olympic discovery of sport's potential to challenge social hierarchies is likewise worth remembering as we continue to struggle with issues of privilege, class, race, and gender. The ancient Greek heritage suggests a genuine link between athletics and virtue, but it also provides an inspiring example of sport's educational and political potential—as long as its connection with philosophy is preserved.

DISCUSSION QUESTIONS

1. In ancient times, athleticism was used to demonstrate rulers' worthiness to lead. Is athletics relevant to leadership in the modern world?
2. The religious context of the ancient Olympic Games inspired a truthseeking attitude toward sport that emphasized impartial judging and accuracy of results. What would be the effect of more religious involvement in the modern Olympic Games?
3. Ancient sport is said to have inspired democracy in part by revealing the worth of people from lower classes. Does sport today provide a similar opportunity for poor people to show their worth, or does it tend to favor the wealthy?
4. Plato promoted athletics for females because he viewed athletics as a form of moral education. What would he say about female participation in school sports today and equal opportunity laws such as the United States' Title IX?
5. Aristotle's ethics emphasizes activity and training. Do you think training for sports can also be a kind of moral training?

Chapter Two

The Modern Olympic Revival

The award-winning movie *Chariots of Fire* offers a glimpse of Olympic sport shortly after its late-nineteenth-century revival in Europe. The story revolves around two British sprinters, a Jew named Harold Abrahams and a Christian named Eric Liddell, both of whom face challenges derived from issues of class and diversity. Abrahams, a Cambridge University student, employs a professional coach to improve his technique. This is considered unethical by the college dons since it runs contrary to the ethos of the gentleman amateur who should rely on his natural athletic gifts and not take sport too seriously. Eric Liddell, meanwhile, finds himself torn between a very strong commitment to his faith and the practical demands of his sport. When the Olympic final for his best event turns out to be on the Sabbath, he chooses not to run, even despite a personal appeal to his patriotism by the Prince of Wales. In the end, Abrahams wins his event, foreshadowing the demise of amateurism. And Liddell, buoyed partly by a note of support from American competitor Jackson Scholz, gains an unexpected victory in his weaker event, the 400 meters—sweet reward for his unwavering dedication to his faith.

On the one hand, these scenes seem very far removed from the Olympic Games of ancient Greece. On the other, we can recognize issues such as religious dedication, aristocratic entitlement, transcendence of social class, and competitive encouragement familiar from our study of ancient Greek sport in chapter 1. But what of Olympic sport's close association with philosophy? What about its role in education? In fact, sport did find its way into schools and universities in both Great Britain and the United States in the modern era. Philosophy had its place in the curriculum as well, but it was now kept separate from sport. College athletics came to be regarded as something detached from academics, and philosophers generally shunned sport as a subject unworthy of serious inquiry. It would not be until the 1970s that the philosophical study of sport was recognized as a legitimate academic field. (A full discussion of the development of philosophy of sport in the academy—including key figures, methods, and resources—is provided in the appendix.)

I think it is fair to claim, nevertheless, that the ancient link between philosophy and sport born in ancient Greece was "revived" with the founding of the modern Olympic Games in 1896. Indeed, the modern Olympic Games may represent the first time in history that a sporting event was self-consciously driven by philosophy. The Games' primary founder, Pierre de Coubertin and his colleagues were interested not only in promoting a sporting event but also in promulgating a set of philosophical ideals that they thought would improve the world. Drawing on ideas from ancient Greece, as well as the contemporary European Enlightenment and British pedagogical thought, Coubertin coined the term "Olympism" to describe this philosophy. Coubertin was not a professional philosopher, and Olympism, arguably, is not a philosophical system, but it does present definite philosophical guidelines for the practice of sport. What is more, these guidelines have endured despite the more than one-hundred-year history of the modern festival and its unprecedented global reach. Modern Olympism's continued appeal is testament, I believe, to the profound link between sport and philosophy discovered in ancient Greece.

An interesting question arises from the study of Olympism as a philosophy of sport—or perhaps from the study of the Olympic Games as a manifestation of that philosophy: what does it mean in practice to adopt a philosophy of sport, and, more specifically, how can a movement spanning so many different epochs and cultures be guided by a single philosophy? Philosophies, like sports, are generally thought to be the products of particular cultures, epochs, and even particular lives. We speak of Confucianism or Kantianism, referring to specific people. Even philosophies with more general names, such as Daoism or utilitarianism are easily linked with a particular time, place, and thinker or group of thinkers. Olympism, in a way, is linked with the time and place of the ancient Olympic Games—but it is not an effort to impose ancient Greek culture and values on the modern world. Rather, it is an attempt at a universal philosophy based upon values common to everyone in the world. In the same way that people all over the world can play the game of soccer, people all over the world are supposed to be able to embrace Olympism. Is such a thing even possible?

OLYMPISM AS A PHILOSOPHY

First we must ask whether *philosophy* itself can be universal, and before we can answer that question we have to ask what is meant by the term. The primary tenet of Olympism, which has endured since the publication of the first Olympic Charter in 1914, clearly presents itself in philosophical terms: "Olympism is a philosophy of life, exalting and combining in a balanced whole the qualities of body, will and mind. Blending sport with culture and education, Olympism seeks to create a way of life based on the joy of effort, the educational value of good example and respect for universal fundamental ethical principles." [1]

Self-declaration does not make something a philosophy in the strict academic sense, and Olympism can be criticized for its lack of systematic propositions. [2] Philosophy—at least in the context of the European Enlightenment familiar to the Olympic founders—should involve a series of clear propositions established through reason and knowledge.

Coubertin's countryman René Descartes is a good example of this conception of philosophy. Descartes developed a philosophical method based on rejecting all previous traditions or opinions and then reconstructing knowledge by solely rational means from the cornerstone of one logically irrefutable truth. [3] This understanding of philosophy would have appealed to the Olympic founders' interest in internationalism because it took itself to be culturally transcendent. Descartes regarded himself as a "citizen of the world" [4] and believed the power of reason was "naturally equal in all men." [5] According to this way of thinking, philosophical propositions based on reason demonstrated through logic are universally valid and applicable across cultures. The problem, however, is that not all cultures and systems of thought regard such clear propositions to be philosophy's goal. The Chinese classic *Daodejing*, for example, seeks to understand the "Way" (*Dao*) but asserts at the beginning that this understanding cannot be explained or even "named" in words. [6]

It seems fair to say that the modern Olympic founders did not have Daoism in mind when they drafted the "Fundamental Principles of Olympism," but it would not be fair to deny that Daoism is indeed a philosophy. After all, Olympism defines its goal as creating a certain "way of life" right after it declares itself to be a philosophy. Indeed, if we define philosophy according to its ancient Greek meaning as the love (*philia*) of wisdom (*sophia*), or characterize it as a disposition for learning and contemplation following Pythagoras (who is said to have coined the word), [7] our understanding becomes compatible not only with European rationalism, but also with Chinese Daoism, and most important with a flexible interpretation of Olympism itself. [8] Olympism may be criticized for changing over time, but other forms of philosophy (i.e., process philosophy) are continual negotiations.[9] Olymp-ism might be eclectic, but eclecticism is itself a nineteenth-century European philosophy that seeks to consolidate and conciliate diverse systems. Olymp-ism need not be the same kind of philosophy as Rationalism or Empiricism in order to be a philosophy.

In fact, the qualities that make Olympism seem weak when tested against some strict definitions of philosophy can explain the strength and endurance of the Games on a global scale. One of these paradoxical strengths comes from the lack of a detailed and definitive text—there is no book in any language that spells out Olympic philosophy at length.[10] If Olympism can be said to have a text, it would be the Olympic Charter, or more specifically, the page in the Olympic Charter that lists the "Fundamental Principles of Olympism," only the first of which (quoted above) can be said to be specifi-cally philosophical. Olympism's principles are sometimes vague and always open to multiple interpretations. Nevertheless, one can discern within Olympism elements of philosophy's traditional branches of metaphysics, ethics, and politics. Each of these branches is discussed more fully in subse-quent sections of this book, but a brief discussion of Olympism in terms of them will help us to see the relationship between philosophy and sport.

OLYMPISM AND METAPHYSICS

Metaphysics is the branch of philosophy that examines the fundamental na-ture of things. What are Olympism's metaphysics? Within the description of Olympism as a philosophy that exalts and combines "in a balanced whole, the qualities of body, will and mind," we recognize a humanistic viewpoint that posits an idealized metaphysics of mankind. It is this aspect that moti-vated professional philosopher and Olympic gold medalist Hans Lenk to interpret Olympism as a philosophical anthropology—that is, a philosophy concerned with the nature and status of humanity.[11] The lack of any clear definition of just what this ideal Olympic human being would be, however, might seem to keep the philosophical anthropology of Olympism from hav-ing much normative force—that is, the ability to bind a person morally to that ideal. How can we use the ideal Olympian as an ethical guide when it is unclear what the ideal Olympian is?

Coubertin, no doubt, was inspired by the Hellenic idea of *aretē* and the images of heroism to be found in ancient Greek poetry and mythology—images like that of Heracles, Achilles, and Odysseus. But any attempt to draw a portrait or even point to an example of the ideal Olympian would run up against the immense diversity of individuals who have exemplified the Olympic ideal over the history of the modern Games. Coubertin's ideal was probably a strapping European male, but tiny female gymnasts and lanky African marathoners have come to exemplify the ideal, as have lithe male figure skaters and husky female shot-putters. The point here is that the *lack* of a strict definition has allowed for a variety of interpretations of the ideal, without leaving it devoid of meaning. In a similar way the simple definition of a goal in soccer can accommodate a variety or playing styles and strategies without sacrificing the notion of excellence.

The language of a balanced "body, will, and mind," on the other hand, seems to evoke a specifically Western metaphysics of mankind derived from medieval Christian philosophy and the Muscular Christianity of Victorian England. In fact, the "ancient Greek" adage of a "sound mind in sound body" only makes sense as a tenet of Olympism when reinterpreted through the eyes of modern British pedagogical thought—where it appears as the slogan on a gymnasium in Henry Fielding's popular novel *The History of Tom Jones*. The Latin saying *mens sana in corpore sano* came from the Roman satirist Juvenal who was talking about prayer—it originally had nothing to do with sports or even exercise.[12] Olympism's ability to reinterpret Juvenal's words into a motto for a physically as well as mentally active lifestyle, however, stands as further evidence for the importance of philosophical flexibility. We can clearly affirm that Olympism is a philosophy that values humanity generally—after all, it identifies as a goal "the harmonious development of mankind"[13]—without definitively articulating the exact image of humanity it promotes.

Indeed Olympism's failure to define its vision for humankind might have inspired its commitment to nondiscrimination. Among the current "Fundamental Principles of Olympism" is the following statement: "Any form of discrimination with regard to a country or a person on grounds of race, religion, politics, gender or otherwise is incompatible with belonging to the Olympic Movement."[14] This declaration flies in the face of modern Olympic Games history. Coubertin himself wished to bar females from the Games, and discrimination and exclusions of all kinds can be found throughout Olympic history. But philosophical ideals should not be derived from the practices of flawed human beings; rather, they should serve as a guide and inspiration to improve those practices over time. The ever-increasing diversity of athletes participating in the Olympic Games today reveals the power of a vague and sketchy philosophical ideal not only to accommodate a variety of interpretations but also to expand our collective conception of an ideal human being. If Olympism is to be a globally relevant philosophy, the ideal image of humanity it presents is best left vague enough to accommodate a variety of interpretations across cultures and over time.

OLYMPISM AND ETHICS

The next question to ask of Olympism as a philosophy is whether its soft metaphysics can support any kind of meaningful ethics. Ethics—the branch of philosophy concerned with right and wrong action—traditionally depends for its normative force on a clear metaphysics. For example, Immanuel Kant's metaphysical understanding of human beings as essentially ends in themselves leads him to assert that it is a moral imperative to always treat humanity, others as well as oneself, as ends and never merely as means to some end.[15] It may be charged that Olympism fails to present a philosophical anthropology or that the image of the ideal human it does present is too vague to have ethical force. But Kant's characterization of human beings as ends in themselves is likewise vague and open to interpretation. Olympism's promotion of an inclusive and holistic ideal of mankind that values harmony and balance as well as excellence is sufficient to support the kinds of ethical principles inscribed in the logic of sport—principles like equality and fairness.

The first Fundamental Principle of Olympism demands "respect for universal fundamental ethical principles" without ever articulating what these principles are. Some would say that ethical principles are always the product of a particular culture, so there can no more be universal ethical principles than there can be a universal culture. Even very general moral guidelines like the Golden Rule or Kant's categorical imperative (discussed in chapter 9) cannot capture the moral beliefs of every culture under the Olympic umbrella. There is something common to all members of the Olympic Movement, however—a sincere value for sport. Sport-related moral principles, such as equality of opportunity and reward according to merit, may therefore be considered universal within the Olympic community. These principles are manifest in the rules of sport. In the 100-meter dash, for example, runners must start from the same line at the same time (equality of opportunity), and the gold medal is awarded to the first athlete across the finish line in the final heat (reward according to merit).

It can be dangerous, however, for Olympism to try and codify these general moral principles into rules and regulations beyond sport. As the sad history of Olympic amateurism shows, some noble ideals quickly lose their moral force once they become written regulations. The ideal of the amateur is an athlete who competes for the love of the sport rather than any external reward—especially money. By defining amateurs in terms of income sources rather than motivation, however, the Olympic Movement promoted a culture of greedily "gaming the system" rather than valuing sport as something to be appreciated as an end in itself. Individual athletes and entire nations responded to amateur regulations by finding clever ways to pay athletes—for example, by giving them special government jobs. Athletes for whom sport was strictly an avocation found it difficult to compete in this environment. And soon the rule designed to *remove* the influence of money on Olympics put money at the center of athletes' and coaches' concerns.

Eastern philosophy could have predicted amateurism's demise. The *Daodejing* of Laozi warns that increasing prohibitions and rules only increases the commission of crimes, and Confucius observes that most people respond to legislation by thinking only about exemptions.[16] Although sports depend for their existence upon rules, Olympism's "universal ethical principles" are better left as general ideas than codified into a specific set of rules. This allows for universal agreement about the importance of ethics, and even about the value of general principles like equality and fairness, without privileging the specific interpretation of any particular culture. The enduring debate about female participation from conservative Muslim countries illustrates the complexity of such issues. Olympism declares sport to be a human right and demands that it be practiced "without discrimination of any kind and in the Olympic spirit, which requires mutual understanding with a spirit of friendship, solidarity and fair play."[17] But does forcing a country like Saudi Arabia to send a certain number of female participants to the Games show friendship and understanding?

Since the postmodern turn in twentieth-century philosophy, there has been a return to the ancient tradition of virtue ethics—a form of moral thought that focuses on persons rather than principles (as in Kantianism) or consequences (as in utilitarianism). A key benefit of virtue ethics for Olympism is that it has roots in both the ancient Greek tradition of Socrates, Plato, and Aristotle and the ancient Chinese tradition of Laozi and Confucius. It even plays an important role in contemporary feminist ethics of care. Perhaps more important, an ethical emphasis on virtue rather than legislation better reflects Olympic values, not least because it looks inward toward personal perfection, rather than outward toward the correction and control of others.[18] Virtue is understood as a kind of "moral force" that is contrasted favorably with physical (and especially violent) force. Virtue is conceived not as a social construction but as an innate disposition that is cultivated, like athletic talent, through intentional training and inspiring examples—a model that well reflects Olympism's professed promotion of the "educational value of good example."

Of course, specific conceptions and lists of virtues vary inevitably across history and cultures. Even though specific virtues typically demanded by Olympic sports—for example, courage and self-control—are universally valued, how these values are expressed might vary from culture to culture. Thus, there is more room for cross-cultural consensus on the question of virtue than may first appear.[19] Olympism may affirm that certain virtues are universal, while allowing for different expressions of them within different activities. A

judo player's courage in facing an opponent's charge is different, for example, from a gymnast's courage in facing the parallel bars—but they are both
forms of courage, and they are valued in Eastern and Western sports alike.
Virtue ethics—as we will see in chapter 10—can help Olympism to accommodate Western demands for philosophical rigor, while respecting Eastern
philosophy's (as well as postmodern philosophy's) skepticism about hard
and fast rules.

OLYMPISM AND POLITICS

Finally, we must acknowledge Olympism's explicitly political dimension in
addition to its metaphysics and ethics—despite the Olympic Movement's
frequent attempts to disassociate itself from politics. International Olympic
Committee (IOC) members swear an oath to keep themselves free of any
political influence.[20] National Olympic committees are instructed to resist
political pressure.[21] Political demonstrations are barred from Olympic sites
or venues.[22] And part of the "Mission and Role of the IOC" is "to oppose any
political or commercial abuse of sport and athletes."[23] Another part, however, is "to place sport at the service of humanity and thereby to promote
peace."[24] Because it promotes a particular vision of community, this is an
explicitly political goal—one that reflects the Fundamental Principles of
Olympism's stated goal of "promoting a peaceful society concerned with the
preservation of human dignity."[25] What is distinctive about Olympism's politics, not unlike its ethics, is its connection to sport. The IOC wants to use
sport rather than conventional governmental means to achieve the political
goal of peace.

    This approach might be unique, but I would not call it innovative. Indeed,
I think it derives from the ancient Olympic Games, whose own association
with peace seems to have not originated as a political decree but rather grown
out of the unifying and pacifying effects of multicultural competition—specifically the ability to set aside differences, treat others as equals, and tolerate
differences.[26] Of course, the ancient Olympic Games—in stark contrast to
the modern festival—were initially open only to Greeks, more specifically
free, male Greeks with enough wealth and leisure time to train and travel to
competitions. But there were real cultural differences between the loosely
organized collection of Greek tribes and city-states—the frequently cited
contrast between Athens and Sparta is just one example. What is more, these
tribes were constantly competing for resources and very often at war with
one another.

    What the Olympic festival did was to give them a religious reason to set
their differences aside, declare a temporary truce (*ekecheiria*), and come

together upon neutral ground to worship a common deity. As we saw in chapter 1, the first footrace was staged at Olympia to select an honoree to light the sacrificial flame.[27] Obviously each tribe would have its own best candidate for the honor; I believe that the footrace functioned as a mutually acceptable way to make this selection without resorting to established social hierarchies or to violence. In order for the selection made by the footrace to be valid (and therefore pleasing to the all-knowing deity), each contestant needed to be given a fair chance—they needed to be treated as equals for the purpose of the race, no matter how much they hated each other outside the sanctuary. In addition, they had to tolerate their differences long enough to live and dine together for the duration of the festival. No doubt there was friendly sharing of songs, stories, food, and wine brought from back home, and it is likely that some of them actually came to value their differences. In this way, the Olympic Games taught ancient Hellenes a political lesson about peace, even though their original purpose was religious.

Because engaging in sport requires us to set aside conflict, treat others as equals under a common set of rules, and at least tolerate if not appreciate our differences, it lays the groundwork for peaceful coexistence. And because the modern Olympic Games do this on a global scale with the whole world looking on, they too can place sport in the service of peace—as the "Fundamental Principles of Olympism" declare. This political philosophy conflicts somewhat with tradition since it relies not on the authority of a civilizing force but rather on the need for cooperative decision making in the *absence* of a single authority. Western philosophers like Thomas Hobbes understand law as something imposed by an authority to overcome our uncivilized and violent natural state. Eastern thought, meanwhile, tends to associate violence with law and authority and seeks peace by "going back" either to Confucianism's remote and idealized past or to Daoism's uncorrupted natural state.[28] What is important for Olympism is not to promote peace through the force of authority, even IOC's own authority, but rather to focus on staging the Games and promoting sport for all, because sport functions as a vehicle for promoting peace precisely by gathering diverse groups together and treating them all as equals in an open, publicly observed forum.

Sport's metaphysical structure provides a better model for Olympism's political goals than does the Games' troubled history. Nationalistic abuse of the Olympic festival by host governments, competing nations, and even terrorist groups has interfered with the movement's larger political goal. The practice of boycotting the Olympic Games—which reached its peak in the 1980s with the Moscow and Los Angeles protests—hampers the Olympics' peace-promoting potential by preventing diverse athletes from interacting. The current practice of housing athletes outside the Olympic Village to avoid distractions that could harm performance has an analogous effect. Other political uses of the Games, such as Tommie Smith and John Carlos's 1968

protest against civil rights abuses in the United States—captured in the famous image of the barefoot athletes raising gloved fists on the Olympic
medals stand—can be interpreted as part and parcel of the Olympic promotion of peace. The United Nations now declares a modern Olympic Truce,
but its principles are widely violated, as when the United States hosted the
Salt Lake Games while fomenting war in Iraq, or when Russia invaded
Georgia nearly simultaneously with the opening ceremony of Beijing's
Games.

Despite such frustrations, what Olympism demands is a nonviolent and
nonauthoritarian philosophy of peace that rejects hegemony and embraces
diverse interpretations. It demands Coubertin's notion of a sincere internationalism, which embraces cultural differences while seeking common
ground, rather than the paradigm of hegemonic cosmopolitanism, which
seeks to impose a single "superior" culture upon all.[29] The ideal is neatly
captured in the contemporary concept of multiculturalism, but the political
dimension of Olympism should perhaps allow even more interpretations than
those limited to the discourse of nations. Recently the IOC committed itself
to the principle of global environmental sustainability—a commitment easily
interpreted as an outgrowth of Olympism's peace-promoting philosophy.
We'll discuss all these issues further in chapter 15.

The political philosophy of the Olympic Games depends on the "Olympic
spirit" that the "Fundamental Principles of Olympism" define in terms of
mutual understanding, friendship, solidarity, and fair play.[30] These terms,
like the rest of the Olympism's language, must be open to translation in
hundreds of languages and to interpretation across history and culture. Such
flexibility and vagueness may disqualify Olympism from the status of a
legitimate philosophy in the academic sense, but it turns out that an enduring
international phenomenon like the Olympic Movement needs philosophical
principles flexible enough to express common values that can be interpreted
in different ways without losing their meaning. Just as Olympic athletes from
diverse cultural backgrounds compete in a common arena, diverse understandings of Olympism can find common ground. Understanding Olympism
as a philosophy, both derived from and expressed through sport, demands a
multicultural approach. In this sense it can teach us something about the
problem of philosophy—and its relation to sport—in the age of globalization.

DISCUSSION QUESTIONS

1. It has been charged that Olympism is not really a philosophy because
   it does not have systematic propositions and it offers only a short and

vague written text. Do you think Olympism should be developed into a more traditional philosophy, or do you think it works well as it is?

2. Olympism is said to promote a particular human ideal. Try naming some people who reflect that ideal. Do they have to be of a certain race, sex, or ethnicity? What do they have in common?

3. Olympism suggests that sport promotes "universal fundamental ethical principles"; a common example is fairness. Can you think of another fundamental ethical principle that is universal (i.e., common across cultures)? Can you think of an ethical principle that is specific to certain cultures and does not cross over?

4. Olympism's political goal is to promote peace, partly by bringing diverse athletes together in an atmosphere of friendship. Do you think this atmosphere is expressed in today's Olympic Games? Are there aspects of the Olympic Games that work against the goal of peace?

II

Metaphysical Issues in Sport

Socrates typically began philosophical discussions with a "What is x?" question—an initial attempt to conceptualize or even define the subject. Metaphysical questions ask about the fundamental nature of things, and so the first question Socrates would ask in a metaphysical discussion of sport would be simply "What is sport?" When I ask my own students this question, they usually answer by listing examples: football, basketball, tennis, high jumping, and so forth; but this approach quickly runs into obstacles. First, there is debate about whether some activities, such as fishing, cheerleading, bowling, and mountaineering, are sports. Then, in order to answer that question, we need to agree upon the characteristics we take to be essential to sport. We need a definition that lists the necessary and sufficient conditions for something to qualify as a sport. So perhaps we go back to the list of things we all agreed to be sports and start looking for characteristics that they all have in common. Do all sports have written rules? Do they all have competition? Do they all require physical prowess?

The question and the process we use to answer it are important because our metaphysical understanding of what sport is directly influences our normative conception of it, that is, our account of what sport should be. Before we can claim that it is wrong to break the rules, to take performance-enhancing drugs, or to run up the score against weaker opponents, we first need an understanding of the nature and purpose of the primary activity. At the same time, in the pursuit of a metaphysical understanding of sport, we must always keep an open mind. For every serious attempt to conclusively define sport, there is a serious contention that sport is, by nature, indefinable.

Some say that an accurate definition of sport is not only impossible but also undesirable, first because we can understand things without defining them (indeed, we need a preexisting understanding just to test the definition), and second because thinking that we do have a definition might lead to the conclusion that we already understand sport and therefore have no need to think about it further. The lesson here is that it is much more important to ask and explore the question "What is sport?" than it is to find a definite answer. Just as dribbling, shooting, and passing comprise the "fundamentals" of basketball, the debate about what is and is not a sport, the negotiation of characteristics essential to sport, and the comparison of theories about the nature of sport comprise the "fundamentals" of sport philosophy.

Applying Socrates's famous "What is" question to sport and athletes yields a variety of answers. In this section we will explore the relationships between sport and play, games, art, and virtue-centered social practices. Sport has important metaphysical relationships with all of these things, but at the same time it is identical with none of them, and to understand it metaphysically we need to consider how these various facets fit together to create sport as we experience it today. We will also consider the metaphysical nature of athletes and observe how contrasting views in the Eastern and Western traditions might affect the practice and understanding of sport. It is from the metaphysical foundations that we establish in this section that we will go on to evaluate the practice of sport in ethical terms. From the fundamental activity of trying to understand essentially what sport is, we can turn to the question of how it should be practiced.

Chapter Three

Sport and Play

One of the first and most influential answers to the metaphysical question "What is sport?" is that sport is a form of play. On some level, this link seems undeniable. No matter how seriously cultures or individuals take their sports we never seem able completely to tear them away from the roots of play. We *play* games, competitors are called *players*, and even the most complex and orchestrated movement is called a great *play*. When a serious professional like Serena Williams plies her trade, we say that she is *playing* the *game* of tennis. At the same time, what Williams is doing seems a far cry from the paradigm of lighthearted child's play. When I was a kid, I used to play with model horses, building them barns out of cardboard boxes, "feeding" them breakfast cereal, and repairing their broken legs with electrical tape bandages. It can be hard to see anything more than a linguistic connection between "playing" model horses and "playing" middle linebacker in the National Football League. But philosophers make a good case for a metaphysical link between sport and play, even if they disagree about what that link is and whether it should be preserved. What is clear is that we cannot deny, and should not ignore, sport's connection to play. Sport may not be identical to play, or even a specific subset of it, but in order to understand what sport is we must first try to understand play.

Reactions to the idea that sport is a form of play are generally of two kinds. First, there are those who believe that it debases or trivializes sport. Sports today, they say, are serious business, in both the psychological and the economic sense. People may play around with sports by tossing a ball in the backyard or staging an informal soccer game on the beach, but competitive sport demands planning, dedication, toil, and persistence. The kind of spontaneous, lighthearted frolicking we associate with play contrasts sharply with the sports ideal of superlative achievement earned through years of training and practice. In real sports, winning is the most important thing, not pleasure. True athletes are not consoled by the refrain "It's only a game!" Sport is rightly taken seriously because it provides important educational and economic benefits. Student athletes play sports to finance their educations. Professional athletes dedicate themselves to sport just as doctors and lawyers dedicate themselves to medicine and law. They make sacrifices, strive for excellence, and earn a living, sometimes even a fortune. It is not child's play! On this view, linking sports with play belittles the efforts of serious athletes and ignores the social importance of athletics. Modern sports, from this perspective, seem to be almost the opposite of play.

On the other hand, there are those who believe that thinking of sport as play actually elevates or ennobles sport. In fact, both Plato and Aristotle exalted play as something higher and better than practical business. Aristotle defined as most noble those actions that are done for their own sake. [1] Most of human activity is done to satisfy our needs, but gods have no needs and so they have the luxury of doing whatever seems pleasant or intrinsically worthwhile. Since humans should privilege their divine rather than their animalistic impulses, they should strive to engage in intrinsically worthwhile activities. Plato declared that "man is made God's plaything, and that is the best part of him." In *Laws*, it is concluded that the best life is one of play:

> Therefore every man and woman should live life accordingly, and play the noblest games and be of another mind from what they are at present. . . . For they deem war a serious thing, though in war there is neither play nor culture worthy of the name, which are the things we deem most serious. Hence all must live in peace as well as they possibly can. What, then, is the right way of living? Life must be lived as play, playing with certain games, making sacrifices, singing and dancing, and then a man will be able to propitiate the gods, and defend himself against his enemies, and win in the contest. [2]

In this view, play is among the highest human functions. The practical business of earning a living, winning honors, and advancing socially are all lower concerns—linked to the survival instinct we share with animals. In fact, in an ideal world where all of our needs are satisfied, we would do nothing but play. The educational and economic benefits of sport would no longer be needed, and our games would be uncorrupted by such concerns. In the end, both philosophers who believe that play trivializes sport and those who believe that play ennobles sport seek to understand the metaphysical link between the two. As philosophers we believe that making the world better begins by understanding it better.

THE CHARACTERISTICS OF PLAY

In attempting to understand sport as a form of play, many philosophers look to Johan Huizinga's 1944 book *Homo Ludens* (Man the Player). Using a historical and sociological approach, Huizinga surveys the play element in culture and notes at the outset that play is in fact older than culture and engaged in by animals and not just human beings.[3] Huizinga discusses modern sports near the end of his book, acknowledging that they have been taken with increasing seriousness since the end of the nineteenth century and, therefore, that "something of the pure play-quality is inevitably lost."[4] It is not Huizinga's discussion of sport on which philosophers focus, however, but rather his definition of play, which is presented in the first chapter.

> Summing up the formal characteristics of play we might call it a free activity standing quite consciously outside "ordinary" life as being "not serious," but at the same time absorbing the player intensely and utterly. It is an activity connected with no material interest, and no profit can be gained by it. It proceeds within its own proper boundaries of time and space according to fixed rules and in an orderly manner.[5]

Here, Huizinga describes play using a kind of *via negativa* similar to the method some medieval philosophers used to describe God—that is, he defines it primarily by specifying what it is not. Play is not necessary, not serious, not ordinary, and not materially productive. Later, Huizinga offers a more positive definition. "Play is a voluntary activity or occupation executed within certain fixed limits of time and place, according to rules freely accepted but absolutely binding, having its aim in itself and accompanied by a feeling of tension, joy, and the consciousness that it is 'different' from 'ordinary life.'"[6]

In 1958, Roger Caillois critically evaluated Huizinga's characterization of play, taking issue with, among other things, its disconnection from material interest.[7] Caillois then turned Huizinga's summary into a six-point list. Play, he says, is "defined as an activity which is essentially:

Free: in which playing is not obligatory; if it were, it would at once lose its attractive and joyous quality as diversion;

Separate: circumscribed within limits of space and time, defined and fixed in advance;

Uncertain: the course of which cannot be determined, nor the result attained beforehand, and some latitude for innovations being left to the player's initiative;

Unproductive: creating neither goods, nor wealth, nor new elements of any kind; and except for the exchange of property among the players, ending in a situation identical to that prevailing at the beginning of the game.

Governed by rules: under conventions that suspend ordinary laws, and for the moment establish new legislation, which alone counts; and

Make-believe: accompanied by a special awareness of a second reality or of a free unreality, as against real life. [8]

It was Caillois's list that John W. Loy Jr. used as a starting point for his 1968 effort to define the nature of sport. [9] Paul Weiss then incorporated both Huizinga and Caillois into his own discussion of play, sport, and games in his book *Sport: A Philosophic Inquiry*.

Philosophers quickly recognized, however, that a philosophical approach to the question of play would have to go beyond external descriptions of the activity itself and account for the internal experience of the agent (the person who plays), that is, the phenomenology of play. As David Roochnik puts it, "Play is a quality of activity; it is a vibrant experience that each one of us has had at some time or another. To deal with it as an objective thing is to contradict what it is, and thus destroy it." [10] Roochnik goes on to characterize play as an orientation toward the world; a kind of chosen attitude or "stance." "Play is a mode of being. It is a way of comporting oneself, a way of approaching and extending oneself to the world. It is a phenomenon that frequently arises in various human activities. But when taken self-consciously, when chosen as the best way to be, play can become more than a sporadic phenomenon; it can become a stance." [11] Drew Hyland picks up on this idea and goes on to develop a theory of play that defines its stance as one of "responsive openness," [12] but his was not the final word. Today there is no universally accepted definition of play in the philosophy of sport literature.

What we can say, however, is that philosophical accounts of play need to synthesize the agent's internal experience with the activity's external qualities. As Angela Schneider puts it, "play is a mode of performing actions rather than a type of action." [13] If we revise Huizinga's and Caillois's lists of (mostly) external qualities according to the internal approaches adopted by such theorists as Roochnik, Hyland, Klaus Meier, Schneider, and Randolph Feezell, we might generate a new characterization of play as voluntary, extraordinary, autotelic, absorbing, and fun. Let us examine each of these as they have been discussed in relation to sport.

VOLUNTARY

"First and foremost," says Huizinga, "all play is a voluntary activity. Play to order is no longer play: it could at best be but a forcible imitation of it." [14] The claim that play must be voluntary is rarely disputed. [15] The paradigm case of play as spontaneous frolic clearly occurs at the will of its participants. Even in more formal activities, it is difficult to imagine what it could mean to play against one's will. We do know of children forced by overbearing parents to play little league baseball, but surely this example is "play" only in a manner of speaking—an unfortunate choice of words that fails to capture the true spirit of play. Once I watched my brother in a youth soccer game happily spearing dried leaves on the spikes of his shoes in an isolated corner of the field. He was playing, but not playing soccer. The child on the baseball diamond and the soccer player on the field might, at some point, "get into the game" and *begin* to play despite their initial reluctance, but until they willingly engage in the activity, they are not playing. As Paul Weiss concludes, "Play . . . must be freely accepted, even when it is not freely entered into or freely ended; it is free in the sense that it is carried on by the player only while he desires to engage in it."[16]

Caillois, in the definition quoted above, describes play as "free" rather than "voluntary." Is there any difference? Caillois says that sport is free in the sense that it is "not obligatory" and explains that players are "free to leave whenever they choose by saying, 'I am not playing anymore.'"[17] Huizinga also seems to equate freedom and voluntariness, by describing play "first and foremost" as "voluntary" and then identifying its first "main characteristic" as freedom.[18] But there are important philosophical differences between the conceptions of freedom and voluntariness. The most obvious is that "freedom" better describes external facts, while "voluntariness" describes internal attitudes. If we think of freedom "negatively" simply as the absence of constraints—as when a person is freed from prison or a student athlete is declared eligible and therefore free to compete—we do not capture the sense in which play is free. The playing of games entails the imposition of constraints—specifically, the constraints spelled out by the rules of the game—not the elimination of them. Even most forms of child's play, as when I played with my model horses or my brothers played at being "superheroes," require an acceptance of the constraints imposed by the make-believe world.

Freedom in play is not so much an external fact as an internal attitude—a *sense* of freedom that is gained, paradoxically, by the voluntary acceptance of boundaries and constraints. According to Hyland, the experience of freedom for finite human beings "must take place within a set of limiting conditions."[19] Sport provides these limiting conditions by marking off a particular place and time, such as the boundaries and time limit of a soccer game, within which we play. Players feel free because these constraints allow them to concentrate fully on the unpredictable events that take place within that time and space. Hyland explains it thus: "The boundaries and time limits of a game perhaps most clearly of all do allow us to focus our consciousness and our bodies in such a way as to pursue to the end a set of possibilities, and so a realm of freedom."[20] There is a sense, as Caillois observes, in which players' actions are free within the limits set by the rules.[21] Realistically, however, athletes' possibilities are limited: I could respond to a tip-off in basketball by performing a backflip—it would even be athletic—but I wouldn't be playing basketball. The freedom we experience by playing sports is primarily *psychological* freedom that depends on voluntary attitudes, not the elimination of external barriers.

This distinction is important for philosophy because we must consider the possibility that all events, including our personal actions, are predetermined. It could be that our course of life is already programmed and we experience it like we experience a movie, under the illusion that the characters are free to do whatever they choose. Freedom, in that case, can be nothing more than a feeling. John Locke illustrated this possibility with the image of a man unknowingly locked in a room with an old friend. He willingly stays to chat with his friend, oblivious to the external fact that he is imprisoned. Locke concludes that liberty is nothing more than being able to do what we choose to do.[22] Perhaps the sense of freedom in sport depends precisely on the choice to play. If so, conscious choice might also transform obligation into freedom as with Albert Camus's Sisyphus, condemned by the gods as his eternal punishment to roll a heavy rock up a mountain, only to have it roll back down to the bottom. Camus imagines Sisyphus liberating himself from his punishment, not by refusing to push the boulder, but by *choosing* to do it.[23] Likewise, a person "made to play," as Weiss says, can play freely if "he willingly does what he must."[24]

Of course, true voluntariness and the sense of freedom that comes from it may not be such an easily controlled choice as Camus makes it out to be. Randolph Feezell, who emphasizes the enjoyment inherent in play, links the experience of freedom not just with willingness but also with an individual's ability to identify with the activity.[25] He thinks that we feel free within the time and space provided by play because it gives us the chance to be who we really are.[26] Drew Hyland likewise believes that we identify with the play experience because it fulfills our human nature as "incomplete and overfull, both given to dominance and to submission, both monadic and relational."[27] The feeling of freedom, characteristic of play, according to both, depends on its voluntariness, and its voluntariness depends on our ability to embrace and identify with what we are doing. Freedom in play is an internal perception more than an external reality.[28] And in rule-governed activities like sport, the sense of freedom depends paradoxically upon the voluntary acceptance of the limitations and constraints imposed by the rules.

EXTRAORDINARY

Huizinga's second defining characteristic of play is that it is "not 'ordinary' or 'real' life, but rather a stepping out of 'real' life into a temporary sphere of activity with a disposition all its own."[29] The distinction between play and ordinary life, on the one hand, reflects the observations of Plato and Aristotle that things done for their own sake are importantly different from things done to satisfy worldly needs and desires—things done because they have to get done. The idea goes back to the ancient Greek myth of Prometheus, who gave humans the spark of divine intelligence so that they could transcend the realm of animals, which is focused only on survival, and create beautiful things like poetry, music, and dance. In this view, play is separate from—and nobler than—work. It is a view at odds with modern industrialism, which tends to privilege work and production. Industrial societies value play only insofar as it refreshes and restores people to a state where they can work more.[30] We might even say that the view of play as nobler than work is not much in favor with modern sports, where a serious approach is demanded, hard work is expected, and financial reward is often sought. Despite this culture (which will be discussed further), the modern sports world does seem to be distinct from ordinary life. As Paul Weiss affirmed, "Sport, athletics, game, and play have in common the idea of being cut off from the workaday world."[31]

How exactly is play "cut off" or "separate" from the ordinary world? A common answer is through spatial and temporal boundaries. Says Caillois, "In effect, play is an essentially separate occasion, carefully isolated from the rest of life, and generally engaged in with precise limits of time and space."[32] Huizinga also associates play's "secludedness" with its "limitedness."[33] He emphasizes here the spatial separation from ordinary life, which in sport is often represented by visible boundaries. The lines that mark off a football field, the plastic tape that carves a mountain-bike course through the woods, and the walls that surround a handball court serve not only to contain the space of play but also to exclude ordinary life. As Huizinga explains, "A closed space is marked out for [play], either materially or ideally, hedged off from the everyday surroundings. Inside this space play proceeds, inside it the rules obtain. Now, the marking out of some sacred spot is also the primary characteristic of every sacred act."[34] The stipulation that the boundaries may be "ideal" and the connection to sacred acts betrays the fact that play's apparent separateness, like its apparent freedom, exists more within the mindset of players than objective reality. The physical boundaries and barriers are symbolic and, like the religious rituals, they serve to get participants into the right mood. Play itself is as much a part of real life as anything else. It is the attitude of the players that makes it extraordinary.

Roochnik insists on this last point and denigrates those who would discount the importance of play by deeming it illusory or separate from the real world. He notes that the feeling of seclusion we experience in play is our own doing and not exclusive to the play activities. "A full involvement in any situation will give rise to a unique world of distinctive temporality and spatiality."[35] Play is extraordinary because we view it as extraordinary or, more accurately, because it is a stance or attitude that is distinct from the stance of ordinary life. Hyland says that in the stance of play "we have a particular relationship with space, time, others, our equipment, etc."[36] He describes this relationship as one of openness (a heightened awareness of our surroundings) and responsiveness (the ability to respond to what happens in those surroundings).[37] It is, of course, the bounded nature of the play world that makes such a focused stance possible; by setting aside the concerns of everyday life, we can give all our attention to the task at hand. "Play is full commitment of body and spirit to the activity," Roochnik reminds us; "it is immersion in the world that is here and now, and it is only this kind of immersion that does full justice to the powers of man to encounter the world."[38] Understood in this way, not as a particular activity, but rather as a focused and committed approach to almost any activity, play is neither illusory nor trivial. In fact, it permits the utmost seriousness within its limited boundaries.[39] Play, then, is extraordinary, both in the sense that it lies beyond the ordinary and in the sense that it is something special that deserves to be valued.

AUTOTELIC

The Greek word *telos* signifies a purpose or end. Aristotle claims that we always act for the sake of some end, and that every end terminates in the final end of happiness (*eudaimonia*), which is desired for its own sake.[40] A thing desired for its own sake, then, is *autotelic*—an end in itself. Play is generally characterized as autotelic because it aims at no end beyond itself—that is, no external or extrinsic end. The goods sought in play are said to be internal and intrinsic to the task—such as the pleasure gained by playing a good game of bridge. Further, play's internal goods should not satisfy preexisting needs or obligations. If I go for a run because I need to release some stress, my activity is not strictly autotelic. As Huizinga explains, "Play is superfluous. . . . It is never imposed by physical necessity or moral duty. It is never a task. It is done at leisure, during 'free time.'"[41]

Early on, autotelicity was widely accepted by philosophers as characteristic of play and valued as a quality of truly worthwhile sport. More recently, however, the nature and scope of autotelicity has been called into question, especially as it applies to sport. If a game is played for the sake of pleasure, is it truly autotelic? What about schoolchildren let out to play at recess so that they can concentrate better when they return to the classroom? Could professional sports ever be autotelic? Caillois revised Huizinga's claim that play should have no material interest to the stipulation that it be "unproductive," thereby including casino games but excluding professional sports."[42] Paul Weiss interprets autotelicity to exclude gamblers, professional athletes, and even fitness buffs. "If engaged in for the sake of health or money," he claims, "play ceases to be play at the point where these objectives dictate what is done."[43] Embedded in Weiss's apparent stringency, however, is an important caveat: it is only when external objectives "dictate" the action that play ceases to be play. Autotelicity, like voluntariness, depends on internal attitudes rather than external circumstances. I may take up tennis in order to improve my health, and in that sense it won't be play. But nothing precludes me from becoming pleasantly absorbed in the activity and thereby achieving a state of play somewhere along the line. The difference is not the activity so much as how I think about it.

We might even say of the first case that I am *using* tennis (to get in shape) rather than *playing* tennis (for no external purpose). Bernard Suits has helped to clear up much of the confusion here. He employs the term "instrumentalism" to describe the use of games to achieve external goods, including but not limited to prizes and salaries.[44] But he distinguishes between instrumental and autotelic activities, not on the basis of the activity, but rather on the motivations of the participant. Echoing erstwhile Olympic ideology, he endorses the amateur attitude of playing "out of love of the game" rather than "love of what the game can produce."[45] But Suits here makes the same mistake that the Olympic Movement did in thinking that external circumstances can reveal internal motivations. The fact that someone dedicates much of her life to achieving excellence in an activity, the fact that she is praised, rewarded, and even paid for performing it publicly, does not entail that she is doing it for the money. In fact, the pursuit of excellence and performance of a task with which one identifies and finds intrinsically rewarding is the hallmark of . . . a professional! We have all done jobs for the money, but serious careers are a matter of passion. Most philosophy professors I know believe this. Feezell states that teaching philosophy is, for him, "more like play than work."[46] Why do we hold athletes to a different standard?

Perhaps we believe that play-type activities lose some of their value when taken too seriously. Suits complains that Olympic athletes, even though technically amateur (in his day), are playing because they are under immense pressure to win—pressure that is simply absent from informal contests like pickup basketball. He argues that "acting under such a compulsion, rather than the desire to win simply because winning defines the activity one is undertaking, is what turns a game that could be play into something that is not play."[47] Athletes often say that no one puts more pressure on them than they put on themselves. I think the pressure Suits has in mind here is external—the pressure to win for the sake of one's team, for the sake of one's country, or for the sake of the honor attached to an Olympic medal. On the other hand, if we require play to have absolutely no external *telos*, it may end up that hardly anyone ever really plays. Engaging recent research in action theory and psychology, Stephen Schmid argues that the autotelicity of play requires both a player's goal (i.e., climbing a rock) and the goal motivation (because it provides a rewarding challenge) to be intrinsic.[48] In reality, most of us have mixed, even complex, sets of reasons for playing sports, which include at least some extrinsic goods.

Autotelicity remains an important characteristic for play, but perhaps it is better regarded as an ideal than a requirement. Instead of insisting that motivations for play be purely autotelic, we might focus on their value or defensibility. Education, for example, is an excellent reason to play sports, and it might be that achieving the responsively open stance of play is one of sports' great educational benefits. Hyland shares this view, but he warns that we actually undermine the educational benefits of play by making education our explicit goal. "[If I say,] 'Today I will play basketball in order to learn about myself': not only am I unlikely to learn much, I almost certainly will fail to attain genuine play."[49] While it is clear that extrinsic goals can compromise or even destroy the experience of play, it is not clear that all extrinsic goals always do. I have met several student athletes who regard their sports as distracting drudgery—something they do only for the scholarship dollars that make their educations possible. I also know student athletes completely engaged in and enthralled by their sports experience. They embody the spirit of play while earning just as many scholarship dollars as those doing sports for the money. As Roochnik concludes on the question of autotelicity, "Play is a stance to be taken that it is characterized by immersion. It does not follow from this that we should be utterly oblivious to the future. Play does not preclude having a *telos*."[50]

FUN

The most obvious intrinsic reason for engaging in play is simply that it is fun. Many philosophies, including Epicureanism and utilitarianism,[51] posit pleasure as the highest good, yet philosophers of sport identify pleasure as a primary characteristic of play less often than one might expect. An exception is Feezell, who says, "We choose to play our games or engage in such activities for no other reason, in many (or most) cases, than the intrinsic enjoyment involved."[52] Pleasure does not appear in Caillois's definition of play or in Huizinga's most frequently quoted summaries of play. But Feezell points out that Huizinga, at one point, calls the fun element "the essence of play."[53] Fun is perhaps overlooked because it is such an obvious feature of play. If I say that I played around all day, the implication is that I had fun. If I say that I played baseball or soccer all day, the implication is not clear because I may just be using the verb "play" as a manner of speaking again. Sports, sometimes, are not fun at all—and we know that going in. But insofar as sports are or can be a form of play, it seems like they should be fun. Sports completely devoid of fun surely are disconnected from play. Feezell claims, in fact, that once pleasure goes out of sports, an athlete will quit playing.[54] This observation seems to be confirmed by the popular athletic saying "I'm going to play until it quits being fun." Fun is essentially pleasant.

Where exactly is the fun in play? We say "baseball is fun," but two kids could be playing the exact same game and one is miserable while the other is happy. Is fun a quality of the activity or of the person participating? Feezell suggests that enjoyment is something intrinsic to play itself. He claims, "Play is engaged in for the sake of the intrinsic enjoyment of play itself" and that this enjoyment makes play "intrinsically valuable."[55] Feezell takes his account to affirm play's autotelicity, but he is challenged by Schmid who claims that it begs the question (that is, it assumes as true what it is trying to prove). On the one hand, to argue that autotelic play is intrinsically valuable because it does not depend on anything else extrinsic to the activity is essentially to say that "autotelic play is intrinsically valuable because it is intrinsically valuable."[56] On the other hand, if play is valued because it produces fun or enjoyment, then "these psychological states are what is intrinsically valuable and one's participation in a sport is a means to this end."[57]

Schmid's challenge seems to reflect Aristotle's claim that happiness is the only thing pursued for its own sake, but in fact Schmid argues that we *can* engage in activities for their own sakes quite independently of any pleasure or enjoyment gained. His real point is that pure autotelic play requires purely intrinsic reasons for participating; pleasure and fun are actually extrinsic reasons. This doesn't mean, however, that fun and pleasure aren't good reasons to engage in playful activities, or even that they aren't essential elements of play. As Feezell admits, it is "from the standpoint of the lived experience of the player [that fun] appears as the irreducible and essential element of his activity."[58] We have returned again to the idea that play is an attitude or stance adopted by a person rather than an externally observable quality of some activity. We further note, with Hyland, that "fun is not the *telos* of sport; [but] when sport works, when it is the best it can be, it is fun. Fun, too, is a distinctive characteristic of that [stance of] responsive openness which informs our sporting play."[59]

ABSORBING

If we accept fun as a distinctive characteristic of play, and we value play as a mode of participation in sport, the question naturally arises, what is it about playful activities that generates fun? Perhaps the connection lies in play's ability to absorb us completely. Huizinga characterized play as "utterly absorbing" in his initial summary, but this characteristic was left off Caillois's list, perhaps because, again, he was trying to describe play as something external rather than an attitude or stance. Weiss recognized that "play is all-absorbing both for the child and the athlete,"[60] but it is the theory of play as a stance that provides the greatest insight into play's capacity to absorb. In Hyland's characterization of play as the stance of responsive openness, we can see how the need to remain open and to respond to whatever happens requires absorption in the activity. Games and sports in particular create the uncertainty identified by Huizinga[61] and the doubt identified by Caillois[62] as features of play activities that grab our attention and pull us away from the ordinary—even away from self-consciousness.

There is a sense in which play demands that we leave behind self-conscious intentions and calculations and simply abandon ourselves to the flow of the activity. As Weiss observes, "He who wants to be refreshed through play must forget about refreshing himself, and just play."[63] Even the early twentieth-century philosopher R. G. Collingwood recognized that play required "capriciousness" in the sense of making decisions "spontaneously or out of habit without any conscious process of reasoning."[64] In 2008, Seth Vannata applied Edmund Husserl's phenomenological insight to play, declaring its "defining trait" to be thoughtlessness. "Like the mundane activities of reading out loud or even finishing a spoken sentence," Vannata explains, "once you are overly conscious of the act, you stumble. In this light, playing can be said to be 'unconscious.'"[65] Absorption in the flow of play activity often manifests itself in sport as the phenomenon of "flow" or "the zone"—a feeling of perfect control and effortlessness even while performing difficult athletic tasks. In fact, psychological studies reveal that the experience of "flow" or "being in the zone" occurs when an athlete's skills reach perfect balance with the challenge presented by the activity.[66] One cannot force oneself, or even will oneself, into flow—it must arise spontaneously.

On the other hand, an athlete must prepare herself to reach the level of skill necessary to experience flow. In Eastern philosophy, the concept of *wu-wei* implies a similar kind of effortlessness, one that comes out as result of training and understanding. The *Daodejing* of Laozi reminds us that

> The most supple things in the world run roughshod over the most rigid.
> That which is not there can enter even when there is no space.

This is how I know the advantages of *wu-wei*!
The teaching that is without words,
The advantages of *wu-wei*
Few in the world attain these.[67]

Getting beyond the self and 'not thinking' are likewise important ideas in Eastern philosophy that can be applied to sport. Vannata recognizes this, adding that the Western tradition of phenomenology, specifically Husserl's idea of passive synthesis, which recognizes the contribution of our prereflective consciousness to experiences such as play, get to the heart of our absorption in play.[68] Approached from an Eastern or Western perspective, absorption seems to be an important characteristic of play.

Hopefully this chapter has improved our understanding of play as a phenomenon related to sport. One thing clear from the discussion is that play isn't always sport and sport isn't always play. But insofar as sport shares some important characteristics with play, we might ask whether those characteristics can have normative application—that is, can they make sport better? First, the connection between voluntariness and the quality of the sports experience is clear. Forcing a child or even oneself to participate in sport is unlikely to result in a positive experience. At the same time, it is possible to willingly accept something forced upon you, as Sisyphus did. But it is always important, in the first place, to understand and value the principle of voluntary participation. Second, we should appreciate the extraordinariness of play and try to make sport a special place apart from ordinary life—even if it is a job. Third, the principle of autotelicity should be viewed as an ideal that might be experienced within play—even if our motivations for entering into sport are often mixed and can be directed at other extrinsic goals. The point is that focusing on those external goals can corrupt the value of play. Fourth, fun is essential to play but not essential to sport. By finding a way to play in sport we are more likely to have fun and maybe to succeed. Fifth, play is all absorbing as is sport performed at the highest levels—especially in "flow." In sport, unlike child's play, this absorption depends on a proper balance between challenge and skill, but it is never a bad idea for an athlete to practice not thinking and just abandon herself to the game.

DISCUSSION QUESTIONS

1. Have you ever felt forced to play a sport against your will? How did it affect your experience? Has sport ever seemed like work to you?
2. In your experience, does having extrinsic goals like prizes or scholarship money inhibit the experience of play in sport?

3. Do you think athletes perform better when they are having fun, or does the experience of fun come from playing well?
4. Have you ever experienced "flow" or "being in the zone" in sport? Did the experience have any of the play characteristics (voluntary, extraordinary, autotelic, absorbing, and fun) discussed in this chapter?

Chapter Four

Sport and Games

The American cyclist Lance Armstrong won seven Tours de France, two more than anyone else in history. He has been accused of cheating in at least one of those Tours by using a banned drug called erythropoietin (EPO). To many, the allegation is not surprising since EPO is believed to have been used widely in the sport as a relatively safe and undetectable crutch to make it through grueling three-week stage races. If the allegation is true and Armstrong intentionally broke an antidoping rule at the Tour, what may we conclude? Should we say he is still the legitimate winner of the race, since such rule breaking was accepted and widespread among pro cyclists at that time? Should we say that he is not the legitimate winner because he intentionally broke a rule and therefore failed to "play the game" as it is defined by the rules? Or should we say that the antidoping rule is a different kind of rule from those that really define the sport—such as the rule that you must complete the course by pedaling a bicycle and not driving a car or flying in a helicopter? Or should we say, most strongly, that that year's Tour de France was not a bicycle race at all because sports are defined by their rules and (at least) one of the sport's rules was broken? Implausible as it sounds, the connection between rules, games, and sports at least suggests this radical conclusion.

SUITS ON GAMES AND RULES

One of the most influential answers to the metaphysical question "What is sport?" is simply that it is a set of rules. The most influential correlation between rules and sport is made by Bernard Suits in the process of defining games. In his seminal work *The Grasshopper*, Suits identifies the elements of

a game as (1) the goal, (2) the means of achieving the goal, (3) the rules, and
(4) the "lusory" attitude.[1] At first blush, this account makes it seem as though
rules are only one among four distinct elements of a game, but it turns out
that the other three elements all depend on the rules. First, there is a game's
goal (i.e., putting a ball in a net or crossing the finish line first), a state of
affairs that Suits designates as "prelusory" because it can be described independently of a game. But of course this state of affairs derives its meaning
from the rules that designate it as a way of winning the game, thereby
transforming it into a "lusory" goal.[2] Game ends are inseparable from rules
for Suits. "If the rules are broken, the original end becomes impossible of
attainment, since one cannot (really) win the game unless one plays it, and
one cannot (really) play the game unless one obeys the rules of the game."[3]
His point here is metaphysical; he is trying to describe the nature of games,
but it has important implications for the ethics of sport as well.

Game rules do more than give meaning to game goals; they actually make
the activity possible. On the face of it, this seems fairly obvious. I cannot
play football without obeying any of the rules. I may be playing with an
object called a football, I may be running around on a field, kicking a ball,
and so on, but I will not be playing the game of football unless I willingly
obey the rules of the game. This feature of game rules makes them different
from, say, moral rules such as the Bible's "Ten Commandments," which I
may choose to follow, but my following them does not make my engagement
in the activity (i.e., loving my neighbor) possible. I'm perfectly capable of
loving my neighbor without such rules. The "Ten Commandments" designate rather than define actions. As Suits concludes, "In morals obedience to
rules makes the action right, but in games it makes the action."[4]

This aspect of game rules not only makes games seem to be essentially
sets of rules but also captures the sense in which playing games must be
voluntary. Play, as we saw in chapter 3, must be voluntary, and to play games
we must voluntarily obey the rules. What is more, our voluntary acceptance
of rules can be withdrawn at any time. As Suits says, "There is always the
possibility of there being some non-game rule to which the game rule may be
subordinated"—as when continuing to play might violate some rule of morality.[5] Suits gives the example of a race car driver who drives off the track to
avoid hitting a baby that has crawled into his path. Of course, the driver at
this point has quit playing the game, not just because his obligation to avoid
running over children is more serious than the game, but also because he has
voluntarily ceased to obey the rules of the game.

Not all games are instances of play, says Suits,[6] but he does believe that
games grow out of play. "[A] game is when unsophisticated play, i.e., kicking a can, is transformed into a sport, i.e., soccer or hockey."[7] Games, however, cease to be play, according to Suits, once they become "instruments for
external purposes (most obviously for acquiring money, as in the form of

salaries drawn by players in the NHL, CFL, and so on)."[8] These professional athletic games are not exactly work either, in Suits's view, because work is something characterized by the employment of efficient means and game rules are distinctive precisely in that they forbid efficient means.[9] If I work at a brewery loading beer barrels onto trucks, I will be forgiven for and even expected to use levers, forklifts, and any other efficient means I can find to accomplish my task. But when beer-barrel loading becomes a game, as it does in some strongman competitions, such efficiencies are explicitly forbidden by the rules. This sense in which athletic games require the voluntary adoption of inefficient means also has important ethical implications for the use and regulation of performance-enhancing technologies. Not only are sports justified in prohibiting certain means of improving performance, but also prohibiting efficient means is a fundamental part of what sport is (this will be discussed further in chapter 9).

Despite their origin in play, difference from work, and link with voluntary choice, games can be (and often are) played with the utmost seriousness. Such seriousness, observes Suits, is a characteristic of the player and not of the game.[10] Nevertheless, Suits does build an intentional condition into his definition of games. He calls it the "lusory attitude" and says it is needed to explain "that curious state of affairs wherein one adopts rules which require one to employ worse rather than better means for reaching an end."[11] As in our discussion of play in chapter 3, the mindset of the agent turns out to be essential to any understanding of the activity. Indeed, Suits's final and extremely influential definition of a game does not describe an object so much as a way of acting—a way of acting that must be understood within the context of rules: "To play a game is to attempt to achieve a specific state of affairs [prelusory goal], using only means permitted by the rules [lusory means], where the rules prohibit use of more efficient in favour of less efficient means [constitutive rules], and where the rules are accepted just because they make possible such activity [lusory attitude]."[12] Suits's definition of games, then, when applied to sport, links sport metaphysically with rules and with a participant's willingness to accept those rules. It shows that rules provide a context without which sport can make no sense. But what is the relationship between rules, games, and sport?

FROM GAMES TO SPORTS

Even if we recognize that games are made possible by the existence and acceptance of rules, more needs to be said about the difference between sport and games. Suits's initial thought was that a game could become a sport by meeting certain requirements, namely, "(1) that the game be a game of skill,

(2) that the skill be physical, (3) that the game have a wide following, and (4) that the following achieve a certain level of stability."[13] In an article entitled "The Tricky Triad," Suits illustrates the relationships among games, play, and sport with a Venn diagram of three intersecting circles that illustrate, among other things, that not all sports are games.[14] For the area of the diagram representing sports that are not games, Suits has in mind performance sports, such as diving and gymnastics, frequently found in the Olympic Games.[15] Since these kinds of events are judged rather than refereed, they seem less defined by their rules and therefore more similar to competitions like beauty contests than to rule-governed games. Nevertheless, he judges them to be sports because of their emphasis on physical skills. In "Tricky Triad," Suits redefines sports as "competitive events involving a variety of physical (usually in combination with other) human skills, where the superior participant is judged to have exhibited those skills in a superior way."[16]

Physical skill is widely regarded as an essential element of sport. It clearly distinguishes sports games like basketball from nonsports games like poker or chess. Even if a game of chess should happen to involve physical skills, as it would when played by moving heavy, life-size pieces around on a giant outdoor board, it would remain a game and not a sport on Suits's definition because the outcome is not dependent on the superior demonstration of physical skills. Meanwhile, if someone were to protest that poker is a sport because it appears on television sports networks or is discussed in the sports section of the newspaper, we would have to wonder what the difference between a sport and game could be. Poker, in this sense, might satisfy Suits's requirement that sports have a wide following, but that criterion is itself controversial. The International Olympic Committee (IOC) requires that potential Olympic sports be "widely practiced by men in at least 75 countries and on four continents and by women in at least 40 countries and on three continents,"[17] but the IOC is not here defining the term "sport"; rather, it is setting up criteria for the kinds of events that should be included in the Olympic Games.

The IOC also requires that candidate sports be backed by strong institutions and institutionalized in the sense of having established norms, codified rules, formal associations, and specific administrative bodies.[18] But the question immediately arises of what such an activity is before it becomes institutionalized. Are we to say, for example, that wrestling was not a sport until some official body was developed to oversee it? Homer's epics depict wrestling events centuries before the Olympic Games were supposed to have begun, and even at the height of ancient athletics, rules seem to have varied between one festival and another. Indeed, the codification of rules and the establishment of modern sports governing bodies (such as FIFA, the international soccer association) took place after the nineteenth-century revival of the Olympic Games revealed that a common understanding was needed. The

American discus thrower Robert Garrett, for example, did not know the weight of the discus he would throw in those first modern Games. The fact that he had trained with a much heavier discus might be one of the reasons he won.[19] Rules might be necessary for sport, but universal institutions that make uniform those rules are not.[20]

It is precisely a difference of rules, furthermore, that motivates Suits's distinction between performance sports and game sports. Specifically, Suits claims that performance sports lack "constitutive" rules.[21] Constitutive rules are distinguished from "rules of skill" or "regulative rules" as those rules that make sports actions (i.e., touchdowns and home runs) possible. Without its constitutive rules, a game could not exist, or at least it wouldn't be the same game. If the rule against handling the ball were eliminated from soccer and players were allowed to pick up the ball and run with it, we would no longer have a game of soccer. Constitutive rules are those upon which, in William Morgan's words, "the very existence of the game is logically dependent."[22] Despite such clear declarations, however, the concept of constitutive rules is hard to apply with precision. Warren Fraleigh, for example, counts the specifications for a sport contest's area and duration as well as the allowable equipment and materials among the constitutive rules.[23] Suits, however, wants to classify such things as "pre-event" rules, admittedly part of performance sports, but distinct from the constitutive rules that characterize game sports.[24]

Are performance sports meaningfully different from games? Klaus Meier and R. Scott Kretchmar think they are not. Meier claims that performance sports like gymnastics do have constitutive rules,[25] and furthermore they satisfy Suits's original four defining characteristics of games: goal, means, rules, and lusory attitude.[26] In fact, the gymnastic event of balance beam seems to Meier to be an excellent example of a game whose rules stipulate the inefficient requirement that certain moves be performed on a narrow platform elevated off the ground.[27] Kretchmar agrees with Meier that sports performances are games but distinguishes them as "beautiful games" because of their emphasis on aesthetic criteria. The real difference between games and performances, says Kretchmar, is that the game player accepts rules in order to make an activity possible, while a performer embraces the rules as necessary for the creation of art.[28] It seems, in the end, that the only thing required to transform a game into a sport is, in Meier's words, "the additional characteristic of requiring physical skill or prowess to be demonstrated by the participants in the pursuit of its goal."[29] Sports are types of games that focus on physical skill.

FORMALISM AND ITS LIMITS

The understanding of sports as games defined exclusively in terms of their formal rules is called "formalism." It is a metaphysical theory about what games are, and it carries important normative implications for how games should be played. Explains William J. Morgan, "[For formalists] what it means to engage in a game, to count as a legitimate instance of a game, to qualify as a bona fide action of a game, and to win a game is to act in accordance with the appropriate rules of that game. All instances and actions that fall outside the rules of the game, therefore, do not count as legitimate instances or actions of a game.[30] This implies that an intentional rule viola-tion, such as Diego Maradona's infamous "hand of god" goal in the 1986 World Cup or even the common practice of fouling to stop the clock in basketball, are effectively failures to play the game that may even have the result of transforming that activity from a game into something else. Predict-ably, this implication has caused much debate about formalism and also about the ethics of rule breaking (which we'll discuss in chapter 9). If sports exist only on account of rules, does breaking one of those rules make the sport cease to exist? How about breaking two of them? We may agree that you can't break *all* of the rules and still call the activity a sport, but where do we draw the metaphysical line?

One response goes back to the concept of "constitutive" rules. Maybe fouling someone to stop the clock in basketball doesn't nullify the game's existence, but handling the ball in soccer does. In the basketball example, there are additional rules that anticipate such violations and prescribe appro-priate penalties. The basketball player who commits the violation does so in full expectation of being penalized. She seems to be working within the framework of the rules and therefore playing the game. Other rules, such as the prohibition on handling the ball in soccer, seem constitutive in that they define the game and distinguish it from other games. If a soccer player catches the ball and starts running with it, we are likely to say that he is playing a different game, perhaps American football, rather than soccer. The temptation is to say that the handball rule is constitutive because it somehow defines the game of soccer, while the basketball fouling rule is merely regu-lative, because it simply regulates actions within the game. As we observed earlier, however, it is not always easy to distinguish "constitutive" from other types of rules.

Perhaps the difference is to be found not in the rule itself but rather in its use. Graham McFee argues that the same rule may be used in a regulative or in a constitutive way. The handball rule can be used to (partially) define soccer, or it can be used to regulate action within a game through the use of penalties.[31] McFee's distinction constitutes a problem for formalism as a metaphysical account of games since it shifts the emphasis from the formal nature of the rules to the way human beings *use* those rules at some particular time. This means that we cannot define an entire game or sport, such as soccer, in terms of its formal rules. What we can do is use the formal rules along with several other factors in trying to make sense of a particular soccer match. We might contend that Maradona's "hand of god" goal or a professional cyclist's use of banned substances invalidates the result of their contests. Indeed athletes' obedience to the formal rules of the game is known to vary according to the style of particular referees, just as highway patrolmen's habits determine the "real" speed limit on a highway. But is the relationship between rules and games so idiosyncratic as all that?

WRITTEN VERSUS UNWRITTEN RULES

One response to the logical incompatibility puzzle produced by formalism (i.e., that you cannot intentionally break a rule and play the game at the same time) is that sports and games should be understood less in terms of their official written rules than in terms of their unofficial, "unwritten rules." Fred D'Agostino calls this the "ethos" of games. He describes it specifically as "that set of unofficial, implicit conventions which determine how the rules of a game are to be applied in concrete circumstances."[32] The written rules of a game may constitute some ideal notion of what, say, a game of baseball should be, but that notion, like a Platonic ideal, is rarely if ever actually obtained. In the real world, a game is played according to its ethos or unwritten rules, which sometimes permit actions that violate the formal rules. D'Agostino's favorite example is baseball's spitball, a very difficult pitch to hit because of the action achieved by a pitcher illegally moistening the ball before he pitches it. For some pitchers, such as Gaylord Perry, the spitball was a specialty, and players expected him to use it even though it was illegal. According to a strict reading of formalism's logical incompatibility thesis, spitballs cannot be part of the game of baseball, and games in which spitballs were thrown are not true instances of the sport. If we account for unwritten rules or ethos in understanding sports, however, the illegal spitball can be included as a kind of intentional rule breaking that is nevertheless "part of the game" because it is accepted as such by the players.

D'Agostino's challenge to the formalist account of games has intuitive appeal, not just because it offers a solution to the logical incompatibility thesis but also because it seems to reflect the actual practice of sports as we experience them. There is a risk, however, that the ethos theory throws the proverbial baby out with its bathwater. If we allow games to be defined by such an amorphous entity as unwritten rules, conventional practice, or what is generally accepted by players, we are left with little basis for discerning a good from a bad game, and perhaps for distinguishing ethical from unethical behavior within the game. When the maximum speed limit in the United States was fifty-five miles per hour on the highway, drivers routinely broke the rule without being ticketed by police. Because the written rule was ignored and the enforced rule was neither posted nor consistent on any given highway on any given day, it became a dangerous guessing game to see how fast one could drive before being pulled over. Perhaps an "ethos" of appropriate speeding, say sixty-five miles per hour, was adopted. But it seems absurd for a driver breaking the law at sixty-five to rebuke as a scofflaw someone who passes him at seventy miles per hour. If written rules are not followed, there seems to be no unbiased standard for distinguishing acceptable from inacceptable actions.

William Morgan describes the problem thus: "By taking as its point of departure convention rather than the internal logic of the game, as revealed by its rules, the critics [of formalism] collapse any meaningful distinction between theory and ideology."[33] Morgan admits that games played in the real world rarely live up to a Platonic ideal in which every written rule is followed perfectly, but he thinks we should stop short of simply accepting these defects as part of the game because rule-breaking behavior is often caused by extraneous economic or political concerns—as such, it is a form of contamination.[34] According to Morgan, we can grant "that games are more than their rules, and that games are played out in rich social textures it would be foolish to ignore," without giving up the metaphysical importance and moral force of constitutive rules.

> An awareness of the social fabric of baseball [does not explain] why a game in which spitballs are thrown is still a game of baseball. We already know the answer to that question: spitball-baseball is a legitimate game because it does not violate the constitutive rules of baseball. The conventions of American baseball may well explain the greater incidence and matter of fact acceptance of such rule violations in this culture as opposed to other cultures, for example Japanese baseball, but it is the formal rule-governed structures of these games that explain to us why both are in fact baseball games.[35]

The formal rules of sport provide what Morgan calls its "deep logic" because they spell out in a public way what the sport is supposed to be. If we put conventionally accepted rule violations like spitballs and offensive holding in American football on the same metaphysical level as the formal rules, we may find ourselves without any critical standard by which to evaluate games.

THE LETTER AND THE SPIRIT

Another response to formalism may be to add a layer on top of the formal rules by arguing that sport consists of an agreement to abide by not just the letter but also the spirit of the rules. As Warren Fraleigh points out, sports are made possible not only by the existence of rules but also by players' agreement to follow them—something implicitly affirmed at the outset of the game.[36] "The rules of sport are not laws imposed upon the individual without his/her direct assent but are laws, the regulatory effect of which the sports participant directly chooses and thus legislates for himself or herself."[37] Even if we play sports for economic or political reasons, and even if breaking rules would help us to advance those extrinsic goals, our actions may be condemned on the basis that we violated the voluntary agreement to abide by the rules implied by our choice to play the game. As Morgan puts it, "Choosing to realize those purposes by playing a game . . . means nothing less than to make the attainment of one's personal goals contingent on the achievement of the formal goal of the game."[38] In other words, we should abide by the rules and the spirit of the game, even if we play it as a means to some further end.

This means that, even if Gaylord Perry made a lucrative career out of throwing spitballs and even if his actions were expected by opponents and officials, every spitball he threw was a condemnable violation of his agreement to play by the rules of baseball. The same goes for doped cyclists. In professional cycling, the use of altitude training, hypobaric chambers, blood transfusions, and drugs like EPO to boost concentrations of oxygen-carrying red blood cells is so widespread that riders often express no moral qualms over doing it. Many consider hematocrit manipulation a necessary and therefore acceptable part of their sport. But when riders test positive for EPO or are caught transfusing blood, they are widely condemned inside and outside the sport for having violated the rules. We can say that Floyd Landis did not legitimately win the Tour de France because he broke the antidoping rules, without committing ourselves to the conclusion that it was not even a bicycle race. On the other hand, if we take what is commonly practiced or accepted among athletes as our only standard for evaluating actions, we have no real basis for condemning athletes who are caught breaking rules that are routinely broken. What we need is some standard that accounts both for rules and for conventions, without being reduced to either of them.

What are we to say if a particular practice seems objectionable but is not against the rules? At the 1984 Olympic Games in Los Angeles, the U.S. cycling team performed secret blood transfusions to improve riders' performance. The technique was very effective. The team won nine medals, including four gold. When it was later revealed that they had engaged in this practice, the medals were not stripped because—at that time—transfusions were undetectable in tests and not explicitly banned. When Athens Olympic medalist Tyler Hamilton was caught twenty years later with blood anomalies that suggested a similar practice, he was penalized heavily and morally condemned. But is the only difference here rules? Many would say that the 1984 cycling team violated the spirit if not the letter of the rules. The spirit of the sport is that you improve your performance through training rather than medical manipulation. The transfusions, although they did not violate the rules of the sport, violated its spirit. Altitude training, because it is a response to training, seems within the spirit of the rules. Hypobaric chambers are against the rules in some countries and accepted in others. The ambiguity illustrates the importance of rules in defining what is and is not acceptable within the spirit of a sport.

Both the spirit and the letter of the rules contribute to our understanding of good games. "The spirit of a sports rule is not what the rule states explicitly; rather, it is the reason why the rules makers made that particular rule a constitutive rule," says Fraleigh. "If participants understand only the letter of the rule, they have a limited base from which to determine how to follow the rules."[39] The 1984 U.S. cycling team may have followed the letter, but their violation of the spirit is clear. The fact that they concealed their transfusions suggests further they knew they were violating the spirit. In some cases, the spirit of the rules may even override the letter. There is a custom in English football of kicking the ball out to stop play when an opposing player is injured. The ball is then thrown back in to the opposing team to restore its possession. This unwritten rule clearly supports the spirit of the game, although there is nothing about it in the rules. I have even heard of motorcycle races in which cheating on engine displacement is tolerated among those using stock equipment in order to make their machines competitive with the factory-sponsored teams—again a violation of the rules that supports the spirit of competition (among the riders if not the machines). At best, however, such practices are corrections to rules problems that allow such challenges to the spirit of sport in the first place. An ideal set of rules would capture a sports spirit and consistently command respect.

The final point is that rules, both in letter and spirit, play an essential role in the metaphysical understanding of sport. We can say this without committing ourselves to the formalist position that written rules actually define sport. Clearly there is more: the *ethos*, the unwritten rules, the spirit behind the rules. According to Graham McFee, the confusion stems from trying to clearly define sport according to one or the other of these things rather than recognizing it as a complex human activity that simply takes account of them. McFee distinguishes rules from rule formulations. He says that the same rule could be formulated in many ways, for example, in a different language; it can also be understood and interpreted in different ways by different people, and this is just what happens. "In fact, the only grounds for classifying a string of words as a rule-formulation (hence what is said in them as a *rule*) is their *use* as a rule: they are sentences (or some such) *used in a particular way*, not sentences with miraculous normative properties."[40] In McFee's view, then, the metaphysical relationship between rules, games, and sports depends not so much on the nature of the rules themselves but rather upon the way these rules are used by people. To be sure, we cannot understand things like "sport" or "rugby" without involving the concept of rules, but it does not follow that these things are nothing more than sets of rules. It seems clear that we need to add people into the mix. Without players who follow them, rules are nothing more than words on paper. Sports are not rules but rather rule-governed activities—something perhaps better understood as social practices.

DISCUSSION QUESTIONS

1. Name a game that is definitely not a sport; then name a game that definitely is a sport. What seems to be the essential difference? Do activities like fishing and hunting have to have rules to be considered sports?
2. The prohibition on handling the ball seems like a constitutive rule in soccer; can you identify a rule in your sport that is similarly constitutive? Can you identify a rule that is not constitutive?
3. Give an example of rule breaking that is socially accepted in your sport (i.e., fouling to stop the clock in basketball). Do you think the sport would be better if people quit breaking that rule? Would it be worse?
4. You can learn a sport's rules by reading them, but how does a player learn the spirit of a sport? Are rules, in fact, learned in a similar way?

Chapter Five

Sport and Social Practices

Everyone has memories of magical moments in sport. One of mine was at the team ski-jumping competition of the 2006 Torino Winter Olympic Games. It was a clear and cold night in Pragelato (which literally means "frozen field"), and my perch high up on a metal grandstand made it colder still. I was mixed in with fans from Norway, Japan, Austria, and many other countries, each of us decorated to support our favorite teams. As the skiers slid down the ramp and then leapt off into the sky, we cheered for our favorites and clapped politely for the others, pausing occasionally to sip hot chocolate or stamp our frozen feet. Then, without warning, one of the jumpers uncorked a great one—we all knew it from the moment he took off. A gasp of giddy excitement enveloped the whole arena as we watched him fly and wondered if he would ever land. When he did land, with a record jump, we all shared in the thrill. Even his competitors seemed filled with joy by his feat, and they rushed over to congratulate him. We all felt like we had some part in his achievement, the athletes most of all, but also the coaches, judges, and even the spectators perched up in the stands. The moment was given meaning not just by its athleticism and beauty but also by its historical context—the stories of the athlete, his team, the sport itself, and the Olympic Games. As a former athlete, the feat also brought back memories of my own (much more modest) triumphs in sport. It is not the sponsorships, prizes, or medals that make sport great, I thought; it is the feeling we get at moments like these.

My reflection, familiar enough to anyone who loves sport, neatly illustrates the philosophical explanation of sport as a social practice and the shared joy of its magical moments of achievement: an "internal good" of that practice. Social practice theory, as expounded by Alasdair MacIntyre in the early 1980s, forms part of a long line of social theories of sport. The debate in chapter 4 about rules versus ethos reveals the intrinsically social nature of sports; as Graham McFee points out, "Rule-following presupposes a rule-following community."[1] But there has been debate over exactly what kind of social entity sport is. Some view sport as a species of social contract akin to the seventeenth-century philosopher Thomas Hobbes's famed characterization of rationally self-interested humans voluntarily giving up a part of their liberty and subjecting themselves to laws for the greater good of peace and harmony.[2] John Rawls's twentieth-century version of the social contract includes notions of equality and fairness readily applicable to sport.[3] Other philosophers view sport as a more specific social relation. Robert Simon defines athletic competition—at least in its most ethically defensible form—as a mutual quest for excellence through challenge.[4] MacIntyre's theory, which understands sports as practice communities within which virtues are cultivated and exercised, has evoked particular interest and debate among sport philosophers.

MACINTYRE'S THEORY

In his 1981 book *After Virtue*, MacIntyre critiques the failure of modern ethical theory to achieve a rational defense of morality and prescribes as a solution an updated version of Aristotelian virtue ethics grounded in what he calls "social practices." The book is not about sport per se, but MacIntyre repeatedly uses games and sports as examples of social practices, which he defines generally as

> any coherent and complex form of socially established co-operative human activity through which goods internal to the form of activity are realized in the course of trying to achieve those standards of excellence which are appropriate to and partly definitive of that form of activity, with the result that human powers to achieve excellence, and human conceptions of the ends and goods involved, are systematically extended.[5]

We have already seen that sports and virtue were linked in ancient Greek thought, so it comes as no surprise that a proposed revival of Aristotelian ethics should identify sport as a place where virtue might be cultivated.

MacIntyre's theory goes beyond a simple restatement of the axiom that sport builds character, however, by offering distinctions and insights useful to the critical assessment of how sports may succeed or fail to build character in a modern context. The distinctions are between internal and external goods, as well as practices and institutions. The insights include the communal nature of sport and its need for moral traditions as well as some conception of a human *telos* to provide context for the virtues. The overriding lesson of social practice theory applied to sport is that we acquire virtue through sport not so much by training and improving our individual performances but rather by participating actively and thoughtfully in communities with histories, traditions, and shared standards of excellence. Since we participate in a variety of social practices in life, the virtues learned in sport can transfer to our participation in other sorts of practice communities and help us to resist the corrupting influence of institutions. Ultimately, social practices provide a flexible but consistent moral framework for living a coherent and meaningful life story.

INTERNAL VERSUS EXTERNAL GOODS

Suspicion that athletes' interest in wealth and honor somehow corrupts sport as a practice is found throughout sport history—especially during the nineteenth-century revival of the Olympic Games, which was motivated largely by values attached to the so-called amateur spirit. MacIntyre's distinction between goods internal and external to practices resonates particularly well in this context since it classifies money, prestige, and social status as *external* goods that can be achieved through any number of activities. More valuable on MacIntyre's scheme are internal goods like the joy I experienced witnessing the ski jumper's achievement at the Torino Olympics, or what the running community experienced when Roger Bannister achieved his four-minute mile. The notion of internal goods derives from Aristotle's claim that the enjoyment supervenes upon achievement in worthwhile activities.[6] MacIntyre adds that internal goods are practice specific, understandable only within the terms of a particular kind of practice, and recognizable only by those familiar with the practice—its particular history and challenges.[7] What is more, internal goods benefit the entire community, even though they are usually products of competition. External goods, by contrast, benefit the individual possessor to the exclusion of all others; prize money, medals, and even records are the property of individuals and teams, not entire communities.[8] This distinction between internal and external goods therefore reflects the paradoxical nature of competition in which resistance to and even defeat of my opponent is actually a form of cooperation that serves to make us both stronger and better.[9]

Whereas external goods can be achieved solely through athletic skill, social virtues are required to realize internal goods. Going back to the four-minute-mile example, it is conceivable that Bannister cared only about the personal glory and pecuniary benefits he would reap from the feat. Some of his rivals, likewise, may have experienced the moment of Bannister's achievement with anger and disgust because the indivisible good of being the first four-minute miler was now lost to them. Experiencing internal goods requires social virtues such as justice, honesty, and courage.[10] Indeed, MacIntyre describes virtue as "an acquired human quality the possession and exercise of which tends to enable us to achieve those goods which are internal to practices and the lack of which effectively prevents us from achieving any such goods."[11] MacIntyre allows for great performances by practitioners who are "vicious and mean-spirited" but points out that they "necessarily rely on the virtues of others for the practices in which they engage to flourish and also deny themselves the experience of achieving those internal goods which may reward even not very good chess-players and violinists."[12] The bitter rival unable to appreciate the beauty of his competitor's performance actually deprives himself of the sport's internal goods because he lacks the requisite virtues. He can train, compete, and even win external goods, but he lacks the social virtues needed to gain access to a sport's internal, community-based, goods.

The flipside of this connection between virtue and internal goods is the implication that focusing on external goods is harmful to both athletes and sport. In fact, persistent problems like doping and other forms of cheating are frequently motivated by emphasis on external goods. As Angela Schneider and Robert Butcher explain, "If one practices a sport for the external rewards it brings, then provided that one can still gain those rewards, there is good reason to use any means to achieve them."[13] An athlete who seeks internal goods, by contrast, will avoid unfair or efficient shortcuts (like advantages gained through doping or special equipment) because she understands that they undermine the joy and satisfaction associated with, for example, a perfectly executed play. "There are good reasons, if one cares about one's sport," say Schneider and Butcher, "both to value victory and to value it only as the outcome of a fair and challenging process."[14] The argument is that the joys of achievement identified as internal goods in MacIntyre's scheme cannot be had by athletes who dope or otherwise cheat. When we dream as children of winning a gold medal in the Olympic Games, we don't imagine achieving it as a result of doping or deceit. I argue that what we really dream of is being the *kind of person* who deserves such a reward because we have acquired the skills and virtues associated with athletic victory.[15] Doping and similar actions can create a competitive advantage over those who eschew them,[16] and it may result in external reward, but it certainly does not help me to become the kind of virtuous person imagined as deserving such rewards. According to these arguments, then, it is the misplaced emphasis on external goods that leads to problems like doping in sport.

Social practice theory has also been used to argue *for* the acceptance of performance-enhancing drugs in sport. W. Miller Brown says that performance-enhancing drugs could increase an athlete's access to the internal goods of a sport, perhaps by allowing her to participate in sports competitively beyond the normal age of retirement. According to Brown, "The constraints of the practice, including the internalizing of the virtues, are compatible with the use of performance-enhancing drugs, novel and risky training regimes, and biomedical or surgical treatments or modifications of practitioners."[17] By banning drugs and other performance-enhancing technologies, he argues, we are cutting individuals off not just from the external goods associated with winning but also from internal goods that are acquired through skilled participation. Part of Brown's point is that the internal/external distinction of goods in sport is too harsh and that in fact goods present themselves in a kind of continuum between the two poles.[18] Some goods are more internal; others, more external, but this distinction does not necessarily dictate their relative value. Brown explains that some external goods "conflict with the continued flourishing or development of the practice itself. Other external goods, such as entertainment, education, training, or protection of others, may not conflict with a practice's conduct but rather be direct consequences of its most capable performance."[19] Brown's argument does not suggest that athletes ought to cheat. His point rather is that some forms of doping are part of a prudent pursuit of internal and external goods in sport and should therefore be permitted.

In short, the ontological distinction between internal and external goods does not, by itself, create the ethical distinction sport philosophers seem to be looking for. In the first place, certain goods classified as external to a sporting practice—such as health, recreation, and education—carry more social value than typical internal goods, such as the joy attending mastery of a difficult skill like pole vaulting. In addition, certain of sports' apparent internal goods are of very dubious social value. I am thinking here of the thrill created in American football by the kinds of solid hits and high-speed tackles that make postgame highlight reels. Few football practitioners would deny that such tough defensive plays are among the internal goods of the game, but even fewer could justify their value or even their moral acceptability outside of the game.

As Graham McFee points out, MacIntyre seems to allow no room for external criticism of a practice's internal goods—even as he admits the possibility of "evil practices."[20] Mike McNamee adds that, in reality, motivations for engaging practices are usually complex; both the internal means of sport and the external rewards of money and prestige can be simultaneously valued.[21] It seems ironic or perhaps arbitrary that in fields such as music or academia we praise "professionalism" as dedication to one's craft, evidenced partly by the fact that one makes one's living from the practice, yet in sports we denigrate professionals for the same reason. There is no guarantee that paid athletes play just for the money, nor is it the case that increases in external rewards cause more athletes to dope and cheat.[22] MacIntyre's internal/external distinction turns out to be a useful but not a decisive tool for the social evaluation of sport.

PRACTICES VERSUS INSTITUTIONS

MacIntyre's privileging of internal goods seems to be based upon their relation to social virtues. He notes that the very same virtues that provide access to internal goods can be an obstacle to achieving external goods.[23] For example, when Luz Long helped his opponent Jesse Owens to qualify for the long-jump finals in the 1936 Olympics, he exercised the social virtue of friendship and set the stage for a close and challenging competition, but he also reduced his own chances of victory. This paradox may seem to devalue virtues that reduce one's chances at victory, but it gains meaning in the distinction between practices, such as ski jumping, and institutions, such as the International Ski Federation, that oversee them. MacIntyre recognizes the necessity of institutions to the continued survival of practices, but he also warns that they threaten the well-being of those practices. "Institutions," MacIntyre points out, "are characteristically and necessarily concerned with what I have called external goods. They are involved in acquiring money and other material goods; they are structured in terms of power and status, and they distribute money, power, and status as rewards."[24] The danger is that institutional values can take over within a practice, thereby eroding the practice's internal goods and eventually leaving practitioners with no reason to participate but external goods. Sports, in this scenario, would be like dead-end jobs, activities done only for the money.

Sports are able to preserve their integrity only insofar as the virtues cultivated within the practice community and embodied by its members resist the corrupting power of institutions. Let us recall some of the social virtues required to appreciate an internal athletic good such as the gesture made by Olympic wrestler Rulon Gardner when he left his shoes on the mat after winning the bronze medal match at the 2004 Games in Athens. First, we need to understand the history and traditions of the sport to even make sense of the gesture; then the sporting contest needs to have been conducted in accordance with certain virtues in order to imbue the gesture with value and meaning. Gardner was symbolically bidding a respectful farewell to his sport at the end of a successful and meaningful career. It was an emotional moment for those who watched, but that positive emotion depends ultimately on the virtues exercised both by the athlete and by his sport. Olympic wrestling needs the virtues of justice to motivate the fair running of the matches, truthfulness to ensure veracity of the results, and courage to face the risk of failure.

If these practice-sustaining virtues are overshadowed or replaced by an institution's characteristic emphasis on external goods, however, we end up with something more like made-for-television "Catch Wrestling" in which standards of fair competition and respect for tradition are sacrificed in favor of sensationalism and profit. As MacIntyre explains, "If in a particular society the pursuit of external goods were to become dominant, the concept of the virtues might suffer first attrition and then perhaps something near total effacement, although simulacra might abound."[25] One may witness the comic-book farewell of a popular professional wrestler, but it would be orchestrated by an institution such as World Wrestling Entertainment for the express purpose of maximizing its entertainment and merchandising value. Institutions threaten practices by privileging external goods and therefore undermining the virtues cultivated through the pursuit of internal goods. These virtues, in turn, encourage athletes to resist the corrupting influence of the institutions, perhaps by donating their time and money to help younger athletes.

Virtues may be associated with sport, but they are something different from athletic skills. Unlike the technical abilities needed for success within a sport—things like leg speed in cycling or batting skill in cricket—virtues are dispositions that can be expressed in a variety of actions and activities. "Someone who genuinely possesses a virtue," says MacIntyre, "can be expected to manifest it in very different types of situation, many of them situations where the practice of a virtue cannot be expected to be effective in the way that we expect a professional skill to be."[26] A virtue such as courage, then, will be exercised not only when a soccer goalie faces a high-speed shot but also when he resists efforts by institutions to enlarge the goal so as to increase scoring and spectator appeal. Practices, likewise, cannot be merely collections of people with shared sets of technical skills; rather, they need to be collections of people joined by shared values. As MacIntyre explains, "What is distinctive of a practice is in part the way in which conceptions of the relevant goods and ends which the technical skills serve—and every practice does require the exercise of technical skills—are transformed and enriched by these extensions of human powers and by that regard for its own internal goods which are partially definitive of each particular practice or type of practice."[27] It is the practitioners' dedication to the internal goods of their practice that enables them to resist the corrupting power of their institutions.

William J. Morgan sees in this antagonistic relationship between practices and institutions nothing less than the potential redemption of sport from the corrupting influences of capitalism: "While much of what is called sport these days is infected with the rational demeanor and ethic of the market, particularly the entertainment market, there is more to sport than is evident in its business side," explains Morgan.[28] Specifically, he refers to the "internal logic of sport" that is inscribed in its rules—a notion that reflects Bernard Suits's definition of game playing as "the voluntary attempt to overcome unnecessary obstacles."[29] The internal logic of sport captures the sense, explored previously, in which sport is a form of gratuitous play that stipulates the adoption of inefficient means to arbitrary goals just because they make the game possible. For example, the goal of soccer, putting a ball into a net, must be achieved using only one's feet—and it is this stipulation of inefficiency (among other rules) that makes the game challenging and interesting to play.

This internal logic of sport is clearly at odds with market values, which seek the most efficient path to monetary goods (we'll return to Morgan's argument in chapter 14). In addition, the focus on attaining ends by any means necessary undermines the very ancient tradition of engaging in sport for the purpose of cultivating and expressing virtues. Practitioners who understand the link between sports' internal logic and its social value are in a position to resist institutions' corrupting tendencies, not least by serving within those institutions as coaches, officials, organizers, and governing body members. The International Cycling Federation's declaration of the "primacy of man over machine" (a principle that bans innumerable technological efficiencies for bicycles) clearly reflects the perspective of practitioners over the interests of institutions and the industry that supports them. Most likely it is an example of virtuous practitioners resisting the corrupting power of institutions from within.

COMMUNITIES AND VIRTUES

It is important in social practice theory to remember the primacy of the community. Our modern tendency to privilege individual liberty over the common good is one of the things MacIntyre wants to resist. A practice like basketball is not an activity so much as a group of people. As MacIntyre explains, "To enter into a practice is to enter into a relationship not only with its contemporary practitioners, but also with those who have preceded us in the practice, particularly those whose achievements extended the reach of the practice to its present point."[30] It is by understanding sports as communities and ourselves as responsible members of those communities that we can best acquire the virtues. Humility and trust, for example, are demanded of an athlete who must acknowledge the inadequacy of her own performance in comparison with the authoritative standards of her sport.

In order to improve, athletes typically work with coaches, thereby subordinating themselves in their relationship to other practitioners and subjecting themselves to a period of apprenticeship that demands respect, courage, and honesty. As MacIntyre explains, "Just so long as we share the standards and purposes characteristic of practices, we define our relationships to each other, whether we acknowledge it or not, by reference to standards of truthfulness and trust, so we define them too by reference to standards of justice and courage."[31] Virtues in sport are cultivated not only by facing the artificial obstacles of the game itself but also by engaging in a community. Indeed, the ancient Greek idea of virtue (*aretē*) is always understood within a community—it derives from the recognition that humans are social animals. Our individual good cannot be separated from the good of our communities.

The teaching of this lesson of community interdependence is a common justification for the educational use of team sports, but individual sports also teach this lesson as long as they are understood as social practices. Peter J. Arnold uses MacIntyre's theory to defend the pedagogical value of sport in the *Journal of Moral Education*. Arnold characterizes sport as a valued social practice that teaches us through experience about the principle of equality and the duty of fair play. Sport, he says, demands that we commit to its internal goals and standards. "This entails acting in accordance with its rules and upholding its best customs, conventions and traditions. It involves exercising those virtues such as honesty, fairness, courage, determination and persistence which not only help characterise sport as a practice, but which are indispensable elements in allowing it to flourish."[32] Sport's efficacy as education in community values is widely doubted however. MacIntyre may be right that isolating oneself from practice communities is "to debar oneself from finding any good outside oneself,"[33] but it seems that people can and often do play sports without engaging meaningfully in sports communities.

Even within teams, individual athletes are often pitted against one another in winner-takes-all contests for starting positions that force them to focus on their personal interests to the exclusion of all others. In fact, individualistic and self-aggrandizing behavior seems more common among team-sport athletes. The game is not supposed to reward such behavior, but the market clearly does. If sports are to serve as education in community values, there must be an effort to manage them toward that end. Schneider and Butcher argue convincingly that athletes may rationally eschew the self-interested benefits of doping to gain the collective good of clean sport, but how many athletes are even aware of such arguments, let alone able to act in accordance with them? "Perhaps," says W. Miller Brown, "we must acknowledge the predominantly individual character of sports and their goods."[34] If the cultivation of virtue through sport depends upon it functioning as a community, the individualistic practice of sport may have no place in education.

TELOS AND LIFE NARRATIVE

A final, often overlooked aspect of internal goods is that they are the product, in MacIntyre's words, "of a certain kind of life."[35] This too resonates with sport; one of the reasons we so appreciate achievements like the four-minute mile or the prodigious ski jump is that we recognize them as products of a valued athletic lifestyle, characterized by virtues like hard work and perseverance. Even in the heavily institutionalized and external goods–focused culture of contemporary sports, talk about virtues such as effort and discipline abounds. To be sure, this is part of the historical narrative of sport itself. Even when the *Chariots of Fire* ethos of natural aristocratic superiority caused athletes to train in secret or disguise their coaches, the connection between training and success was acknowledged by athletes. Today's popular culture likes to portray successful athletes as privileged playboys, but athletic achievement still depends, as it always has, on a particular way of life. In the documentary *Hoop Dreams*, a concerned mother explains the failure of her elder son, once a blue-chip basketball prospect, with a sigh: "Curtis's idea of being good," she says, "is that you don't have to follow the rules."[36] Whatever skills or virtues enabled Curtis to reach the athletic level he did failed to protect him from the temptations of success and also failed to transfer to other areas of his life. Why is this so often the case?

We have already observed that the athletic skills necessary to achieve a sport's external goods are not the same as the virtues nurtured and preserved by engagement in a practice. And just as skills like dribbling and shooting a basketball are essentially useless off the court, virtues like hard work and self-discipline are useless if a person is incapable of applying them outside sport. In fact, MacIntyre wouldn't call them virtues at all in this case. If a person really possesses the virtue of self-discipline, it will manifest itself in all aspects of her life because it will be understood as a feature of, in MacIntyre's words, "a social and moral life in terms of which it has to be defined and explained."[37] In other words, for athletic virtues to be authentic and not what MacIntyre calls "simulacra," they must manifest themselves within a unified and goal-directed life narrative.

The goal or *telos* here cannot be simply an athletic goal, even a big athletic goal like winning an Olympic gold medal. It must, in MacIntyre's words, "transcend the limited goods of practices by constituting the good of a whole human life, the good of a human life conceived as a unity."[38] This unity, in turn, is characterized by a particular virtue: integrity, constancy, or singleness of purpose—a virtue that "cannot be specified at all except with reference to the wholeness of human life," according to MacIntyre.[39] This unified life may be different for different people at different times in different cultural contexts, but it will involve the same sorts of virtues. Indeed, it is plausible that the virtues of an ancient Olympic champion such as Milo of Kroton were not so very different from those of Olympic wrestling champions today. Virtues like courage and justice don't change, but they are expressed differently in different contexts and different activities. Ultimately in social practice theory, they are directed at nothing less than a good life, understood as a kind of narrative to be written by each of us in our particular context.[40]

MacIntyre's refusal to spell out a universal idea of virtue, relying instead on dynamically different practice communities, is appealing for its flexibility, but some remain frustrated by its apparent inconsistency. Graham McFee says that "MacIntyre's ideas cannot explain the normativity inherent in a practice but, instead, depend on it."[41] He allows that sport may teach us to follow rules, but worries that rule-following may be nothing more than habit. Sport should do more than train us to do an action. It should foster an understanding of why we do that action.[42] MacIntyre's social practice theory also demands such understanding. To fit MacIntyre's requirements for a valued social practice that cultivates virtues aimed at a unified, good life, sport must further promote an understanding of *why* we do sport as part of that life. Too often, this connection between sport, virtue, and life purpose is regarded as automatic or empty. Social theories of sport, and social practice theory in particular, provide a framework for understanding and eventually fostering sport's ability to cultivate virtue.

DISCUSSION QUESTIONS

1. Give an example of an internal good in your sport—a special moment that comes from achievement according to the sport's standards of excellence. Do these goods motivate you as much or more than external goods?
2. The logic and values of sport are sometimes at odds with the values of the institutions that govern them. Can you think of an example where a sports institution changed the rules for external reasons, such as money or popularity, harming the internal values of the sport?
3. Do you think team sports or individual sports are better for developing social and community virtues like friendship and fairness?
4. If the virtues cultivated through sport are supposed to be expressed throughout a person's life, why do so many athletes get into trouble outside of sport?

Chapter Six

Sport and Art

Not all theories of sport are based on rules and communities; many philosophers view sport rather as a form of art. In thinking about the relationship between sport and art, an image likely to come to mind is that of an ancient Greek athletic sculpture such as Myron's famous *Discus Thrower*. Such statues can seem so real as to be living, but at the same time their beauty derives from their *not* being alive—that is, that they are not imperfect human beings but rather representations of perfect ideal types. In fact, the *Discus Thrower* statues that we see today in the British Museum or Rome's Museo Nazionale are already representations of a representation of a representation. They are marble copies of the original bronze, long since lost, which was probably a "copy" of some nameless athletic model, who posed for the portrait of a famous Olympic victor at a particular moment in a particular competition, to be erected at Olympia or some other athletic sanctuary. Like Pindar's poetic victory odes, however, such statues were not meant to be realistic portraits of particular winners so much as generalized celebrations of an ideal cultural type. In this way, the *Discus Thrower* represents something particular and at the same time expresses the general cultural ideal of beauty and goodness called *kalokagathia*. It is this intersection between the particular and the ideal that gives athletic art its power, and it is the mind of the spectator that brings those realms together. The interesting question, however, is not whether athletic statues and poetry are art. They are. It is whether sport itself can be art.

There are artistic sports. Some, such as artistic gymnastics, even carry the designation in their name. Many others—such as figure skating, ice dancing, diving, and synchronized swimming—employ aesthetic criteria or even "artistic merit" as standards of evaluation. Sports are usually performed, furthermore, in venues specially designed or demarcated for spectatorship. And all sports—even rough games like rugby—can be appreciated aesthetically by knowledgeable spectators in the right context. These parallels between sport and art, however, do not answer the question of when and if sport can *be* art—a question further complicated by continuing debate over the definition, and even the definability, of both sport and art. Perhaps the best response is simply an exploration of the affinities between sport and art and, more precisely, sport's aesthetic nature. What is the relationship between sport and beauty? What is the aesthetic value of athletics? Can spectators appreciate sport as art? Can athletes be artists, or even their own works of art? The question of whether sport is art may never be settled, but we can learn much about the metaphysical nature of sport by examining its relationships with art and the aesthetic.

SHARED ANCESTRY

Philosophical discussion about the relationship between sport and art grows out of sport's affinity with play. Friedrich von Schiller claimed in a nine-teenth-century letter that beauty is the object of the play instinct.[1] Schiller located this play instinct at the intersection of the rational, ideal, or formal aspect of life and the aesthetic, real, material aspect: "There shall be a communion between the formal impulse and the material impulse—that is, there shall be a play instinct—because it is only the unity of reality with the form, of the accidental with the necessary, of the passive state with freedom, that the conception of humanity is completed."[2] Beauty, Schiller concluded, is produced through the playful unification of material and ideal. "The beautiful must not only be life and form, but a living form," he says.[3] Of course, Schiller's location of beauty in play and the living form does not automatically turn sport (or even play) into art. More accurately, it identifies play as a common ontological ancestor of both sport and art, and it points to the importance of the human mind in the creation of beauty. Based on chapter 3, we might also observe the play characteristics of being voluntary, extraordinary, autotelic, fun, and absorbing as frequently manifest in both art and sport. Such a "genetic" link based on play can account for the occasional resemblance between sport and art without implying their identity. It is sport's natural playfulness, explains Joseph Kupfer, that lends it so readily to aesthetic appreciation.[4]

Just as the seriousness of competitive sport creates problems for its categorization as play, however, it also seems to wreak havoc on sport's affinity with art. Karl Groos identifies the joy "rooted in playful experimentation and imitation" as a cause of full-fledged art.[5] The joy of sport seems rooted in different causes. Unlike art, sport is rarely made for the specific purpose of creating beauty, or even a significant aesthetic experience.[6] An Olympic figure skater may don a theatrical costume and execute a meticulously choreographed routine, but she is primarily pursuing points for the purpose of winning a competition and only coincidentally creating aesthetic value. Not all definitions of art depend on the intentions of the artist, however. Essentialists look for something intrinsic to the work, while contextualists define art largely by its relation to other works of art.[7] There is also an antiessentialist movement that rejects all efforts to define art in terms of any particular function. Clearly, if absolutely anything can be art, sport can also be art. But this trivial kind of identity doesn't tell us anything new or interesting about the nature of sport. For that, we need to ask philosophical questions about the similarities and differences between sport and art.

The affinity between sport and art is based on shared ancestry: both are descendants of play, and they share certain play characteristics that condition the spectator's aesthetic experience. First, they are both extraordinary—set apart from everyday life, often by explicit boundaries of space and time. Even when an ordinary object such as a soup can is presented as an artwork, it is made so precisely by removing it from its ordinary setting. This aesthetic transformation, which takes place in the mind of the beholder, depends on not just spectator pleasure but also particular kinds of knowledge and understanding. Second, both art and sport are autotelic—they are valued for their own sakes or as ends in themselves rather than as means to practical ends. Although both sport and art can be bought and sold for money, financial gain is not (or at least should not be) their primary purpose, and indeed the instrumental exploitation of both sport and art seem to diminish their aesthetic value. This reveals that both sport and art embody a moral dimension that informs their aesthetic value. Finally, this moral dimension raises questions about the roles of sport and art in education. Ancient Greek philosophers such as Plato saw a deep conceptual link between beauty and goodness, which was manifest in the educational ideal of *kalokagathia*. Modern thinker Karl Groos, meanwhile, identifies the "moral elevation and profound insight into life" as factors that enable art to transcend the realm of "mere" play.[8] In this view, the link between sport and art goes beyond play and even aesthetics into the moral realm of intentions, ends, and finally social value. Where, then, does it start?

FRAMING: THE MIND OF THE BEHOLDER

Sport and art, observes Christopher Cordner, share the play characteristics of being "separated from the everyday world, whether by the frame around the canvas, or the touchline, the edge of the hockey rink, or the stage in the theatre."[9] These boundaries have a lot to do with aesthetic enjoyment, perhaps because they impose a rational limit upon the otherwise free-flowing chaos of life. Aristotle claims that beauty depends on order,[10] and Nietzsche identifies the beauty of tragedy in the tension between Apollonian order and Dionysian chaos.[11] Perhaps what boundaries do is act as a signal to adopt an aesthetic attitude to whatever they catch in their frame, as when a photographer chooses some section of a visual field to create an artistic image. Just as artwork is frequently concocted from everyday objects, images, sounds, and experiences, the raw human movements that make up sport also derive from common experience. It is the spatial and temporal frame circumscribing the object—the chalk lines on the field, the opening and closing whistles of a ball game, and the rising and falling of the curtain on the stage—that bring it out of the realm of the ordinary and offer it up as a package for aesthetic appreciation and enjoyment.

The framing of sport and art create what Marjorie Fisher calls "aesthetic situations"—interactions between spectators and artists (or artworks) that bring the best out of the performers by poising the audience to appreciate their work.[12] This can be seen in the architectural similarities of theaters and stadiums, or even in the way that museums invite spectators to interface with their artworks. An argument can be made that certain ordinary objects, such as Andy Warhol's famed Brillo Box, are made into art by being in a museum. It seems, rather, that the spectator makes that transformation by adopting an aesthetic attitude. As Arthur Danto said, "To see something as art requires something that the eye cannot descry—an atmosphere of artistic theory, a knowledge of the history of art: an artworld."[13] This is not to say that for sport to be art we simply need to put it in a museum. In fact, sporting events such as fencing tournaments are often performed in theaters built for the performing arts. What it does suggest is that the aesthetic value of sport, like art, depends at least partially on the attitude of the spectators and their willingness and ability to view the athletic performance aesthetically—as something set off from the ordinary.

The aesthetic framing of sport and art have been interpreted as a manipulation of time and space contrived specifically to raise awareness of freedom and possibility. Consider the moments leading up to the start of an athletic game or dramatic performance. We experience what Drew Hyland calls "the powerful thematizing, as opposed to the simple presence of the finitude of temporality and spatiality." This heightened awareness, in turn, challenges us to "turn that finitude into possibility."[14] The passage from ordinary life to the extraordinary realm of the aesthetic can be as simple as blowing an opening whistle, or it might involve music, lighting, and rituals such as playing the national anthem. What is important to accomplish is a transformation of the "real world" with its stifling predictability and unrelenting inevitability into a "play world" characterized by possibility and opportunity—what philosophers sometimes call the "sweet tension" of uncertainty so characteristic of sport. The sense of possibility created by this framing might even transcend the game or performance. The opening ceremonies of the Olympic Games seek to create the mindset that the historical anomaly of enduring world peace is somehow within our grasp. By setting sport and art apart from the ordinary, we, in Jean-Paul Sartre's words, "strip the real of its reality,"[15] thereby carving out a mental space where we are open to possibility.

There does seem to be a conflict, however, between aesthetic values and athletic values. Danto's artworld is not the sportworld, and even if one were to evaluate a sporting performance from within the artworld—perhaps by critically reviewing the drama of a game as if it were a tragedy—one would not thereby transform sport into art. The aesthetic value of the athletic maneuvers seems distinct from, and sometimes at odds with, their competitive purpose. Fans may delight in the spectacle of an American football player kicking out his toes as he runs away from a defender, but the player might simply be trying to avoid being tackled from behind. And if the player *is* performing a kind of dance for the audience, he is likely to be chastised in the sportsworld for "showboating" rather than focusing on the game. Some sports even have rules against athletes playing too much to the audience, and all sports by nature penalize athletes who fail to focus on the game. Furthermore, a sports fan interested primarily in the outcome of the game (or perhaps the outcome of his wager) may be insensitive to or even resentful of such artistic flair. We might say, because of this, that the fan lacks artistic sensitivity, but we would hardly say that he fails to appreciate sports.

What are we to say, then, about sports audiences who favor artistic considerations over athletic ones? The Olympic sport of ice dancing is famous for this. At the 1984 Sarajevo Winter Olympic Games, Christopher Dean and Jayne Torvill exploited loopholes in the competition rules to achieve such explicitly artistic goals as mesmerizing the audience, telling an archetypal story, and interpreting the music of Ravel's *Bolero*.[16] In Sarajevo, they won the favor of the crowd and a controversial gold medal. In the 1994 Lillehammer Games, the crowd awarded Torvill and Dean with a longer standing ovation than all other pairs, but the competition judges awarded them only a bronze medal. In this case, the purely aesthetic appreciation of their performance conflicted with competitive practicality as defined by the contest rules. Whatever the artistic value of Torvill and Dean's performance to the audience, its athletic worth was something different. Ice dancing may be both sport and art, but it does not follow that sport and art are the same thing.

On the other hand, sophisticated spectators of sport can find aesthetic value in a specifically competitive context. In this view, a highly experienced and knowledgeable spectator, such as an Olympic judge, is better suited to evaluate the aesthetic value of a performance than audience members who have never competed in and maybe rarely witness the sport. To be sure, the ability to recognize a beautifully executed, strategic play in team sports, like basketball, requires a trained eye and a good understanding of the game. Furthermore, experiencing the full emotional power of something like the decisive goal in the 1980 Olympic hockey semifinal between the United States and the USSR depends on not only the competitive context of that game but also its relation to other famous events in the history of hockey and the Olympic Games.[17] Similar claims can be made about art. For example, full appreciation of a Greek tragedy demands knowledge of history and mythology. Similarly, athletic aesthetics seem to demand sport-specific knowledge. In fact, knowledgeable spectators can take aesthetic pleasure in an efficient though not conventionally beautiful motion precisely because of its competitive value. Olympic champion Michael Johnson, for example, had an unusual but highly effective gait that some compared to the waddling of a duck. Casual spectators deemed it ugly, while true running aficionados found beauty in its genius and economy.

Athletic aesthetics may demand sport-specific knowledge, but it seems too strong to say that it simply reduces to competitive efficiency. As Lesley Wright explains, "We need to be more receptive to aesthetic possibilities, acknowledging that the aesthetic in sport is far ranging, involving an emotional response and not just the recognition of a technically efficient or functionally excellent performance."[18] Sport and art share the play characteristic of being set apart from ordinary life, and they both create aesthetic situations that bring artist (or artifact) and spectator together. Art is sometimes distinguished from sport on the basis of the intellectual engagement of the spectator. According to Karl Groos, this intellectual aspect is what elevates art beyond the merely aesthetic toward the "richer spiritual effect" that is "perceptible only to the higher senses."[19] But intellectual engagement is a property of the spectator, not the object, and it is just as relevant to sport as it is to art. The content of the spectator's knowledge may be different in art and sport, but in both cases, beauty is truly in the mind of the beholder. It is not by applying artistic standards of beauty to sport that we appreciate it aesthetically; rather, it is by appreciating sport within an informed athletic framework that we imbue it with aesthetic and potentially artistic value.

ENDS AND MEANS

The second affinity shared by art and sport is the play characteristic of autotelicity. As Robert Stecker says in his book *Aesthetics and the Philosophy of Art*, "When we value something as aesthetically good, we value it for its own sake or as an end rather than for something else it brings about or as a means."[20] Sport, insofar as it is play, is likewise an end in itself. But some thinkers such as David Best take the inseparability of means and ends to be something that *distinguishes* art from sport. According to Best, "Where art, or more generally the aesthetic is concerned, the distinction between means and end is inapplicable."[21] What he means is that a beautiful touchdown and an ugly one count the same in football, but a beautiful and ugly painting could never have the same artistic worth. There is an end or purpose to sporting movement (i.e., scoring points or winning games) that transcends the manner of achievement. Best admits that "aesthetic sports"—such as gymnastics, diving, and figure skating—resemble the arts "in that their purpose cannot be considered apart from the manner of achieving it."[22] But he concludes that such sports still are not art because "the means never quite reaches the ultimate of complete identification with the end which is such an important distinguishing feature of the concept of art."[23] A poem, for example, may be entered in a contest, but it would be absurd to say that what mattered was whether the poem won and not how it was written. Winning ugly, it seems, has no place in art contests.

On the other hand, the very existence of the phrase "winning ugly" suggests that athletes are at least aware of the aesthetic value of their performances. "A win is a win," they say. That's true of wins *generally speaking*. But a *particular* win, it seems, may be ugly or beautiful—and beauty will add to its worth. Terry Roberts claims, in fact, that Best's means-end distinction between sport and art errs precisely in its equivocation between the general and the particular. Roberts argues that Best is describing sports generally and art particularly, and that when we consider both practices in the same way, the means-end distinction disappears. "Whether the aim, purpose, or meaning of a work of art can be identified independently of the way it is accomplished is not a function of the nature of the an art work itself," says Roberts, "but rather it is a function of the way it is described, particularly or generally."[24] For example, we can describe a soccer goal generally as putting the ball into the goal under certain conditions; likewise, we can describe a song generally as putting musical notes in a certain order according to certain conditions. But if we discuss a particular goal in a particular game or a particular song performed at a particular concert, we will evaluate its aesthetic worth according to the manner in which it was performed. The value of a sporting performance, like an artistic performance, transcends statistical evaluation.

As we saw in the previous section, competitive concerns inform the aesthetic value of sport, but only partially. Particular sport performances, even entire games or seasons, gain aesthetic value from the manner of their execution, their dramatic and historical context, and even the symbolic value projected on to them by spectators. To say that a symbolic sporting moment, such as Bob Beamon's record long jump in the 1968 Olympics, was nothing more than a leap of 29 feet 2 1/2 inches (8.9 meters) would be an impoverished understanding of a rich and meaningful moment. As Terry Roberts says, "Just as we should not let the jaded interest of so-called 'typical' fans determine the place of scoring within the logic of sport, we would not let such generalized, and in that sense trivial, accounts determine the place of meaning within the arts."[25] Sporting actions like shooting a basketball may have an explicit purpose, such as scoring, but that purpose is internal to the game and therefore within the autotelic boundaries of play. Sport is not, like cars and telephones, something made purely to serve external ends.[26] Like art, it is an end in itself and even the often-criticized goal of winning is nothing more than an internal part of the game.

The instrumental use of art and sport, furthermore, seems independent from their autotelicity. The payment earned by a musician does not prevent his performance from being art; likewise, the buying and selling of an athletic performance does not (necessarily) prevent it from being sport. The fact that an athlete or artist is paid does not imply that they perform solely for the money. Even if they are motivated to perform by the promise of earnings, the performance itself can still be autotelic. The presence of external motivations does not necessitate the absence of internal ones. People can and clearly do act out of complex motivations. As Christopher Cordner observes, "In both spheres an indefinitely wide range of motives is operative. An artist, like a sports player, may be moved by the desire to be the best in a given field, to make something perfect, to earn fame and fortune, to please an audience, or *épater le bourgeois*. Or he/she may just love painting or writing or running or baseball."[27] There is nothing that prevents a professional musician from performing out of simultaneous desires for money, fame, beauty, social commentary, and sheer unadulterated joy. Likewise, there is nothing that prevents a professional athlete from performing for the same complex of reasons. Professional basketball player Bill Bradley claims that he often played for the "pure pleasure" of it, sometimes forgetting the score, even in important games.[28]

What threatens aesthetic values is not so much the use of sport or art for external ends but rather its exploitation: the selling out of a practice's internal values in order to pursue external ends. It is one thing to be paid or patronized as an actor, musician, or artist and another thing to tailor one's art specifically to the market's or patron's interests. The boxer who intentionally loses a match in order to gain gambling revenue is exploiting his sport because he sacrifices the internal demand that he try to win for the external goal of revenue. The boxer who receives a monetary prize for winning makes no such sacrifice. The boxer who "takes a dive" is furthermore subject to moral condemnation; he has immorally exploited his sport by violating its internal requirements. His action is characterized as "an ugly thing to do," and he himself is likely to be disgusted by the prospect of performing it. The difference between use and exploitation is a moral one, and our reaction to it suggests that morality does have an effect on aesthetic value—in sport as well as art.

Stephen Mumford uses Diego Maradona's "hand of god" goal (which was later revealed to be an illegal handball) and Ben Johnson's steroid-fueled 100-meter race at the 1988 Seoul Olympics to illustrate the connection between moral and aesthetic value. However beautiful these things may have been to witness at the time, their beauty is diminished—and perhaps turned to disgust—by the discovery of their (im)moral context. Mumford compares these with Leni Riefensthal's famous film *Olympia*, which was visually stunning and inaugurated a variety of creative cinematographic techniques but ultimately celebrated dubious Nazi principles and supported their immoral regime. According to Mumford, the aesthetic value of the film, like the sports examples, is diminished by its moral context. [29] To some, the sport example will seem to involve more aesthetic diminishment than the art one. To others, neither example will seem aesthetically diminished by its moral context. But the difference will not depend on whether we make a moral distinction between ends and means so much as on whether we make a conceptual connection between beauty and morality.

ART AND SPORT TRANSCENDING PLAY

It was noted above by Karl Groos that the moral connection is what elevates art (and sport) above the realm of mere play. One form of this elevation is just putting such practices into the service of social and humanistic ends, especially education. The ancient Greek use of sport for education pivoted upon a strong conceptual connection between beauty and morality. *Kalokagathia*, which combines the ideals of beauty and goodness, was the driving force of not only Greek athletic art but also the gymnastic education that aimed to cultivate both simultaneously. Plato's Academy is perhaps the most famous example of such gymnasia. In the context of Plato's philosophy, the ideal or "form" of the good is closely connected with that of beauty. In *Hippias Major*, for example, Plato says, "Then if beauty is the cause of goodness, the good comes into being through beauty. That is why we fervently pursue thinking and all other beautiful things—because their offspring, the good, is worthy of our zeal. Based on what we are discovering, the beautiful is a kind of father to the good." [30] It is the understanding of these forms of goodness and beauty that both results in and is cultivated by performing beautiful bodily movements. Dancing, in particular, requires aesthetic as well as athletic sensibilities, and it employs such moral virtues as courage and self-control. By performing visually beautiful and controlled movements in Plato's Academy, students were prepared to perform morally beautiful and controlled actions in their civic lives.[31]

The roles of art and sport in education are less well defined today, but it seems at least possible that they might inform moral education. Immanuel Kant valued fine art because it seeks to engage our higher cognitive powers. An artist, according to Cordner, "seeks to produce something for contemplation."[32] Adds Best, "It is distinctive of any art form that its conventions allow for the possibility of the expression of a conception of life situations."[33] And though some find it difficult to imagine an athlete designing his performance to express his conception of contemporary moral, social, and political problems,[34] sports can and often do inspire such contemplation among knowledgeable spectators. In fact, athletics have been used to express conceptions of virtue and morality since their discernible origins in ancient Egypt and Mesopotamia, and the ancient Greek contests at the root of modern sport were explicitly tied to moral ideals.[35] As we saw in chapter 1, the athletic displays of kings and pharaohs weren't contests at all but performances intentionally designed to convey political messages about leaders' moral worthiness and divine favor. Athletics always have and still do "enact or realize life-values," says Cordner, and this is a quality they share with art.[36]

Moreover, great artists and athletes attract us for the same reason: "The distinctiveness of their genius."[37] Whether they intend it to be so or not, athletes' performances can be objects of intellectual contemplation and social criticism. Nadia Comaneci's "perfect 10" performance on the uneven parallel bars at the 1976 Olympic Games inspired people to contemplate the possibility of human perfection. Meanwhile, Hassiba Boulmerka's performance at the 1992 Olympic Games inspired social commentary on attitudes toward females and female bodies in conservative Islamic countries.[38] To say that these performances are not worthy of such contemplation because they were not intended by the athletes to be so is to call a great many objects of inspiration and contemplation unworthy. At the same time, to call them worthy of contemplation is to put them on a level with art without insisting that they are art. Art and sport share the ability to open our minds to possibility.[39] At the same time, intellectual contemplation of them engages the higher cognitive faculties capable of reflecting on such important conceptions as beauty and goodness.

For those who believe that beauty in sport is confined to the beauty of athletes' bodies, or perhaps the grace of their movement, it is worth recalling that Greece's ancient athletic stadiums and gymnasia (like ancient theaters) were located in notoriously beautiful natural environments. Aristophanes likens Plato's Academy to a paradise: "You shall descend to the Academy and run races beneath the sacred olives along with some modest compeer, crowned with white reeds, redolent of yew, and careless ease, of leaf-shedding white poplar, rejoicing in the season of spring, when the plane-tree whispers to the elm."[40] The uncommon natural beauty of athletic settings such as Olympia, Nemea, and Delphi can be appreciated even today. What we have lost is the idea that immersion in beauty leads to an aesthetic appreciation of goodness and perhaps even the ability to develop aesthetic sensitivity as part of a good moral education—an education aimed at *kalokagathia*. The beauty of the ancient Greek athletic form represents such moral virtues as self-control, such religious virtues as humility, and such civic virtues as liberty. In this sense, the athlete's body is his or her own work of art. According to Fisher, "Athletes are artists both in so far as they perfect their own bodies, but also the forms of their game."[41] Cordner identifies grace as "a total harmony of being," located in the person and not just her movement and ultimately linked to the moral realm.[42] What is more, athletic grace for Cordner is not just a matter of physical movement but also a manifestation of how the athletic aesthetic of grace is linked ultimately to the moral realm. As in the Platonic idea of *kalokagathia*, one cannot strive for true beauty without also striving for goodness. Just as the birth of a child or the donation of organs is considered a morally beautiful act regardless of its visual repugnancy, virtue adds value to athletic victory, and beauty to the athletic form. Though also present in art, the link between moral and aesthetic value is especially strong in sport.

All of this brings us back to our *Discus Thrower* and his enduring artistic value. The statue can be seen as the legitimate offspring of art and sport, two activities that are not identical but nevertheless share the common ancestor of play and manifest many of its genetic characteristics. They are metaphysically intermediate between the ideal and real, the formal and the material, and the universal and particular, and are therefore capable of expressing as well as representing beauty. They can both be appreciated aesthetically—simply as a form of pleasure or, when understood in their dramatic and historical contexts, as forms of symbolic meaning. They are both, at least ideally, autotelic—in need of no justification beyond themselves. Although diving gives style points and swimming doesn't, beauty can and ought to be valued in them both. And while both sport and art can be used for external ends, it is their intrinsic moral worth that informs their aesthetic value. Finally, the educational value of sport and art demands the same engagement of higher cognitive powers needed to understand their moral dimension and to appreciate their aesthetic beauty. Not just performances, but also the athletes themselves, can and ought to be appreciated as objects of intellectual and even ethical contemplation. This is, after all, the Hellenic heritage of modern sport and the genetic destiny it shares with art, as a legitimate and beautiful offspring of play.

DISCUSSION QUESTIONS

1. Compare your experience playing sports with your experience creating art. How are the experiences similar? How different?
2. Imagine a "beautiful play" in your favorite sport. How much of its beauty depends on an understanding of the competitive purpose of the game? Would a person unfamiliar with sport see the same beauty?
3. Does finding out that an athlete did something immoral diminish your aesthetic appreciation of their feat? For example, do Marion Jones's Olympic performances seem less beautiful because she later admitted to doping?
4. Moral goodness is said to make art and athletes more beautiful. Does this also go for romance? Is a person made more attractive by their moral qualities?

Chapter Seven

Mind and Body

The downhill skier's eyes are closed, and she seems completely detached from reality. The television camera zooms in close as she twists her body and curves her hands, while she races down a course that exists only in her mind. What exactly is going on in this moment, and how does it relate to the metaphysics of sport? We might say simply that the skier's visualization technique is an invention of sport psychology—a way to habituate the mind to the challenge that lies ahead and a means of building confidence, overcoming fear, and improving physical performance. But buried within our answer are metaphysical assumptions about the nature of the athlete and athletic performance that have far-reaching consequences for the practice of sport. Most notably, the language we use to describe the training technique breaks the athlete up into separate parts: a part that thinks, a part that feels, and a part that actually skis. With no more than a moment's reflection, however, we realize that all three parts must be involved in the skiing, otherwise why involve them all in training? It must be an accident of linguistic convention that we use terms like "physical performance" and "physical education"—we know these things involve more than physical matter, more than the body, or do we?

The metaphysical nature of athletes, which is to say, the nature of persons, is infrequently discussed in the philosophy of sport literature. Our experience of ourselves as athletes, meanwhile, frequently seems at odds with traditional explanations of the nature of persons, which often differ significantly according to culture and even gender. The metaphysical question "What am I?" is intimately connected to the personal identity question "Who am I?" And the way that we approach and eventually answer these questions has profound implications not just for athletes' experiences in sport but also for such enduring issues as the role of sport in education, the impact of gender on sport participation, eating disorders, the use of drugs and genetic technologies, and even the enduring myth of the dumb jock. In short, our metaphysical understanding of athletes has as big an influence on sporting practice as our metaphysical understanding of sport itself. At a minimum, we should seek to understand the variety of metaphysical conceptions of persons and their potential influence on the practice of sport. The purpose of this chapter is not to promote a particular metaphysical account but rather to inspire and enrich philosophical discussion and thereby to improve our understanding not just of athletes but also of sport as an enduring human practice.

Philosophical theories of persons in both Eastern and Western traditions usually center on the relationship between mind and body. Human experience, almost universally, takes note of these two aspects of personhood. How human beings understand them, however, is anything but universal. If we project the two concepts onto the dichotomy between material and nonmaterial existence, three possibilities emerge: both mind and body are nonmaterial (idealism), both are material (physicalism), or one is material while the other is nonmaterial (dualism). The fourth possibility, that each has both material and nonmaterial aspects or qualities, is rarely discussed in the Western philosophical tradition, but is assumed in the Eastern tradition, or, to be more precise, a strict dichotomy between material and nonmaterial existence does not condition the traditional Eastern view. Meanwhile, a later Western approach called phenomenology leaves the dichotomy to one side, focusing rather on our experience as human beings in which we are always both mind and body or, to use the technical term, embodied. Metaphysical theories about persons are almost as varied and old as philosophy itself.

THE WESTERN DUALIST HERITAGE

Western philosophy debated the metaphysical nature of human beings almost from the start. There was general acceptance of the material nature of the body (*sōma*), but opinions differed about the *psychē*—a word conventionally translated as mind or soul but understood also as the source of bodily appetites and movement. Some of the earliest philosophers, known collectively as the "pre-Socratics," were physicalists. Democritus, for example, theorized that everything was made of atoms (Greek for "uncuttables"), material particles assembled into objects that could be broken down and reformed into new entities like so many interchangeable Lego blocks. Early physicalists did not necessarily deny the existence of gods and minds. They simply understood those things to be particular configurations of matter. Perhaps this was not so much of a stretch for them, given the anthropomorphic understanding of most ancient gods. The belief that gods and souls were immaterial proved more popular over time, however. Part of the appeal may have come from Pythagoras's theory that human souls were not only immaterial but also immortal and therefore capable of transmigrating from one body to another—even to other species.

At this early stage in Western philosophy, theories of mind-body dualism did not seem to denigrate sport. On the contrary, Pythagorean athletes were famously successful at the Olympic Games. They included the great runner Astylos, winner of three Olympic *stade* (200-meter sprint) races, and the imposing wrestler Milo, who prevailed at Olympia six times in a twenty-four-year span. Plato compliments Ikkos of Taranto, a Pythagorean runner and coach known for his chastity and self-discipline.[1] Plato appears to have embraced Pythagoras's understanding of mind-body dualism as well as his enthusiasm for athletics. In *Republic*, gymnastics are advocated primarily as training for the soul and not for the body,[2] and in the dialogue's concluding "Myth of Er," the soul of the athletic female Atalanta is depicted as choosing a male body for her next incarnation, because she is attracted by the honors afforded to champion athletes.[3] In the *Laws*, gymnastic education and athletic festivals are part and parcel of communitywide education, for males and females focused on *aretē*, something Plato believed to depend on the *psychē*. And in real life, when Plato set up his school in a gymnasium called the Academy, there is no evidence that he discouraged or even deemphasized the athletic activities traditionally associated with that place.

Unfortunately for sport, however, it was Plato's *Phaedo* that had the biggest influence on Western attitudes toward the mind and the body. *Phaedo* depicts Socrates just before his execution trying to console his distraught friends with the notion that his mind/soul (*psychē*) will endure and even prosper after death. He argues that the *psychē* must be immaterial, and therefore indestructible, because it is the organ that perceives perfect ideas—that is, the Platonic "forms"—which are themselves the unchanging immaterial prototypes of which all material things are imperfect copies.[4] In fact, Socrates argues, the mind/soul's affinity with the forms makes the body a distraction or even impediment to understanding them. The body acts like a prison that the *psychē* must escape if truth is to be known.[5] This argument meshed well with the Western religious traditions of Judaism, Christianity, and Islam—all of which recommend spiritual and intellectual paths for coming to know God. The corollary idea that the body is a "prison" or at least hindrance to spiritual and intellectual development can be seen in the religious emphasis on the afterlife and in these religions' attempts to transcend and sometimes even denigrate the body.

It was the radical substance dualism of René Descartes, however, that had the biggest influence on modern Western ideas about the metaphysics of persons. It was not so much Descartes's distinction between body and mind that challenged sport, as the Greeks had accepted dualism while promoting athletics. It was rather the identification of our human essence as *thinking* (understood narrowly as rational cognition) that hung athletics out to dry. The Greek *psychē* had been a much richer and complex concept than Descartes's mind, not least because of its intimate connection to the body. This should not be a surprise. Descartes was a rationalist in search of one logically indubitable proposition when he arrived at his famous cogito: "I think, therefore I am."[6] Since the information available to him about the external world, including his body, was always filtered through the senses, which were unreliable, knowledge was possible only through reason. He calculated that, as long as he was thinking, it must also be true that he exists. Since Descartes's theory identified thinking as the most—indeed the only—certain thing about human existence, he declared us to be essentially "thinking things." It was a declaration different from Aristotle's classification of humans as "rational animals"; in that case, we are corporeal, distinguished from other animals by our capacity for reason. In Descartes's view, we are essentially incorporeal minds, and our bodies are just another doubtful feature of a world to which we lack certain access.

This dualistic legacy has profoundly affected the way we think and talk in the West about human beings generally and sport more specifically. Our minds are characterized as knowing subjects that move passive, corporeal bodies. Our bodies are compared to irrational animals or, worse, unthinking machines. Juvenal's Roman-era saying "*mens sana in corpore sano*" (sound mind in sound body) has been interpreted in modern times as a Hellenic approach to a balanced education, but Juvenal wasn't talking about sport or athletics at all—just mental and physical health.[7] The very idea that we need a balance between mental and physical education assumes that body and mind are educated separately—an idea that follows from a metaphysical understanding of the mind as essentially a thinking thing detached from the body, and by the understanding of physical movement as somehow independent from thinking.

THE CHALLENGE OF THE BODY

When Paul Weiss wrote the first major philosophical work dedicated to sport, he brought the Western dualistic heritage with him. The body, as he described it, presented "a challenge" to be overcome at least partially through the medium of sport. Weiss begins by arguing that the body needs to be considered as much a part of the human being as the mind, but the very fact that he needs to argue this point shows the force of the dualistic heritage. "Only a man intoxicated with a Cartesian, or similar, idea that he is to be identified with his mind will deny that he is a body too," says Weiss.[8] He goes on to endorse the holistic philosophy of Maurice Merleau-Ponty (discussed below) and to discredit physicalists with the quip "since they have at least mind enough to think there is nothing more than a body, I have no mind to follow them."[9] Weiss does not deny the primacy of intellectual activity in human life, and (following Aristotle) he believes that the "full use" of either mind or body precludes the "full use" of the other at any given time. Nevertheless, believing that both should be cultivated, he says, "A career devoted to one alone is possible to only half a man."[10]

Weiss sees athletics as a way to unify mind and body. Sport and art require controlled expression of the emotions, which he understands to be the intermediaries between minds and bodies. He says these activities "offer excellent agencies for unifying men" by "making it possible for minds and bodies to be harmonized clearly and intensely."[11] Weiss explains the process using the mathematical concept of a vector—a quantity having direction and magnitude. He envisions the mind as providing a vector, that is, a future direction, for the body. Through training, a "man uses his mind to dictate what his body is to do," and the body slowly adapts to the desired vector thereby "correcting the disequilibrium between mind and body."[12]

Weiss's use of masculine pronouns here is not gender neutral. He believes that sports are more amenable to males because "the young woman's body does not challenge her the way in which the young man's body challenges him. She does not face it as something to be conquered, since she has already conquered it in the course of her coming of age."[13] Weiss has been criticized for writing a book about sport without having been an athlete (something he admits at the outset of the book). We might add that he also lacks the experience of having been female. And, as we shall see, this lack of experience could be one reason his philosophy of sport preserves such a strong dualism. Nevertheless, Weiss turns the philosophical tide against the dismissal and denigration of the body and grants it newfound importance in the understanding of human nature.

Forty years after Weiss's book, his dualistic theory of mind and body in sport was revived and revised by Daniel Dombrowski in *Contemporary Athletics and Ancient Greek Ideals*. Dombrowski rejects most of Weiss's claims about women and athletics as defective. He compares them dialectically with the views of philosophers such as Jane English, who do have the relevant experience.[14] He then injects Weiss's semi-Cartesian dualism with the ancient Greek concepts of *dunamis* (power) and hylomorphism to transform Weiss's characterization of athletics as the pursuit of bodily excellence into a more holistic, but still dualist, idea of athletics simply as the pursuit of excellence (*aretē*).

Weiss had theorized that athletics gave men the opportunity to become excellent in something they could actually master at a young age.[15] This set the stage for the pursuit of excellence in other activities later on. Dombrowski also recognizes this educational function as essential to sport's social value: "If we do not take it to be our main task to have athletes become excellent," he says, "we come to treat them as workers or appendages."[16] But if we understand human beings metaphysically as hylomorphs—from the Greek *hyle* (matter) and *morphē* (the form or structure given to matter by the mind)—and we understand *aretē* (excellence) as a *dunamis* (power), we can value the cultivation of athletic excellence as education for virtues transferable to activities beyond sport. Dombrowski calls this process "dynamic hylomorphism."[17] Western dualism applied to sport, then, need not exclude the mind or denigrate the body as some religious and Cartesian doctrines imply. In fact, the transfer of virtues cultivated in sport to nonathletic activities seems to require a close link between mind and body.

IDEALISM AND PHYSICALISM

Just as Cartesian dualism found its critics within philosophy of sport, it was challenged within mainstream philosophy as well—first by the empiricists, who held (in opposition to rationalists like Descartes) that all knowledge comes to us through the senses. Empiricists such as George Berkeley shared Descartes's concerns about our senses' ability to deceive and began to question the independent existence of matter itself. If a tree falls in the woods and no one is there to hear it, suggests Berkeley, not only does it not make a sound, but also it might not even exist.[18] Berkeley's theory that only ideas exist is called idealism, and it implies not only that people are essentially immaterial thinking things but also that people are deity dependent—they are ideas in the mind of god. Such strong idealism was embraced by relatively few, but the notion of human beings bereft of material existence led to a focus on immediate experience as the true source of identity. David Hume argued that we are nothing more than a "bundle of impressions" as if our existence amounted to nothing more than a stack of mental photographs tied together with a temporal string.[19] Physical bodies seemed to have no role at all in the modern debate about the nature of human beings.

If the discussion takes place among physicalists, however, human beings are understood as nothing more than bodies, or at least nothing more than physical matter. The term "physicalism" (as opposed to materialism) also betrays a link with the late nineteenth- and early twentieth-century rise of physical sciences. Since such sciences are not equipped to measure immaterial entities, the motivation to deny those entities' existence was enhanced. Indeed, the ancient Greek and Roman Epicurean philosophers were also physicalists, and they devoted much of their studies to natural phenomena in order to liberate themselves from the fear and anxiety caused by mysterious beliefs about immaterial gods and other supernatural forces. Modern physicalists, in general, do not deny the existence of entities like minds, thoughts, or emotions; they simply believe that such phenomena depend or "supervene" upon physical phenomena such as brains, firing neurons, and chemical reactions. As with dualism, there is nothing intrinsic to physicalism that is incompatible with sport, but there is an accompanying attitude that affects the way we view sport.

The attitude toward sport and humanity characteristic of physicalism is an emphasis on the body and a narrowly physiological approach to training. I once had a cycling coach who used to select athletes based on physical data such as watt generation and oxygen uptake; he wasn't interested in past racing results. Such body focus has its own philosophical tradition. In reaction to what he saw as religion's overemphasis on souls and the afterlife, Friedrich Nietzsche denigrates the "despisers of the body" and has his character Zarathustra declare, "Body am I and nothing else; and soul is only a word for something about the body."[20] Physicalism within the realm of sport, however, is usually a response to scientific observation rather than religious doctrine. Empirical science has already learned so much about the structure and behavior of physical organisms that a purely physiological explanation for everything attributed to the human mind seems inevitable.

Attempts to reproduce human intelligence in computers, however, have revealed, as much as anything, how complex the human mind actually is. Thinking—narrowly understood as calculation, recall, and organization of ideas—is quite easily reproduced by machines. But our experiences of so-called qualia—things like sound, color, or smells—are difficult to duplicate in machines, because machines lack consciousness. To be sure, a radio can decode music, an electric eye can detect color, and an alarm can be tripped by the presence of smoke, but these objects do not experience what we experience mentally in the presence of the same phenomena. This suggests that our minds are more than machines, or at least that human brains are importantly different from machines.

But what about our bodies? In comparison with human minds, our bodies seem relatively simple and predictable—maybe more so even than some modern electronic machines. Within sport there is a culture of treating one's body as a machine—sometimes even an expendable machine—one that can be repaired if broken and, once worn-out, can be discarded. Athletes are described and think of themselves in terms of numerical specifications: height, weight, body-fat percentage, squat kilograms, 40-meter time, VO^2 max, batting average, and win-loss record. Training is approached scientifically, like the calculated tuning of a high-tech machine—efforts are measured and monitored with sophisticated sensors and then the numbers are crunched by computers to reveal every possible advantage. Chemical and even genetic manipulation are not excluded; the body is a specimen, the site of an experiment, aimed at discovering and even transcending human capabilities. In his book *Mortal Engines*, John Hoberman identifies the nineteenth-century development of ergometers, devices that quantify athletic performance, as the dawn of an era that would come to view athletes themselves as machines.[21] To be sure that era has not yet come to a close.

KINAESTHETIC INTELLIGENCE

Paradoxically, physicalism's scientific orientation, when applied to sport, separates the body more radically from the mind even as it grants both equal ontological status. That is to say, it not only regards movement as somehow a self-contained function of the body but also views thinking as somehow a self-contained function of the mind-brain that has little or nothing to do with the rest of the body. In fact, the dumb-jock myth has thrived under physicalist hegemony. Now that superior scientific brains can take charge of training and preparation, an athlete's own mind is allocated a diminished role in his or her performance. Even decisions of tactics and strategy within a contest are now often radioed to the athletes from coaches on the sidelines. Of course, as long as athletes' minds are neglected in their training, the dumb-jock theory turns from a myth into a self-fulfilling prophecy. At the same time though, athletes' minds may find new ways to express themselves. Scientific and strategic thinking are not the only forms of human intelligence. As R. Scott Kretchmar points out in *Practical Philosophy of Sport*, intelligent qualities such as creativity, inventiveness, and insightfulness can be expressed in athletic performance.[22] There is no reason to think of rhetoric, mathematics, poetry, painting, and music as legitimate modes of expressing intelligence while excluding athletic movement.

Maxine Sheets-Johnstone takes the connection between human bodies and intelligence even further. She claims that human rationality itself has its origin in the body's movement—that is, in kinaesthetic ways of learning and knowing. In a special issue of the *Journal of the Philosophy of Sport*, Sheets-Johnstone uses the scientific approach of evolutionary biology to argue against the mind-body dichotomy at virtually every level.[23] She argues, first of all, that all human beings begin our lives in infancy by learning about our bodies and our world, or more specifically, how to move our bodies within our world. "Our first sense of ourselves," she says, "is as tactile-kinaesthetic bodies."[24] Furthermore, this is a universal experience for human beings that generates certain body-anchored common understandings that transcend cultural differences. What we call rationality—that quality Aristotle used to distinguish humans from other animals—turns out to be anchored in this kinaesthetic making sense of the world that we undergo as infants. To deny this, Sheets-Johnstone concludes, is to be "so wedded to culture that we deny the common nature that binds us in a common humanity."[25] She concludes that reason, the characteristic so tightly identified with the human mind as to be its essence, originates in and depends upon a "bodily logos."[26] Physicalism, then, while endorsing a more scientific approach to sport and granting ontological identity to mind and body, does little to heal the conceptual mind-body split. Even scientists must give up the assumption that minds and bodies are radically different in order to understand their cooperative role in human existence.

HOLISM AND EASTERN IDEALS

Regardless of the metaphysical makeup of the human mind and body, it is clear that the conceptual separation of the two has been the real source of problems for philosophy of sport—at least in the West. The Eastern philosophical tradition asserts no such essential separation between mind and body, or between subject and object.[27] The entire approach is more holistic— a focus on the connections between things rather than an analysis of their differences. In the words of the Chinese philosopher Zhuangzi, "Heaven and earth were born when I was born; the ten thousand things and I among them are but one thing."[28] In Eastern philosophy, knowledge of truth is often understood as a psychophysical awareness that transcends mere intellection; in this way, it connects the practical and theoretical, thereby healing any illusions of a mind-body split.[29] At the same time, Eastern philosophy does not take mind-body unity (or human-cosmos unity) to be given as metaphysical fact; rather, it regards these as an achievement—a form of wisdom that is, itself, cultivated and expressed through bodily movement. This achievement of mind-body unity is among the express purposes of martial arts training.

As with Greek, the Chinese terms for mind and body do not line up cleanly with the corresponding modern Western concepts. As Chung-Ying Cheng explains, the Chinese term *ti* represents human corporeality at its most basic level, but it understands the body in terms of systems, functions, and vital spirit rather than inert matter or substance. "It may be said that by virtue of the form of the physical body, *ti* realizes its living spirit and vitality, and by virtue of the living spirit and vitality, the physical body maintains its organic unity and organization."[30] Whereas Westerners tend to think of the body mechanically, in terms of muscles and levers, Easterners tend to focus on the internal flow of blood (*xue*) and energy (*qi*).[31] Meanwhile, the Chinese *xin* is usually translated as "heart-mind," not only because it is responsible for both cognitive and affective states, but also because it is thought to be located in the middle of the body, rather than the head.[32] In addition, there is no clear Chinese counterpart to the Western faculty of reason that acquires pieces of truth through logic or apprehension. Knowledge is something closer to wisdom or understanding, an achievement that represents harmony both within oneself and with one's world. A wise person not only recognizes the interconnectedness of everything but also lives, acts, and moves accordingly. This achievement is called *de*—a kind of virtue very similar to the Greek *aretē*, and linked explicitly, like its Hellenic counterpart, with action and movement.

It is inconceivable from an Eastern point of view that human virtue (*de*) could exist without embodiment. As Cheng explains, "Virtue is not a matter of abstract understanding, but a matter of embodiment of a value in life practice and a matter of forming one's personality and spirit. It is in terms of the bodily and actual practice that knowledge can be said to be genuine."[33] As a result, the cultivation of *de* is fundamentally linked with physical action. In Confucianism, the performance of ritual (*li*) habituates body and mind together toward the proper orientation toward the world.[34] Meanwhile, martial arts such as wushu, chi-gong, tai chi, bushido, and the more familiar karate and judo are traditionally directed toward the explicit goal of cultivating *de*, a process that includes not just disciplined movement but also the development of insight about the universe and one's connection to it (more on this in chapter 10).[35] Eastern thinkers often criticize Western sports, at least in their modern practice, for lacking any such effort. Charges Yasuo Yuasa, "Training in [Western] sports aims at developing the body's capacity, or more specifically, the motor capacity of the muscles in the four limbs, and does not include the spiritual meaning or training of the mind's capacity."[36] Is this a fair charge?

WESTERN SPORTS AND PHENOMENOLOGY

To be sure, metaphysical assumptions about the nature of athletes, particularly the mind-body relationship, condition how sports are practiced and interpreted. It is not a lock-step connection, however. Eastern martial arts can be—and often are—practiced according to the Western focus on physical domination and victory, rather than the Eastern emphasis on yielding and enlightenment. This philosophical contrast was illustrated by the popular *Karate Kid* movies, in which a traditionally trained youth is set against bullies who abuse martial arts techniques. In reality, athletes can—and often do—approach their Western sports with a holistic attitude toward mind and body. Indeed, the *experience* of sport, in its Eastern and Western forms, seems to lend itself to the holistic approach. American philosopher and former collegiate basketball player Drew Hyland is a good example. "As I move toward the basket, see my teammate cut, and throw him a pass," Hyland asks, "am I 'thinking' or 'physically acting'? The only sensible answer seems to be both, together, as one."[37] Another American basketball player, later a famous coach, has effectively applied the principles of Eastern philosophy to his sport. In *Sacred Hoops*, Phil Jackson identifies the secret of basketball success as "not thinking."[38]

One need not embrace Eastern philosophy in order to approach sport holistically. Hyland points to the holism embraced by the twentieth-century Western philosophical movement known as phenomenology. After Immanuel Kant identified as insurmountable the gulf between our experience of things (phenomena) and things as they are in themselves (noumena)—another distinction absent from Eastern philosophy—phenomenology responded by focusing only on phenomena. And in athletic experience, humans experience themselves as both mind and body. The French philosopher Maurice Merleau-Ponty challenged Descartes's characterization of the "I" as a disembodied "thinking thing" by declaring, "I am my body." He explains that the "experience of one's own body runs counter to the reflective procedure which detaches subject and object from each other, and which gives us only the thought about the body, or the body as an idea, and not the experience of the body or the body in reality."[39] Hyland observes that this phenomenological holism better reflects the experience of skilled athletes than struggling beginners, concluding that "the lived body unity is a superior achievement, something for which we should strive as the explicit overcoming of the mind/body dualism which we often experience as alienating."[40] Athletics is the striving of whole persons to actualize their wholeness.

Another incongruity between athletic experience and the Cartesian heritage of mind-body separation is the notion that sports performance is a result of conscious cognitive calculation. The difference may be illustrated by contrasting the strict regimentation of a sport like American football—where plays are carefully scripted, called, and executed—with the more intuitive flow of a game like soccer, also a Western sport, but one with more universal appeal. Yuasa blames the calculating approach to sport on Western mind-body dualism and its assumption that training proceeds from mind to body. "Contrary to this order," he says, "the tradition of Eastern self-cultivation places importance on entering the mind from the body or form. That is, it attempts to train the mind by training the body."[41] Yuasa admits that certain Western athletic values, such as perseverance in training, may have the effect of spiritual training, but only if we consciously embrace that objective and cease to view sport merely in terms of health and leisure.[42] Central to this change in attitude is an understanding that the human mind "is not simply consciousness nor is it constant and unchangeable, but rather it is that which is transformed through training the body."[43]

So the metaphysical understanding of athletes, that is to say, of persons, especially in relation to the nature of their minds and bodies, is a crucial issue in the metaphysics of sport primarily because it affects our attitude toward sport and the people who practice it. The Western heritage of mind-body dualism drifted from a complex idea of hylomorphism toward a narrow understanding of the mind as purely rational and the body as mechanically physical. This attitude has had profound effects on sport, including the separation of mental and physical education, a disconnection between sport and spirituality, and an emphasis on the scientific production of performance that tends to view athletes as body-objects rather than persons. The paucity of sporting opportunities for females, the disabled, and even able but physically inferior males can be traced to this attitude, as can the myth of the dumb jock and athletes' own obsession with their physical performance—a preoccupation that can lead to such ills as drug abuse and eating disorders.

I have heard it argued that traditional Eastern sports are free from all these problems because their philosophical heritage unites body and mind and links athletic training explicitly to the cultivation of spiritual virtue. We will explore this charge further in chapter 10. Globalization affects sport as well as economies, however, and neither Asian athletes nor traditional martial arts are immune from the problems of modern sport. It is much easier for individuals to change their philosophical orientations than entire cultures or practice communities. Individual athletes and coaches can adopt an attitude and approach to sport that rejects a strong Cartesian dualism and adopts a constructive holism. Metaphysical holism has roots in both Eastern and Western tradition and can be applied to Eastern and Western sports by both Eastern and Western athletes.

DISCUSSION QUESTIONS

1. Imagine an athletic action, such as a golfer hitting a drive. Would you say the mind is simply controlling the body here, or is the body also informing the mind?
2. Physicalism leads to a focus on measurable statistics, like size, speed, or on-base percentage. Since Billy Beane's success with the Oakland A's (depicted in the book and movie *Moneyball*), statistical analysis has also become very popular in sports management. Do you think something in sport is lost by looking at athletes primarily in terms of numbers?
3. The "dumb jock" myth is said to be a consequence of both dualism and physicalism. Do you think this myth still exists? Do you think the

intellectual parts of sport (i.e., training theory, game strategy, and play calling) should be taken away from the athletes?

4. Based on your experiences with martial arts, or maybe just movies about them like *The Karate Kid*, would you say there are important differences between Western and Eastern sports in attitudes toward the body and mind?

III

Ethical Issues in Sport

Looking at sports today, a cynic might conclude that the phrase "sports ethics" must be an oxymoron. Ethics may be defined as the moral expectations of a civil society, but sport is often viewed as something separate from civil society—an escape from socially imposed restrictions that prevent us from expressing our authentic selves. Spectators cheer fights at hockey games, media outlets replay "highlights" of violent hits in American football, and soccer players intentionally deceive referees by strategically faking injury.

One gets the feeling that sports ethics, whatever they are, must somehow be separate from the moral conventions of society—some of the actions performed in a boxing match, for example, would be illegal if performed outside the ring in the very same place. Furthermore, actions like doping may be widespread and accepted within a particular sport's culture but lead nevertheless to civil prosecution, as the cases of Barry Bonds and Marion Jones have shown. So, sports ethics is not identical to social ethics, but neither can it be completely independent. We might accept deception in baseball while condemning it in government, but that doesn't mean that there need be no moral agreement between sports and society. On the contrary, sports ethics can demand more universality than social ethics. The international nature of Olympic sports requires ethical standards that can apply across vast social and cultural differences. You simply cannot play a water polo game without some agreement as to how players ought and ought not to behave.

The study of sports ethics reflects a central tension in ethical theory more generally: ethics are in some sense conditioned by individual social and cultural beliefs, but they also need some common ground from which to stage meaningful debate about the moral acceptability of individual behavior. If moral relativism is the case and ethics simply collapses to each particular group's conventions—or perhaps any individual's moral opinion, it is hard to see how a community might condemn even the most horrifying actions, such as murdering an opponent in order to win. On the other hand, if sports ethics depends on a particular cultural ethos, say the nineteenth-century English gentleman's idea of amateurism, how can morality they be anything other than a tool for cultural hegemony? Finally, does a community's acceptance of an action make it morally right? Doping seems to be widespread and accepted among athletes in certain sports; is it therefore morally justified in those sports?

Our study of sports ethics is not designed to find definitive answers to these and other ethical questions surrounding sport. Its purpose is to develop skills in moral reasoning and to understand the theories and principles used in that science. We will consider a variety of ethical issues in sport, such as doping, cheating, violence, and commercialism, and we will use a variety of traditional ethical theories such as utilitarianism, deontology, virtue ethics, and even moral aesthetics. But what will make our project specifically one of sports ethics is that we will be looking back to the metaphysical issues we discussed in the first section and trying to discern their moral implications for sport. We will contrast the metaphysical ideal of play with a win-at-all-costs attitude; we will consider the issue of cheating in light of the role that rules play in the construction of games; we will explore the connection between virtues and social practices while considering sport's apparent encouragement of vices like deception and violence; and finally, we will examine the relationship between sport and art in light of ethical issues derived from the use of sports as commercial entertainment. Sports ethics are detached from neither social ethics nor mainstream moral theory and reasoning, but they are at least conditioned by the metaphysical nature of sport, and it is in this context that we shall explore them.

Chapter Eight

Consequentialism and Play

Barry Bonds, by almost any measure, is one of the best athletes ever to play the game of baseball, but in 2011 he was convicted of perjury and obstruction of justice during the investigation of a company charged with trafficking performance-enhancing drugs. The charge that Bonds used steroids and human growth hormone was supported by eyewitness accounts and various other forms of physical and anecdotal evidence—including his seemingly superhuman performance. His criminal conviction, however, was not for using the drugs but rather for lying about it to a grand jury. The lying probably cannot be ethically defended, but what about the doping? Does Bonds's case simply reflect a moral disconnect between sports ethics, as represented by his actions, and social ethics, as represented by the face he tried to present to the outside world? What if the steroids were administered to Bonds without his knowledge, as he claimed? What if the substances were used only therapeutically to help recover from injury and actually contributed to his health? What if steroid use was so widespread in the sport that Bonds was convinced he had to dope just in order to be competitive? What if doping was encouraged to restore the spectator appeal of baseball and keep it from dying completely? How can we explore a sports ethics issue like doping in a way that takes account of social ethics but also accommodates the particular milieu of sport? One way is to evaluate Bonds's actions from a consequentialist point of view—that is, by looking at the effects of Bonds's actions on the community of baseball.

Let us explore Bonds's case using the mainstream ethical theory of utilitarianism along with sport-specific criteria derived from our early discussion about the relationship between sport and play. This discussion will focus on consequences rather than principles or virtues, since utilitarianism is a consequentialist ethical theory and play, as we discovered in chapter 3, describes a desirable state of affairs that can be brought about by sport. Utilitarianism is a moral theory that characterizes right action as that which produces the greatest good for the greatest number. Of course, there is widespread debate about how to define and measure that good, as well as how to define the affected community. But let us bypass that debate for the purposes of our experiment by defining our community as the practice community of the sport of baseball and defining the good in terms of play characteristics— voluntariness, extraordinariness, autotelicity, absorption, and fun. This approach allows us to set aside the question of whether doping violates the deontological principle of fairness (to be discussed in the next chapter). Fairness is a question closely allied with rules, and in fact, steroids were not explicitly against the rules of Major League Baseball for at least part of the time that Bonds is supposed to have taken them. What we're going to look at here is whether Bonds's use of steroids can be ethically defended because it produced more good than bad, or if it should be ethically condemned because it produced more bad than good, in terms of play characteristics within the sport of baseball.

It may seem as if we are stacking the deck against Bonds by using play characteristics as an ethical measure for his actions. A critic might object that we are talking about a professional athlete in serious pursuit of long-standing performance records and huge financial payoffs. Baseball is called a game and games are rooted in play, but play can hardly be a valid criterion for judging the ethics of a professional athlete. An equally strong criticism might be made, however, that such serious professionalism is precisely the cause of immorality in modern sport. Just as Plato and Aristotle thought autotelic play to be more noble and important than work, or politics, or even war, so sport should strive to be as "playful" as possible in order to resist the corrupting influences of professionalism. Many critics think the problem with sports today is that we take them too seriously, focus too much on winning, and pay too high a price to obtain it. Using play as a moral criterion can address that concern—but let's not beg the question by assuming that utilitarian play standards will condemn doping or even professionalism. In fact, the first characteristic of play, that it is voluntary and free, suggests that doping is just another thing that athletes should be free to do.

FREEDOM OR COERCION?

The first characteristic of play is that it is voluntary and free. Sport exhibits this characteristic because participation is always voluntary and athletes often experience a sense of freedom while playing their sports. Freedom is likewise prized in utilitarian ethical theory. John Stuart Mill, one of the founding fathers of utilitarianism, wrote a famous essay called *On Liberty* that argues that the freedom of individuals, in terms of both thought and action, is one of the greatest goods that a community can provide. People need freedom to develop and thrive and so do their communities. People whose lives are closely directed by rules and restrictions develop no greater faculty, says Mill, "than the ape-like one of imitation."[1] Those who are given freedom may make bad choices, acknowledges Mill, but "genius thrives in an atmosphere of freedom."[2] Thriving communities, according to Mill's utilitarianism, will maximize the liberty of their members. Thriving sports communities wishing to maximize their play characteristics should do likewise. Should that liberty include the permission to dope?

Some sport philosophers, such as W. Miller Brown, have argued that sport should allow doping, using Mill's conception of paternalism as support.[3] In *On Liberty*, Mill spells out the rare conditions under which paternalism—that is, the restriction of a person's liberty against their will—is permitted. He says, "The only purpose for which power can be rightfully exercised over any member of a civilized community, against his will, is to prevent harm to others."[4] Applied to the question of doping in sport, this so-called harm principle suggests that doping should not be prohibited for any reason other than to prevent them from harming others, and it is difficult to see how Bonds's taking steroids, the argument goes, actually harmed anyone else. Mill does permit paternalism in the case of children or adults who are incapable of making informed choices about the risks and consequences of their actions. For that reason, Brown supports bans on drugs in youth and scholastic sports. But Bonds is an adult and a professional, with access to the best medical and athletic training advice. Even if he was motivated by greed and vanity, he is hardly an innocent child in need of protection from society. Brown concludes that those who advocate bans on drugs claim to be protecting sport's ability to promote values like autonomy and self-reliance, but ironically by banning drugs they actually deny those things to athletes.[5] It would seem, in Brown's view, that doping should be permitted in order to maximize the play characteristics of freedom and voluntary choice.

Returning to the relationship between play and freedom, however, we might recall another irony—or at least a paradox—from our earlier discussion of play. That is, that the freedom experienced in sport and play depends precisely on limitations and constraints. The play world is set apart from the ordinary world by boundaries of time and space. Sometimes these are formal and visible, as in the walls of a racquetball court and the specific time allotted to play a game. Sometimes they are imaginary, as when a child creates a make-believe house under the dining-room table. These boundaries create a sense of freedom, not least by creating separation from the ordinary world beyond them. When I step into the racquetball court, I am, in a sense, stepping out of my workaday life with its obligations and demands. The boundaries carve out a space within which I feel free because I adopt a different attitude within them: a particular kind of stance toward the world. Drew Hyland, as we saw, calls this the "stance of play" and notes that both sport and art manipulate space and time precisely to raise our awareness of freedom and possibility.[6]

As Eleanor Metheny explains, the rules that are characteristic of sport perform a similar paradoxical function to boundaries of time and space:

> These rules [of sport] are paradoxical. They restrict in order to free. They impose restrictions on human behavior, and they limit human action; but within those restrictions they offer every man an opportunity to know the feeling of being wholly free to go all out—free to do his utmost—free to use himself fully in the performance of one self-chosen human action.[7]

So if the sense of freedom and voluntariness characteristic of play depends not on the absence of external restrictions but rather on the presence of constraints such as rules and boundaries, then perhaps the imposition of rules banning doping ultimately creates a greater sense of freedom and voluntariness for the athletes. How could that be? Imagine that it becomes technically legal to attach a small motor to your bike in a cycling race. Many riders object to the practice and continue to race without the motors, but they find that they are quickly dropped from the pack. At that point, they feel forced to use a motor or to abandon the sport because they cannot be competitive without it. In a similar way, if steroids are permitted in sport and they offer a significant competitive advantage, many athletes will feel as if they have no option but to use them. They won't feel as if they are exercising free choice; rather, they will feel coerced by the *lack* of regulation.

In one of the first philosophical articles about doping in sport, Warren Fraleigh argues that legalizing drugs would increase coercion upon athletes to use them.[8] Former competitive powerlifter Mark Holowchak agrees and adds that such "coercive constraints" expose athletes to undue health risks.[9] Robert Simon questions whether "coercion" is too strong a term if we mean by it that athletes have no acceptable alternative—after all, sport participation is always voluntary.[10] Empirical and anecdotal evidence suggests, however, that many athletes already feel coerced to choose between doping and sport. Verner Moller's interviews with elite athletes reveal that many of them regard doping as a necessary precondition for achieving the athletic goals they have already invested their lifetimes in pursuing. In the words of one athlete, "I have not [competed] for so many years just to stop now that I have reached a point when the dream can be lived out in reality."[11] Former U.S. Olympic Committee doctor Robert Voy confirms Moller's findings. "[I] know, after working elbow-to-elbow with elite-level athletes, that many drug users do not *want* to use drugs but feel they *have* to to stay even with everyone else."[12] Meanwhile, numerous athletes have quit their sports because of a wish not to dope. According to former track-and-field champion Katherine Hamilton, "There is an untold story about all the thousands [who] just drop out because they're just not willing to do the things to your body and to go down that road."[13] In the end, Major League Baseball's earlier refusal to ban and test for steroids arguably made athletes like Bonds feel that they had less freedom of choice about whether to dope, not more. Permission, in this case, actually reduces freedom.

EXTRAORDINARY SERIOUSNESS

A second characteristic of play associated with sport is its extraordinariness: its distinction from ordinary life, in particular, work. This aspect is linked both to the boundaries discussed above and to the quality of autotelicity—that is, play being an end in itself instead of a means to some other end. A key idea here is that play as well as sport should not be taken too seriously. Paul Weiss says that play can be serious, "though not serious in the sense in which ordinary activities are."[14] He observes that "a child is at its best when it plays, [but] a mature man who plays is always less than what a man might be." Weiss thinks that a young man should play, but not all of the time, because there are "other, more useful or noble things he could do."[15] Randolph Feezell adds that play can have an internal seriousness, but it is not a serious matter "when contrasted to the world of work and human suffering."[16] One response to Bonds's case is to blame his doping on professionalism. Because playing baseball is his job, he is entitled to take it seriously and to use any means legally necessary to achieve his goals. Perhaps the ethical issue in this case is not so much doping as it is seriousness and professionalism.

The refrain is often heard that what modern sports needs is a return to amateurism, perhaps as depicted in the movie *Chariots of Fire*, especially by the fictional character of Lord Andrew Lindsay, a member of the English nobility with such an extraordinarily playful attitude toward sport that he is shown practicing hurdles with glasses of champagne balanced on them.[17] The word *amateurism* derives from the Latin root for love and is supposed to designate athletes who play sport for love rather than work. Amateurism was a big part of the early Olympic Movement, and Olympic athletes were subject to strict amateur regulations as recently as the 1980s. Some of the most famous Olympic athletes have run afoul of these regulations, including Jim Thorpe, Paavo Nurmi, and Bill Toomey. Advocates like Avery Brundage refer to ancient Greek athletes in their defense of amateurism, but in fact ancient Greek athletes were not unpaid, and the idea of amateurism derives rather from Victorian England, where an effort was made to exclude the working classes from sport.[18] Over time, attitudes changed. In 1986, the word *amateur* was eliminated from the Olympic Charter, and amateurism's rules in American collegiate sports are currently undergoing criticism and legal challenges.[19]

What does all that mean for the ethics of sport and doping?

Perhaps the demise of amateurism and the rise of professionalism in sports—even at the scholastic level—mean that doping will inevitably increase. Voy identified the amount of money in international sports as one of the causes of doping problems during his tenure (the 1980s), but those were the latter days of amateur regulation and the money was corrupting the promoters, not the athletes, by discouraging them from effectively testing for the drugs.[20] Among athletes, it is far from clear that professionalism actually increases the likelihood of doping. According to International Olympic Committee (IOC) president Jacques Rogge, "The IOC's statistics and those in countries where the authorities perform tests at competitions or during training show that top level athletes, whether amateur or professional, dope less than the mainly amateur athletes at ordinary national level."[21] What all this shows, however, is that classifying athletes according to whether or not they get paid does not automatically determine their attitude toward sport, much less their propensity to dope.

As with freedom, the play characteristic of extraordinariness is a matter of internal attitudes rather than external facts. In chapter 3, we learned that the experience of play as extraordinary was not only an attitude but also an attitude we freely choose.[22] This suggests, from an ethical point of view, that we are responsible for adopting that attitude or failing to do so. Can we say therefore that Bonds's doping was unethical because it represents his failure to adopt a properly playful attitude toward sport? Are seriousness and professionalism improper attitudes for sport more generally? Miller Brown, who supports legalization of doping, believes that the use of drugs in sport is most often motivated by attitudes "characteristic of professionalism."[23] Robert Simon, likewise, compares employees at a firm who use stimulants to work longer hours while competing for promotions to athletes who take drugs.[24] Is the use of coffee or even dangerous prescription drugs for the purposes of advancing one's career importantly different from using performance-enhancing drugs in sport? Perhaps it is the serious, professional attitude that threatens sport's play characteristics—regardless of the level at which the attitude is adopted.

Again, however, this preliminary conclusion is revealed to be hasty by closer scrutiny. Returning to the characteristics of the extraordinary playful attitude, we recall that Roochnik described it as "a full commitment of body and spirit to the activity."[25] Feezell added that the attitude expresses personal identity: "Far from being unimportant or frivolous, the free activity of play expresses some aspect of myself that I take to be 'real' or 'authentic.'"[26] But isn't an attitude in which we are fully committed to an activity that expresses our true identity characteristic of professionalism? Isn't the professional a person who pursues her career with heart and commitment because it represents *who she is*? Isn't she furthermore committed to her profession because she sees some intrinsic value in it apart from whatever extrinsic rewards she might gain from it? To be sure, professionals are of course paid for their work, but mere "jobs" are what people do "for the money." I would argue that a sincere professional attitude better expresses the relevant play characteristic. But would a sincere professional dope?

INTRINSIC VERSUS EXTRINSIC VALUES

Perhaps the problem is not professionalism as an attitude but rather that a professional attitude should be wasted on an unproductive, autotelic activity that lacks extrinsic value. Although Aristotle and Plato argued that autotelic activities like play are actually nobler than productive tasks, Klaus Meier observes that, in cultures that value work, play is often regarded as "being aimless, wasteful, and non serious; a form of idleness, trifling, or sloth abhorrent to productive personality; or, perhaps, even as a morally unseemly enterprise characterized by profligate indulgence."[27] Perhaps Bonds's doping is morally reprehensible precisely because he took such risks and put such effort into an ultimately meaningless activity. Complaints about the exorbitant salaries paid to athletes like Bonds for "playing a stupid game" abound in modern media. These salaries reflect the exchange value of major professional sports as media entertainment, but that is something different from the intrinsic or social value implied by autotelicity. Pornography also has entertainment value and is a big-money business, but that fact does not imply that it has intrinsic worth.

A further complaint, perhaps more relevant to the ethical point, is that sports like professional baseball *may* have intrinsic worth (or, to use the social practice theory term, internal goods), but practitioners like Bonds are focused only on extrinsic goods like money and fame. Sigmund Loland describes this understanding of sport as "relativist" in that it considers the internal norms and values of sport only insofar as they serve to realize external goals. "Sport relativism," says Loland, "is an expression of pure instrumentalism."[28] In this view of sport, doping is logical just so long as it results in the relevant external rewards. If Bonds viewed baseball this way and his goal was primarily money and fame, his choice to dope was understandable, even successful. But what if he didn't care about external rewards so much as apparently internal goals, like winning and setting records? He did achieve both the season-long and lifetime home-run records. Loland associates such goals with what he calls the "narrow view," under which "sport is linked to the exploration and transcendence of the limits of performance."[29] Again, given the records, Bonds's doping may be understandable here.[30]

Preferring what he calls a "wide theory" within which sport has meaning over and above mere performance, however, Loland himself rejects the relativistic and narrow views of sport.[31] He argues that sport's meaning not only is derived from its internal norms and values but also has a connection to deeper sociocultural and moral values. Doping is much more difficult to defend in a wide view of sport, because it privileges community goods such as education over individual goals like victory and profits. For doping to be justified on a wide view, it would have to have obvious social benefits over and above financial and entertainment value.

Loland's wide theory of sport seems consistent with Drew Hyland's account of the value of play. Hyland claims that play itself is "value neutral," but the *stance of play* may be valuable, depending on what we do while in that stance.[32] It is easy to see how qualities that make someone a good player, such as awareness, focus, courage, and perseverance, might also make him a good thief. What matters is that we put our play skills and activities in the service of valuable social goals. The ethics of Barry Bonds's doping, under this scheme, would depend upon the social benefits generated from it, and in his case, it is hard to imagine what those would be. If it turns out that Lance Armstrong doped in his pursuit of seven Tour de France victories, however, the social benefit he provided by inspiring cancer survivors as part of that campaign would need to be weighed in the balance.

From a conventional utilitarian standpoint, the calculation of social benefit makes sense. But whatever happened to the criterion of autotelicity? Isn't sport, insofar as it reflects the ideal of play, supposed to be valuable in and of itself? Wasn't the final point that it is absorbing and fun and does not need external justification? Our study of autotelicity showed that it was more an ideal than a reality and that people have complex motivations to play. Again, the key for play is a participant's particular attitude, his absorption in the activity, not the presence or absence of any additional goals.[33] To be absorbed by playing a sport and to be able to enjoy it completely are clearly intrinsic values. Athletes' experiences of "flow" or being in "the zone" might be the highest expression of playful absorption and enjoyment in sport. What we know about the zone is that it cannot be achieved on demand but rather results from a balance of skill and challenge.[34] Enhancing one's performance with drugs, focusing on victory, and pursuing external goods do not produce more enjoyment in sport or more frequent experiences of the zone. If anything, they interfere with these play-like benefits. The autotelic value of sport, it turns out, depends on training and competing the old fashioned way.

In this chapter we have explored the ethics of doping in sports by combining the consequentialist ethical theory of utilitarianism, which seeks the greatest good for the greatest number, with the sport-specific criteria of goodness provided by sport's metaphysical connection with play. Specifically, we looked at whether Barry Bonds's drug use could be ethically justified using the criteria of playful sports experiences such as freedom, extraordinariness, and autotelicity. What we found was that even though freedom might seem to be best served by the legalization of drugs in sport, in fact it is the rules and constraints characteristic of play that enable a sense of freedom in sport. Ironically, the permission to dope, on account of the concomitant harm linked with use of such drugs, seems to result in less freedom for athletes to do as they wish.

Using the criterion of play as extraordinary and set apart from life, we then explored whether seriousness and professionalism were at odds with the attitude of play. We found, instead, that if we understand professionalism as a commitment to and identification with a particular activity, it closely matches the attitude characteristic of play. It is the unprofessional exploitation of sport for extrinsic purposes like wealth and fame—commonly known as instrumentalism—that seems to challenge the spirit of play and motivate the taking of steroids and other performance-enhancing substances. Although sport can be viewed as a means to external ends or even as a way to discover the limits of human possibility, those conceptions challenge the intrinsic worth or autotelicity associated with play. Intrinsically valuable experiences such as fun and "flow" do not preclude external motivations—whether socially valuable, like education, or socially damaging, like greed—but external motives can interfere with our ability to experience these intrinsic goods in sport by pushing us toward unnecessarily risky behaviors like taking steroids.

DISCUSSION QUESTIONS

1. It was argued that the ban on drugs in sport actually increases athletes' freedom. Do you think the same would be true of a ban on dietary supplements such as creatine? Why or why not?
2. How do you explain Jacques Rogge's claim that amateur athletes are more likely to dope than professionals? Is a more serious athlete more or less likely to dope than a less serious one?
3. If you were a coach and one of your athletes told you he wanted to take a drug that could guarantee victory, even if it would cause his death a short time later, what would be your reaction?

4. What are some of the social benefits of sport that might justify our taking it seriously according to the "wide theory"? Does doping negate any of these benefits? How?

Chapter Nine

Deontology and Fairness

At the 2011 World Fencing Championships in Catania, Italy, a top African fencer from Tunisia named Sarra Besbes mounted the platform to face Noam Mills of Israel, but she didn't compete. Instead, she passively received the requisite number of touches, losing the round in such a way that caused Mills, the *winner*, to burst into tears.[1] Besbes was not the first athlete to refuse to compete with an Israeli—an Iranian refused to face an Israeli in the same tournament. But Besbes's case is different because she *did* enter the contest; she just refused to play the game and therefore intentionally lost. She didn't break any rules and was neither eliminated from the tournament nor sanctioned by the international or national governing body of her sport—in fact, it was the latter that asked her not to compete.[2] "I did my duty," Besbes said later in an interview, noting that she had remained passive rather than withdrawing in order to avoid sanction.[3] Leaving aside the political issues underpinning this incident, what can we say about it from the perspective of sports ethics? The athlete didn't cheat, she broke no rules, she took no drugs, and she did not use violence or even foul language. Still, many would say that she failed to act ethically as an athlete, her behavior was not sporting, and she did not play fair. To understand why they might say these things we need to examine the deontological principles implied by sport.

Deontological ethical theories, such as that of Immanuel Kant, focus on moral laws or principles rather than the virtues of individual agents or the consequences of their actions. Kant's categorical imperative, "I ought never to act except in such a way that I can also will that my maxim should become a universal law,"[4] is presented as a moral duty discovered and legislated by reason. In the same way that Newton discovered laws of the physical universe (phenomenal realm), Kant took himself to have discovered moral laws for practical concerns in the noumenal realm of thought. Applied to a case of

107

cheating in sport, such as a fencer using an illegal foil to increase his chances of scoring, the categorical imperative would permit this only if he could rationally will that all others use the illegal equipment in the same way. But such a wish seems inherently irrational since any advantage gained by the special equipment would be wiped out if it were universally used. Furthermore, since the equipment in question is barred by the rules of the sport, using it ethically would entail willing that everyone disregard the rules—a situation that, taken to its logical extreme, would eliminate sport altogether. What would fencing be if no one followed any of the rules? As we saw in chapter 4, rules are central to the metaphysical nature of games, and they need to be obeyed just to make sport possible.

But sports are also more than rules, which explains why we should be troubled by Sarra Besbes's action in the fencing tournament even though technically it broke no rules. Sports are conditioned by a certain spirit or ethos, commonly called *fair play*, which encourages or proscribes actions not specifically discussed in the rulebook. The postgame handshake is encouraged by this ethos; spitting on your hand in the line is prohibited. Deontological ethical principles likewise carry general implications for our treatment of others. The third formulation of Kant's imperative, which Kant thought was equivalent to the first, demands that we treat humanity "never simply as a means, but always at the same time as an end."[5] Because Besbes's refusal to compete breaks an implicit promise between athletic competitors to at least try to win, it is a mistreatment or abuse of another person. Besbes used her opponent merely as a means to make a political point. Likewise, the authorities who asked Besbes to forfeit her match treated *her* as a means to political ends, rather than an end in herself.

In this chapter, we will combine the structure of deontological ethics with the metaphysics of sports as rule-governed games to explore their moral implications. Bernard Suits, we recall, identified four elements of a game: the goal, the means, the rules, and the attitude. Might these elements carry normative implications for sport? If so, what would they be?

THE GOAL OF VICTORY

"Winning isn't everything," the saying goes; "it's the only thing." This quote, popularly attributed to the American football coach Vince Lombardi, summarizes either the true spirit of sports or the main thing that is wrong with sports—depending on where you stand. A viable ethics of sport must take account of the role of winning in sport, and if we ground ethics in metaphysics, the role of winning in games and sport is central. Suits places "the goal" at the top of his list of game characteristics, explaining it first as a general state of affairs that might be achievable outside a game (the *prelusory* goal), and then within the context of the game as the *lusory* goal, namely, the state of affairs that constitutes winning the game. So my goal in a swimming race is not simply to reach the far edge of the pool (a *prelusory* goal) but also to do so by swimming freestyle the length of the pool according to the other rules prescribed by the game, thereby winning the race (the *lusory* goal). If we combine this metaphysical aspect of games with Kant's categorical imperative, we arrive at an ethical principle that suggests everyone who plays games, including sports, ought to try to win, and furthermore they ought to *will* that everyone else who plays, including their opponents, tries to win, too.

Of course, we cannot logically say that everyone who plays games *ought* to win, since in all competitive games someone has to lose. Furthermore, we must admit, as a matter of fact, that winning may not be the primary motivation or objective of many sports participants. As Warren Fraleigh explains, "The ends of achieving a specific state of affairs, of winning and of trying to win, are all necessary [but] it is not necessary that all participants adopt the end of winning as their personal intended end."[6] This means that, even if your primary purpose for playing a game of tennis is to improve your fitness or perhaps just to have fun, by agreeing to play the game you commit yourself to *contesting*: to using your own skills and challenging your opponent's skills in a genuine effort at victory. If, on the other hand, I go with a friend to the tennis court purely for purposes of fitness and fun and we just try to see how many times we can volley the ball without hitting it out of bounds, you can say we are engaging in a worthwhile activity, maybe even playing a game, but we are not playing the game of tennis. So aiming to win is one of the principles underpinning ethical sports participation, and Sarra Besbes broke this principle by standing passively in her match at the World Fencing Championships. Her opponent, furthermore, was justifiably upset despite winning the match because she had been mistreated ethically.

Yet Noam Mills *won* the match and achieved her goal, so why should she be upset? The victory for her must have lacked meaning because it did not represent what victory is supposed to represent, namely, demonstrated athletic superiority. While it makes sense to say that all (or most) athletes hope to win by demonstrating athletic superiority, we cannot say that all (or most) athletes hope to win because their opponents provided no resistance. One of the things most athletic games test is a competitor's ability to overcome her opponent's resistance. If that resistance is not provided, the test was not really carried out, and the victory therefore loses its value. In fact, there are many circumstances under which victory in an athletic contest fails to indicate athletic superiority. Nicholas Dixon lists bad refereeing, cheating, gamesmanship, bad luck, and even subpar performances by superior athletes or teams among common causes of such "hollow" victories.[7] His conclusion is that winning does not reliably indicate athletic superiority and, as Edwin Delattre had warned nearly twenty-five years earlier, we should not put so much emphasis on victory in sports: "To stress victory to the point of over-looking quality of performance is to impoverish our sense of success in competitive athletics."[8]

A rich understanding of athletic success should also transcend physical performance to encompass moral virtues and consistency over time. Even when athletes exhibit such virtues, however, the objective *value* of athletic victory, and especially the pride they take in it, is easily questioned. David Carr points out that taking pride in the discovery of a cure for disease seems more justified than pride in athletic achievements, the social value of which is much more difficult to justify.[9] It is when the virtues that (with imperfect reliability) lead to athletic victory are applied to more valuable social projects that athletics best defends its worth, especially as education. Said one American football coach recently, "I told the guys if I had one wish, it would be to put that scoreboard to death, because that really shouldn't be the standard. The standard should be excellence. I think it's a much better thing to live by than the scoreboard because that will help them more in life, as a dad, as a husband, as an employee and as a neighbor."[10] Winning does matter, then, but only insofar as it motivates the cultivation of noble qualities. So striving to win, rather than winning itself, is a moral obligation for athletes, and Vince Lombardi got it right when he explained that what he meant was "winning isn't everything—but making the effort to win is."[11]

INEFFICIENT MEANS

Late in 2009, FINA, the international swimming federation, banned the full-body hydrodynamic swimsuits that were threatening to turn their sport into a competition among manufacturers rather than athletes. In 2008, 105 world records were broken, 79 of them by swimmers wearing one particular brand of high-tech suit. At the Beijing Olympics alone, 94 percent of the gold medals were won by swimmers using the same suit.[12] Foremost in that group was Michael Phelps, but he eventually came to resent the suits and threatened to boycott the world championships the next year if they weren't banned. When they were banned, he expressed relief: "It's going to be cool come Jan. 1 to be able to have all of us pretty much wearing the same suit . . . then we're going to be able to talk about swimming again, not suits."[13] Since the hydrodynamic bodysuits began showing up in competitions in the early 1990s, they had caused improved times as well as controversy—not least because the early versions were custom made for top stars and not available to everyone. As Sigmund Loland points out in discussing the ethics of performance-enhancing technologies, "A key principle to reach fair and valid outcomes seems to be that of *equality of opportunity to perform*."[14] With time, though, the suits became cheaper and more widely available. Makers even supplied free suits to Olympic swimmers who couldn't afford them. If everyone has equal access to a legal performance-enhancing technology, what could be the ethical problem? Furthermore, why should a champion like Michael Phelps, who was winning anyway, complain about it?

One explanation is that Phelps's complaint was sour grapes because his suit was no longer the fastest and he had recently lost races to less-heralded competitors.[15] He wanted to win and the object of the sport is to win by swimming faster, so he was just jealous that some competitors were swimming faster than him. A better answer, however, is that he cares about his sport and he recognizes the value of its *inefficiency*. Swimming in a pool is a notoriously inefficient way to move from one point to the next—most swimmers could run faster along the deck than they can swim in the water, and with less energy expended. But this inefficiency, according to Suits's account of games, is precisely what makes the activity a sport. "To play a game is to attempt to achieve a specific state of affairs, using only means permitted by the rules, *where the rules prohibit use of more efficient in favour of less efficient means*, and where the rules are accepted just because they make possible such activity" (emphasis mine).[16] Certain inefficiencies form part of the metaphysics of games and sports, and when combined with deontological ethical principles, they carry moral weight.

Sports equipment that improves the efficiency of achieving the lusory goal of a contest (i.e., that makes it easier to win), cannot be willed rationally to be a universal law according to Kant's categorical imperative because, again, if an athlete's objective is to win, he cannot rationally will that any advantage he gets from his equipment is also available to his competitors because it would cancel out that advantage. Once everyone has the hydrodynamic swimsuits, we still have the same sport, only the records are at risk because everyone gets to the finish line sooner. But getting to the finish quickly is not, by itself, the objective of the sport of swimming. The point is to get to the finish as quickly as possible, given the inefficiencies imposed by the rules, and it is the job of the rule makers to impose reasonable inefficiencies in a way that preserves the intrinsic values of that sport. It might be unreasonable, for example, to make swimmers tie one hand behind their backs, or drag small boats through the water, simply for the sake of inefficiency. But it is not unreasonable, and indeed it might be imperative, to deny them such efficiencies as motors, flippers, or hydrodynamic bodysuits. Why? What's the difference?

The inefficiencies embedded in the rules of sport are not merely arbitrary; rather, they are designed to bring out through challenge certain skills and virtues that an athlete might possess. The breaststroke, for example, is one of the slowest and least efficient competitive swimming strokes. For a time, swimmers found that they could win breaststroke races by remaining under water as long as possible and actually *avoiding* the traditional stroke. This was a skill, but not the skill to be tested in the race, so FINA changed the rules to limit the distance that can be swum underwater in those races. Skills and virtues make up only part of an athletic performance. Access to good coaching, quality food, and facilities also contributes, as does equipment, weather, and even luck.

What ethical sport ought to do, to use Loland's terms, is "eliminate or compensate for essential inequalities between persons that cannot be controlled or influenced by individuals in any significant way and for which individuals cannot be deemed responsible."[17] In basketball, for example, the uncontrollable inequality of height presents an advantage. But rule makers were able to compensate for that somewhat by giving extra value to shots made from a greater distance, thereby diminishing the importance of height in favor of shooting ability—a valued skill that can be influenced through training and practice. Efforts to make equipment and technology identical for all competitors, or at least to standardize it as much as possible, achieve a similar purpose.[18] Certainly there is room for equipment differences that help individuals to compensate for uncontrollable inequalities. Fiberglass vaulting poles, for example, made that sport more accessible to women and smaller athletes. But insofar as performance-enhancing technologies reduce or eliminate the trainable skills and virtues at the center of sport, or render the opportunity to perform less equal, they should be banned.

THE RULES: LETTER AND SPIRIT

The rules, Suits's third characteristic of games, have obvious ethical import as we saw in chapter 4. It makes no sense in Kantian terms to break the rules of the sport without willing that such rule breaking become a universal law. But might there be cases where certain kinds of rule breaking can be willed universally? The formalist approach to sports ethics, as we saw, holds the "logical incompatibility thesis," according to which players who intentionally violate rules fail to play the game. This position suggests that all intentional rule violations, however innocuous, are cheating. To many, this position seems untenable. John Russell points out that inconsequential rule violations are left uncalled in many sports, and he even goes so far as to claim that basketball "cannot be played without constantly breaking rules."[19] Indeed, the foul to stop the clock in basketball is a paradigm example of the intentional rule violations that are accepted as a legitimate part of the game. Players who commit such fouls rarely try to conceal their actions and willingly accept the penalty. In these two details, strategic rules violations reflect Martin Luther King Jr.'s definition of morally justified civil disobedience.[20] But civil disobedience employs the intentional breaking of unjust laws for promoting justice in society and the integrity of law more generally. That goal seems a bit loftier than trying to win a game, and it certainly is not the case that strategic fouls are committed to draw attention to and remove unjust rules. Nevertheless, the idea that all intentional violations of rules are cheating seems too strict.

On the other hand, to define cheating only in terms of rule breaking may not be strict enough. Often, apparently immoral acts in sport are not technically illegal—as we observed with the fencing example at the opening of this chapter, and in chapter 4 with the U.S. cycling team's use of performance-enhancing blood transfusions before the 1984 Olympic Games. The steroid scandal that rocked professional baseball dates back to a time before drug bans in that sport and involves dietary supplements and testosterone precursors that are still widely available in retail markets. The fact that such "legal" performance-enhancing techniques are nevertheless concealed by their perpetrators suggests an awareness of their immorality. But it might also just be strategic—an attempt to gain a legal advantage over competitors without their knowledge. All kinds of legal actions in sport are concealed from opponents. Teams often practice in secret and routinely conceal their communications during games—sometimes employing secret signs and signals. In most baseball and softball leagues, stealing signs is not prohibited by the rules as long as video technology is not employed. Still, the practice is morally controversial because many players and coaches believe that it interferes with the game's test of the athletes' skills.

A formalist response to cases in which apparently immoral actions are legal is simply to write rules against them. For a long time, the penalty in soccer for handling the ball or tackling an opponent near the goal was a penalty kick, but under these conditions it made strategic sense to commit the foul intentionally in order to prevent what would otherwise be a certain goal, as the chances of the penalty kick going in were lower. Recognizing this problem, FIFA changed the rule from a mere penalty kick to a red card, which ejects the offending player from the game and forces their team to play shorthanded. In this way, they eliminated the strategic motivation for the foul. The idea of perfecting the rules has some appeal, but there are at least two problems with it. First, as Robert Simon points out, the very recognition that there is a problem with the rules entails some morally relevant sense of the game beyond the rules—but if games are nothing more than their rules, where do we get such a standard?[21]

Second, as the ancient Chinese philosopher Laozi understood, moral behavior is difficult to legislate. On the contrary, the accumulation of rules and laws only decreases people's respect for them. As Laozi says, "The more prohibitions and rules, the poorer people become . . . the more elaborate the laws, the more they commit crimes."[22] In fact, the current state of professional European soccer seems to bear out that thesis. Because the referee is incapable of monitoring the entire field at once, players engage in all kinds of illicit behavior behind his back—often in full view of the television cameras. The attitude seems to be that "it isn't cheating if you don't get caught"—a blatant rationalization for immorality. Actions such as Thierry Henry's intentional handball in a World Cup qualifying match, furthermore, are sometimes regarded with admiration. Said Henry of the incident, "I will be honest, it was a handball. But I'm not the ref. I played it, the ref allowed it. That's a question you should ask him."[23]

Even sports officials, however, should be able to see that sports ethics involves more than just rules and penalization. In arguing that rules are not all that umpires have to work with, John Russell recalls a case in Major League Baseball where George Brett had a potentially game-winning two-run homerun disallowed because the pine-tar resin spread on the bottom of his bat for grip exceeded the maximum eighteen inches allowed by the rules.[24] It was recognized later that the excess pine-tar resin would have been, if anything, a disadvantage for the purposes of hitting a home run and that disallowing the hit on the basis of that technicality amounted, in effect, to putting the rules ahead of the game itself. To the formalist way of thinking, that last statement is nonsensical because the game is nothing more than rules, but Russell and many others argue that there is something more: an intrinsic logic, perhaps best understood in terms of fair-play principles, that underlies and informs the rules of sport. Russell suggests that sports rules be interpreted according to these principles, which he enumerates as excellence, competitive balance, fair play, and the good conduct of games.[25] Whether or not this list accurately captures the principle or ethos of fair play that underlies sport, we can recognize that there is such a thing and that it should be taken into account when making ethical decisions in sports. Rules are only part of the story.

THE LUSORY ATTITUDE: RESPECT FOR THE GAME

The final frontier of sports ethics, unsurprisingly, is attitude. Suits argued that the "lusory attitude" was what made game playing possible, and Graham McFee claimed that what made rules actually function as rules was nothing other than people choosing to use them that way.[26] It should be no surprise that the aforementioned pine-tar incident was instigated by the opposing team's manager, Billy Martin, who requested after the home run was hit that Brett's bat be inspected. According to at least one account, Martin had noticed the pine-tar violation much earlier in the season but was waiting for a strategic moment to point it out.[27] Such legalistic strategizing seems to involve a willful ignorance of the ethos, spirit, or unwritten rules of the sport, motivated by a narrow focus on winning. Renowned moral philosopher Peter Singer observes that partisanship appears to have trumped morality in pro soccer for both players and fans. "Fans don't seem to mind if members of their own team cheat successfully," he says; "they only object when the other side cheats. That is not an ethical attitude."[28] So what *is* an ethical attitude toward sport, given that sport itself depends in so many ways upon attitude?

Let us return again to Kant, whose categorical imperative prohibited me, in its first formulation, from making moral exceptions for myself, and in its third formulation obliged me to treat others never merely as means but always also as ends in themselves. In short, Kant's deontology demands an attitude of respect toward others and toward what he calls the "universal law." Applied to sport and in particular to Suits's concept of the "lusory attitude," we might summarize an ethical attitude in sport as one of respect for the game. Suits claimed that the lusory attitude was that element of games that "unifies the other elements into a single formula,"[29] and he characterized it as an attitude directed at the process, rather than the goal, "since it willingly accepts rules that make achieving the goal harder."[30] Respecting the game means, first of all, respecting the rules of that game, but it also requires us to respect the other elements of the game discussed above: striving for victory and accepting the inefficiency of means. In short, we need to respect the *process* of playing the game. Furthermore, it demands that we recognize other players' stakes in the game and our own role in facilitating their participation. Treating others as ends and not means when playing games requires us to recognize them as colleagues or co-strivers (this is the root meaning *com-petitor*), rather than obstacles to be eliminated in pursuit of our own goals.

As Robert Butcher and Angela Schneider conclude in their account of fair play as respect for the game, "The athlete who respects the game wishes to play as well as possible against a worthy opponent playing as well as possible. . . . This means that you allow your opponent every opportunity—as defined by the game—to play his or her best."[31] While this attitude makes sense in terms of sports ethics, it may seem foreign to athletes who are more used to *denying* competitors the opportunity to play their best. Psychological tactics such as "trash talking" or "sledging" are adopted precisely for the purpose of putting competitors "off their game." In American football, it is popular to "ice the kicker" by calling a time-out just as the opposing team attempts a field goal in order to interrupt a kicker's rhythm and give him time to doubt himself. Tennis players, too, have been known to stall or delay their play in order to interrupt the rhythm of opponents. These sorts of tactics are sometimes considered part of the game, and a player's ability to resist them may be counted among her athletic skills as long as they don't descend below the level of basic respect for persons, as some incidents of trash talking are known to do.

Worse are sports strategies that actually deny athletes the opportunity to test their skills. The strategy in baseball of intentionally walking batters by pitching the ball so far outside the strike zone that it is virtually impossible to hit appears to be one such practice. The rules provide for an advantage to be granted to the walked batter—but the practice circumvents the testing of both the hitter's and pitcher's skills as intended by the game. In cricket, there is a similar strategy of bowling underarm to batters as a way of preventing multiple runs—especially in situations where multiple runs might win the game. This practice is routinely jeered by spectators, as is stalling by kicking the ball back to the goalkeeper in soccer, or taking a knee to run out the clock in American football. Graham McFee says that knowledgeable audiences are right to express their disapproval of what they recognize as inappropriate ways of playing a game. He calls such play "spoiling" because, even though it is technically permitted by the rules, it denies opponents the "possibility of playing the game according to its spirit."[32] On occasion it is an ally rather than an opponent whose opportunity to play is spoiled, as when cyclists are asked to sacrifice their own chances for victory by towing team leaders in their slipstream to the front of the pack, or when runners pursuing new record times are paced by "rabbits" who set a competitively untenable pace and then withdraw before the end of the race. None of these actions is against the rules of sport, but they all, in some sense, fail to respect its spirit.

Fair play is sometimes understood as the application of moral principles to the realm of sport. Research suggests, however, that it was rather the structure of sport that gave rise to the ideal of fair play, which then became part of social morality.[33] Fairness as an ethical principle originates in the metaphysics of sports and games, and for that reason it makes sense to see what a combination of Suits's definition of games and Kant's deontological ethics can tell us about moral behavior in sport. The initial result is paradoxical, since it points to winning as the end of the athletic contest but notes that winning can't be universalized in Kantian terms: we can't logically will that everyone win a game that only designates one victor. We can, however, rationally will that everyone *strive* to win the game and in this way arrive at a viable sports ethics principle. We quickly learn, however, that this striving to win means that we must respect the rules of the game and, more specifically, the skill-testing inefficiencies that the rules prescribe since it is those inefficiencies that make the activity a game in the first place. We also saw that rules, by themselves, do not dictate the morality of a game, but that deeper principles underpin them that should govern their application and interpretation. Finally, we learned that fair play is, most of all, an attitude. It is an attitude of respect toward the game and toward others that calls into question such common practices as intentional walks and running out the clock but also affirms the athletic spirit of playing one's best and valuing one's successes in sport.

DISCUSSION QUESTIONS

1. Do you think there was anything morally wrong with Besbes's refusal to compete in a fencing match? If so, how might the fencing federation discourage such behavior in the future?
2. Use an example to illustrate the difference between the following versions of Lombardi's statement: "Winning isn't everything; it's the only thing" and "Winning isn't everything, but making the effort to win is."
3. Do you think there is a moral difference between an advantage gained through equipment, such as a hydrodynamic swimsuit, and an advantage gained through nature, such as height or talent?
4. It was argued that attempts to interfere with an opponent's demonstration of skills (intentional walks or running out the clock) go against the spirit of the game. Can you make an argument for the opposing view—that such actions are consistent with the spirit of the game?

Chapter Ten

Virtues and Vices

In the spring of 2011, the Japanese Sumo Wrestling Association made the extraordinary decision to cancel a grand tournament in the wake of a scandal. The problem was not violence, gambling, or associations with organized crime; rather, it was evidence in the form of cell-phone messages that revealed what had long been suspected, that sumo wrestlers were throwing matches to opponents who would otherwise finish with a losing record and therefore be demoted through the ranks. By Western sport scandal standards this may seem mild. But the Japanese prime minister Naoto Kan called it "a very serious betrayal of the people," not least because sumo is the national sport and it represents a traditional ideal of virtue.[1] A serious effort is made to keep the sport morally pure and separate from the corrupting realities of modern life. Wrestlers live and train in so-called stables, are expected to show indifference toward victory, and conduct solemn religious rituals as part of their contests. Whereas the unscrupulous shenanigans of Western sports stars are so common as to be expected, immoral behavior in traditional Eastern sports, especially among the revered masters, is a serious affront. After all, the martial arts are traditionally valued as a means of cultivating virtue, and that value is often projected onto other athletic activities as well. In the East, champion athletes are also expected to be champions of virtue. In the West, by contrast, sports stars seem rather to be champions of vice. "The way to virtue in sport," argues Allan Bäck, "is to abandon [Western] sports— and perhaps to practice a martial art instead."[2]

The empirical data tracking sport and moral development in the West suggest that athletic competition not only fails to cultivate virtue but also actually promotes vice.[3] Indeed, some view the scandals in Japanese sumo as evidence for how the trappings of Western-style sport can corrupt ancient athletic practices steeped in a tradition of moral purity. Traditionalists cite increasing money, media attention, and the influx of foreign wrestlers as causes of sumo's problems.[4] Purists, meanwhile, question sumo's status as a true martial art because of its emphasis on competition.[5] In fact, many were relieved when wushu, traditional Chinese martial arts, was denied status as an Olympic sport. The fear was that the Olympics, despite their ancient Greek athletic heritage, would ruin wushu's focus on the cultivation of virtue. "When Wushu tried to go Olympic," says champion Zhao Changjun, "somehow they lost the character of what Wushu really is."[6] In fact, the transformation of wushu into a competitive sport has coincided with a rise in corruption, including bribing judges and fixing matches.[7] Despite all this, many philosophers of Western sport including Paul Weiss, Warren Fraleigh, Robert Simon, Mike McNamee, Mark Holowchak, and myself continue to extol sport as a way of promoting virtue. So, which is it? Does competitive sport cultivate virtue, or does it promote vice? Perhaps more to the point, under what conditions does sport promote virtue rather than vice?

The ethical question here is not just about people's behavior but also about whether and how the practice of sport and its supporting institutions facilitate and reward the cultivation of virtue or vice. The metaphysical theory of sport as a social practice discussed in chapter 5 tapped into the ancient theories of virtue ethics to be found both in Greek thinkers like Plato and Aristotle and in the Chinese philosophers Laozi and Confucius. Virtue ethics focuses on the moral character of the person who acts rather than his principles (as in Immanuel Kant's deontology) or the consequences of his action (as in John Stuart Mill's utilitarianism). Virtue, in both the Greek and Chinese traditions, is understood as the disposition or power to perform good actions, and virtue ethics generally involves extended discussion of how such dispositions are cultivated.[8] Aristotle identified training (*ethos*) as the source of character (*ēthos*), reflecting the traditional association between virtue (psychical excellence) and athletic training (physical excellence) in his culture.[9] Confucius, likewise, associated the cultivation of virtue with ritual practice.[10] Plato set up his Academy in a gymnasium, and Laozi's Daoism forms the foundation of several martial arts. In modern times, Alasdair MacIntyre's social practice theory has revived virtue ethics, not least in its relation to sport. Perhaps if we combine traditional virtue ethics with the metaphysical understanding of sports as social practices, we will understand when and why sports and martial arts succeed or fail to promote virtue. From there, we may be able to identify ways to improve these practices.

To begin, let us recall that MacIntyre described a social practice as a cooperative activity that realizes internal goods through the pursuit and achievement of standards of excellence in that activity.[11] Practices generate practice communities, and it is by thoughtful participation in these communities that social virtues such as honesty, justice, and courage are exercised and cultivated.[12] Eastern philosophy has long been lauded for its priority on community, but Aristotle also emphasized the communal aspect of virtue ethics, categorizing human beings as "political animals"[13] and asserting that the purpose of communities is to facilitate virtuous action.[14] Participating in a practice community entails relationships with not only contemporary practitioners, like teammates and opponents, but also previous practitioners, like coaches and historical champions, whose achievements have helped to establish the traditional standards of technical and ethical excellence for which practitioners strive.[15]

It's worth reflecting, furthermore, that our own technical and ethical achievements form part of the standards for future generations. What all this entails ultimately is that we *think* about practices like sport as ethical, not merely technical, and that we take the end of our participation in them to be virtue. Bäck claims that traditional martial arts do this by nature, while the focus on winning Western sports makes them "hazardous to your moral health."[16] In what follows, we will compare sports with martial arts in terms of their theoretical potential to produce MacIntyre's list of virtues—honesty, justice, courage, and integrity—in contrast to apparently vicious athletic phenomena such as deception, egoism, violence, and the failure to transfer athletic virtues beyond the field of play.

HONESTY VERSUS DECEPTION

Let us begin with the virtue of honesty or truthfulness. Confucius counts honesty among the five key virtues, while Mengzi claimed that virtuous people are ashamed to have their reputation exceed their actual worth.[17] Aristotle, likewise, praised truthfulness (*apseudeia*) as a mean between the excess of boastfulness and the deficiency of self-deprecation with respect to a person's self-assessment, as well as his behavior and speech.[18] MacIntyre thinks honesty is essential to the relationships embedded within social practices; without it, we would not be able to achieve the relevant standards of excellence, and that renders the practice "pointless, except as a device for achieving external goods."[19]

If we think about the important relationships an athlete has in sports—with coaches, officials, and even opponents—we can see how honesty is important in each of them. In martial arts, the key relationship is with one's master, and honesty seems fundamental here. There is a story in the book *Zen in the Art of Archery* in which author Eugen Herrigel decides secretly to disregard his master's instructions to focus only on becoming selfless and instead works on aiming at the target. Not only does the master immediately recognize the deception and punish him for it, but also Herrigel discovers that his efforts at aiming were indeed counterproductive.[20] Sport, likewise, generally rewards athletes who are honest with their coaches and punishes those who are not. In a basketball team, for example, a player who covers up her injury to try to get more playing time ultimately hurts the team's chances at victory, as does a self-deprecating player who defers to less-qualified teammates. Occasionally a coach might deceive a player in order to encourage him, for example, by telling a runner he's closer to the leaders than he is. But the coach-athlete relationship depends heavily on trust, and dishonesty almost always undermines trust. So at least as far as teammate and coaching relationships are concerned, the virtue of honesty seems to be rewarded by achievement in sports, as it is in martial arts.

The case of officials is a little different. The official's job, of course, is to enforce the rules (letter and spirit) of the game. Players who interfere with enforcement by using deception can be said, in effect, to be cheating. Traditional martial arts emphasize honor, have few rules, and have little need for officials.[21] Golf is similar in that players are expected to call penalties on themselves—a tradition that illustrates shared interest in a fairly played game. In 2010, professional golfer Brian Davis called a two-stroke penalty on himself for a minor infraction that required a slow-motion replay to confirm. By doing so, he gave up his first PGA Tour victory and the million-plus-dollar prize that went with it.[22] Davis's action attracted attention because of the stakes involved, not because self-called penalties are rare. They are as common in golf as they are unthinkable in the professional soccer world discussed previously. This shows not that golf is nobler than Karate-do but rather that virtues and vices are cultivated in communities and, as Aristotle said, the whole community benefits from their exercise. Insofar as a sports community values its standards of excellence, it wants those standards to be accurately measured. Some might be tempted to consider the strategic deception of referees among the skills to be tested by the game. Onlookers joke that soccer players who fake injuries to interrupt play or draw penalties should be given awards for their acting, and admittedly, the game sometimes rewards such actions. But the mere strategic effectiveness of such antics does not transform them into game skills any more than other forms of cheating. A community that condones such tactics actually undermines its own practice. The sports community should do everything it can to discourage deceiving officials.

Deception of opponents, by contrast, seems to be part of most sports. Even Sunzi, a philosophical father of the martial arts, endorses it. He declares that "all warfare is based on deception."[23] Deception in the form of feints and misleading cues is expected, condoned, and rewarded in almost all games, albeit within the limits established by the rules. It is acceptable in baseball, for example, to discourage a runner from stealing a base or taking off before the pitch is released by faking a throw to the baseman, who might then tag the runner out. But there are strict and complicated limits to this tactic.

Why is such deception allowed, and what is the reason for limiting it? First, while deception is generally a vice, the ability to recognize it in others and to respond accordingly is certainly a skill worth having. This is also true in the martial arts. According to this line of reasoning, deception should be allowed and expected between opponents in sport because it enables players to cultivate the quality of not being easily deceived. One may even argue that deception could be used as a virtue under certain circumstances—as when I must deceive a would-be kidnapper about the presence of a child in my house in order to prevent the crime. In fact, Plato understood lying as a skill that could be put to either virtuous or vicious uses.[24] Deceiving competitors in sport may be allowed insofar as it cultivates useful skills, but it should be banned insofar as it interferes with other skills being tested. The balk rule in baseball, discussed earlier, seems designed to prevent the game of deception from overtaking the sport's fundamental skills of pitching and hitting.

In the end, the virtue of honesty in sport should be understood as Mengzi and Aristotle saw it—as a value for the accurate assessment of one's ability or worth. Insofar as sports and the martial arts seek to test the evolving skills of their participants, they fundamentally support this kind of honesty. By the same token, insofar as it interferes with the game—that is, the accurate assessment of relevant skills—strategic deception needs to be discouraged by the reward structure of the game. This is not always easy to do, as the case of faking injuries in professional soccer attests—officials can't simply ignore such displays since the player may in fact need medical attention. Neither, however, should a player's ability to deceive the officials in this way be considered a legitimate part of the sport. It is an abuse of rules designed to protect players' safety.

Deception among players, on the other hand, is considered by some as a "legitimate" sports skill—especially insofar as it contributes to players' ability to avoid being deceived. It is an expected part of the competitive relationship that certain forms of deception, such as head fakes or feinted throws, will be used. But even though deception of coaches or officials, along with some surreptitious forms of opponent deception, such as faking injury, may increase one's chances at victory, these should be regarded as flaws in the game. Victories that come about through the cultivation of vice have no worth to the practice or to the practitioner, both of which should aim at the cultivation of virtue. As such they should not be valued or celebrated within the practice community, and as far as possible, they should be prohibited by the rules of the game.[25]

JUSTICE VERSUS ADVANTAGE

At the opening of Plato's *Republic*, the sophist Thrasymachus defines justice as "the advantage of the stronger."[26] It is a familiar characterization, supported by cynical observation of how the world often works. Today people express a similar idea with the comment "might makes right." Of course, Plato does not endorse this view—rather, he uses it as a provocative starting point from which to expound a theory of justice as the supreme virtue of city-states, and individuals as well. When MacIntyre counts justice among the social virtues needed to experience the internal goods of a social practice, he too is thinking of a property of persons rather than games or institutions.[27] Aristotle characterizes justice as the virtue that concerns our dealings with others, summarizing it as "treating equals equally and unequals unequally in proportion to their relevant differences."[28] This description jibes well with the logic and structure of sports, which provide an equal opportunity for all participants and attempt to reward according to merit. A just athlete might accordingly be one who respects competitors as equals and graciously recognizes the merit of the winner—that is, an athlete who displays "good sportsmanship." But the reality of competitive attitudes in sport seems to better resemble Thrasymachus's definition: you use every advantage you can to win the game and prove your superiority over others. The very fact that athletes need to be exhorted to "be a good sport" reveals an apparent conflict between the natural emotions of competition and the moral expectations of justice, understood as the virtue of sportsmanship.

Perhaps the problem is competition itself. Most social practices, like traditional martial arts, do not emphasize competition the way sports do. Perhaps the virtue of justice in sports actually runs counter to the competitive spirit, and sportsmanship is really just indifference toward competition. Maybe the good sport, like Confucius's gentleman, "never competes."[29] He may participate in a game of archery, but he is uninterested in the outcome. Traditional martial arts reflect this attitude by avoiding competition. Indeed, Bäck claims that if sports want to cultivate virtues like justice, they need to leave competition behind.[30]

To some degree this contrast in attitudes toward competition seems to be cultural. The movie *Running Brave* tells the true story of Native American runner Billy Mills and his struggle to adapt to the ruthless competitiveness of college athletics. Growing up on the reservation, Mills would run just hard enough to win races, thereby avoiding the humiliation of his competitors by a wide victory margin. When he lets a fellow Indian runner catch up toward the end of a college race, however, his university coach scolds him despite the victory. "You gotta crush him, so he knows you're better!" the coach bellows.[31] Mills is at first put off by this attitude, but he eventually assimilates to the cut-throat style of American sports and scores a surprising gold medal in the 1964 Olympic Games despite fierce opponents who jostle him to the edge of the track. The moral of the story is clear: real competitors give no quarter; nice guys finish last.

In the West, even children are taught to compete this way—sometimes to the point of running up the score against lesser opponents in a way that provokes humiliation and tears. High school basketball scores of 110–22 are commonly displayed on the Friday night sports roundup in my supposedly kind-and-gentle home state of Iowa. Philosophers debating the morality of this phenomenon point out, on the one hand, that the losers in such blowouts should not feel humiliated as long as they play to the best of their ability[32] and, on the other hand, that athletes who suffer from pretension may benefit from mild humiliation in sport.[33] Arguably, a just athlete simply wants accurate contest results. If a result is laughably lopsided, so be it. Sports, after all, are knowledge-seeking activities.[34] Knowledge that embarrasses people is still knowledge.

But surely the disposition to enjoy seeing competitors humiliated is not a virtuous one. Taking pleasure in another's suffering (*Schadenfreude*) is, as Mike McNamee observes, "too active, too destructive of human sympathy, to be evidence of a love of justice."[35] A just athlete values justice generally, and not merely, like Thrasymachus, in terms of advantage. Blowouts are the result of unjust matchups—contests that fail to take fair account of the relative merits and compatibility of the competitors going in. Whatever accuracy the scores show in reflecting this disparity does not justify the contest's worth, and just athletes do not place much stock in such contests' results, even when the result is victory. It is not inconsistent with justice to make less than a full effort once victory is assured, or even to end clearly flawed contests early.

In order for sport to promote the virtue of justice, it need not abandon competition completely. Rather, it needs to emphasize *good* competition. The best contests, those that exercise the virtues and produce internal goods such as "flow," are almost always evenly matched.[36] Asian cultures prefer evenly matched contests, observes Bäck, noting that Thai boxers who dominate opponents are forced to retire for lack of bouts.[37] That claim seems to imply that Western sports and athletes generally prefer easy victories, those that do not challenge one's skills or, perhaps, are gained through an opponent's misfortune.[38] There certainly are such cases. I recall my father, a dedicated University of Southern California football fan, declaring at the beginning of one Rose Bowl, "I don't want it to be a good game. I don't want it to be close. I want a blowout!" It was an understandable emotion but not a sober reflection on sport—even though it did show that he at least *knew* what "a good game" was.

Furthermore, his emotion was that of a fan, whose potential payoff is primarily pleasure, as opposed to the athlete, who stands to learn and grow more from a closely fought game. It is easy to forget that an athlete's life is usually dominated by training rather than contests. They train not just for the end goal of victory, else they would only enter contests against much lesser opponents—a practice derided even in Western sports as "cherry picking." Rather, they train to improve their competitive excellence, and they seek contests where that excellence will be justly tested. To say that competitive athletes only want to win is akin to saying that martial artists only want to fight. What they want is to possess the virtues associated with a just victory over a worthy opponent. This desire itself reflects the virtue of justice.

COURAGE VERSUS HUBRIS

Competition in sport has also been lauded for its ability to cultivate the virtue of courage. Because athletes must face the risk of losing and often face the risk of physical harm, competition demands virtues like courage, and in that way can serve as a means of Aristotelian-style virtue training. But there is a sense in which real-world risk is something quite different from sporting risk. You risk losing, but you only risk losing a game. You risk injury, but there is (usually) a trained medic waiting on the sidelines to attend to your needs. Unlike the potentially lethal fight that traditional martial artists train for but hope never actually to experience, modern athletes almost never face anyone trying to kill them.[39] There is a serious question about whether the courage cultivated within sport is in fact the same virtue needed in real life. Martial arts have a danger, in Bäck's view, that is lacking in sport and play.[40] They are designed to cultivate a kind of real-world courage appropriate for serious risks: a courage that does not promote violence and dominance over others but rather seeks to eliminate it. Bäck explains, "[A] martial art has the goal of dealing with violence by transforming the situation so that the violence and conflict with another completely disappear."[41] The image of the master martial artist is certainly not one of aggression and violence, and the Eastern philosophical principle of *yin*, or strength in yielding, can be appreciated even in Western sport. But is it true that the separate and playful nature of Western sports tranquilizes us about violence and actually prevents cultivation of the virtue of courage?

Part of this depends, of course, on what we mean by courage. MacIntyre does not seem to have had swordfights in mind when he counted courage among the virtues needed in social practices; rather, he mentions the need to "take self-endangering risks" and to "listen carefully to what we are told about our inadequacies."[42] Stating that it was not simply an absence of fear, since it may be virtuous to fear some things, such as disgrace,[43] Aristotle identified courage as the mean between (over)confidence and fear.[44] This clarification reflects Plato's discussion of courage as wise endurance in the pursuit of noble goals,[45] or that quality of the spirited part of the soul that enables it to follow reason's lead.[46] In all these cases, courage relies heavily on intellectual discernment plus the ability—cultivated through practice—to follow through with rational decisions despite emotions like fear. In this sense, it reflects martial arts training's goal of liberation from the fear of death. But in the context of Zen Buddhism, that would be liberation from all *selfish* desires—including fame, fortune, and victory.[47] The goal is a state of *mushin* (no mind) that is characterized by a *lack* of self-regard and the *absence* of preoccupation about contest results. In discussing the value of dangerous sport from a Western perspective, by contrast, John Russell and Norman Fischer identify self-affirmation and self-possession as the primary benefits.[48] Does the contrast between Eastern selflessness and Western selfishness suggest that the "courage" cultivated in competitive sports is not a virtue at all?

In fact, *hubris* or overconfidence would be the vice corresponding to courage on Aristotle's chart. There does seem to be a connection between the more violent Western sports, like boxing and football, and ego-puffing displays of bravado by athletes. Boxing is one of the world's oldest sports, predating even the Olympic Games, but it has struggled for legitimacy in the eyes of sport philosophers because its lusory goal, to use Bernard Suits's term, is actually the injury or disabling of one's opponent—that is, knocking him out so that he is unable to continue. If we define violence as the use of force with intent to harm, we can conclude that the sport of boxing condones violence. Traditional martial arts may also train practitioners to use force with the intent to harm but only in order to protect themselves or their communities in response to a violent attack, not just for sport or to win a game. Courage in the martial arts context concerns a real-life threat. But the courage required for boxing is bound up with the creation of an occasion for violence that has no good reason and is therefore morally unacceptable.[49] The ancient Greek vice of hubris involved excessive confidence or pride, especially in the willingness to violate socially accepted norms involving violence.[50] In effect, it represents the mistaken assumption that the normal rules don't apply to you. Since violence is generally prohibited in civil society, boxing's promotion of it can be seen to cultivate the vice of hubris rather than the virtue of courage.

It should be noted, however, that not all use of force in sport is violent and, in almost every other sport besides boxing, it is regulated in such a way as to *prevent* intentional harm or disabling of competitors. Meanwhile, the risks inherent in athletic competition do have the potential to cultivate the kind of wisdom-based courage described by Plato and Aristotle. The risk of

losing, just for starters, fosters the humility foundational to Socrates's understanding of wisdom, as knowing that one doesn't know, as well as Laozi's
enabling condition for greatness, namely, never considering oneself great.[51]
It takes courage to confront one's fallibility by entering the contest, and it
also takes courage to explore the limits of one's capabilities. Russell's defense of dangerous sports as a means of self-affirmation is based on their
ability "to confront and push back the boundaries of the self by creating
contexts in which some of the ordinary bounds of our lives can be challenged."[52] Russell may discount the idea that dangerous sports produce courage, but the benefits he sees in them seem to depend on courage.

What about the vice of hubris? Mike McNamee argues effectively that
sports can go a long way to preventing it. He recounts a famous boxing
match between Sugar Ray Leonard and Roberto Duran in which the former's
technical superiority so embarrassed the latter that he conceded the match,
although he was unhurt. According to McNamee, Duran's hubris, in the form
of egotistical posturing and derisive rhetoric, set him up for this fall, which
was deserved.[53] If indeed boxing promotes the vice of hubris by sanctioning
violence, it is also capable of correcting that vice and promoting real courage
as a competitive sport.

INTEGRITY VERSUS ISOLATION

Even if a case can be made that sport cultivates or exercises virtues such as
honesty, justice, and courage, these virtues have limited worth if they are
confined just to sport. Many athletes, it seems, exhibit their virtues only in
training and competition. I remember once watching one of my student athletes at practice. Her behavior was exemplary: she arrived early, interacted
constructively with her teammates, set an example of concentration and hard
work in every drill, and asked good questions of the coaches that clarified
everyone's understanding. She did all this despite suffering with the flu. At
one point, she pulled out of a drill to vomit in a trash can and then returned
and kept practicing. In the classroom, by contrast, she was a different person
from the gym. She would miss class for the slightest reason or arrive late and
unprepared. Avoiding interaction with fellow students and the professor, she
sat in the back and kept to herself. She almost never turned in an assignment
on time, and even when she did, the work was sloppy and riddled with errors.
Needless to say, her great success in sport was accompanied by constant
academic struggle. What are we to say about cases like these? Where did my
student's athletic virtues go? Are we to say that she selectively manifested
her virtues in the gymnasium but chose not to exercise them elsewhere in her

life? Or is she incapable of expressing them elsewhere? Are athletic virtues isolated to sport?

If they are isolated to one activity, they're not genuine virtues at all. "Someone who genuinely possesses a virtue," says MacIntyre, "can be expected to manifest it in very different types of situation."[54] The virtues cultivated through martial arts do not suffer from isolation, according to Bäck, because martial arts itself is not isolated from the rest of one's life. It is a lifetime pursuit, undertaken deliberately as a path to spiritual enlightenment.[55] Because the sports arena is an artificial environment, Bäck continues, "excellence in the sport, even if attained, may thereby, for many people, be restricted to this artificial setting with its artificial rules."[56] Insofar as sport is play, set apart from the serious business of work and survival, Bäck concludes, "it is somewhat strange to talk of producing virtues for our whole life in a sport."[57]

In my student athlete's case, it was more like sport was the serious part of her life, and school was just a necessary evil that made sport possible. Other student athletes view sport as a necessary evil that makes college possible. Either way, there is a clear divide between their personalities as athletes and their personalities as students, and this divide affects the authenticity of their virtues. For MacIntyre, authentic virtues are understood as features of a "social and moral life in terms of which [they have] to be defined and explained."[58] They must "transcend the limited goods of practices by constituting the good of a whole human life, the good of a human life conceived as a unity." Conceiving of one's life in this way requires an additional virtue, which he describes as "integrity, constancy, or singleness of purpose."[59]

Although, as we have seen, sport is marked off from the rest of life by certain boundaries of space and time as well as attitudes and rituals, there's no reason it has to be *thought of* as something separate and isolated from an individual's life. Many aspects of human life are similarly framed. Religion and family come immediately to mind. But to say that the special sense we get when entering our church or our childhood home (or I daresay a martial arts dojo) makes these things somehow separate from our lives is nonsensical. These distinctive realms and activities combine rather to *make up* our lives. We are fundamentally the same person in all of them.

Different environments and activities call for different behaviors, and the challenges faced in a practice like psychology demand a slightly different set of virtues than the challenges faced in rock climbing. But people who fail to manifest basic virtues like honesty or self-discipline in the different practices that call for them must be thinking differently about these activities. My student athlete would probably say that sport *is* her life. She did not conceive of her life as a unity, which in MacIntyre's terms means that she did not have the additional virtue of integrity. What, however, if sport really is her life and she shows integrity, constancy, and singleness of purpose *within* sport? This would be to make the erroneous assumption that one particular activity *could* constitute an entire life and furthermore that excellence in one activity to the detriment of all others should be the end or *telos* of one's life. As Aristotle explains in *Nicomachean Ethics*, every activity aims at some good, and the final good or end is *eudaimonia*, a happiness or thriving that can only be understood in terms of a complete lifetime. [60]

It is therefore an error to think of one's life only in terms of a sport or to think of sport as something separate from one's life. Having the virtue of integrity means understanding one's life and all of its activities as aimed at a particular end. In effect, it requires us to integrate the various aspects of our lives into a coherent whole. Because happiness is the product of virtuous action, according to Aristotle, [61] we must select and engage in activities in such a way as to cultivate and exercise the virtues. This is precisely the reason that people engage in traditional martial arts, according to Bäck. But based on what we've seen so far, it can also be the reason that people engage in Western-style athletics as well. On a virtue-ethics scheme, the cultivation and exercise of virtue should be the reason for engaging in all sorts of activities, not just sports or martial arts. Likewise, a person with MacIntyre's virtue of integrity will at least try to perform every action virtuously—even those that he doesn't particularly enjoy. We might think back to Albert Camus's Sisyphus, who found a way to voluntarily perform his eternal punishment of rolling a boulder up a hill, and therefore found happiness. [62] Having integrity means choosing to do everything with virtue because it is part of your life and who you are as a person.

The question remains whether sport actually rewards this kind of virtue, and the answer, regrettably, is that often it does not. Student athletes in particular are asked to perform simultaneously two very different practices, and yet the reward structure for athletic performance—for example, scholarships, playing time, and starting positions—is clearly tied to excellence, while the expectations for academics are minimized—a passing grade-point average and progress toward a degree. Many student athletes exhibit virtue in both areas, but the reward system clearly favors isolation rather than integrity.

If the Japanese sumo scandal recounted at the start of the chapter reveals that even virtue-directed martial arts can be corrupted by Western-style athletic values, our subsequent discussion of virtue in sport suggests that Western-style sports might benefit from a virtue-directed approach. The most convincing aspect of Bäck's argument that traditional martial arts are more capable of cultivating virtue than is sport is that traditional martial arts, by his definition, are consciously undertaken for that purpose. Bäck claims that there is something about the practice itself, "the ritual, the formal exercises, the formal patterns (*kata*), the direct connection with ordinary life," that accounts for martial arts' virtue-producing capacity.[63] But these aspects are included (though, perhaps, deemphasized) when martial arts are "corrupted" by being made into sports. The issue from a virtue-ethics point of view is not so much the nature of the practice. Almost any practice with standards of excellence can be used to cultivate virtue, and almost any activity can be done virtuously. The issue is how we *think about* the practice and how we integrate it into our lives.

In a book entitled *Aretism: An Ancient Sports Philosophy for the Modern Sports World*, I and M. Andrew Holowchak argue that, in order for sport to be a good, it must be undertaken for the purpose of cultivating virtues that benefit not only the participant but also the greater community by producing more virtuous citizens.[64] In doing so, we follow contemporary philosophers of sport such as Fraleigh, Simon, and McNamee, as well as ancient virtue ethicists such as Plato, Aristotle, Laozi, and Confucius. Sport, as practiced in the modern world, does not reliably incentivize and reward the virtues, but then a virtuous person should not be motivated by external goods like money and status. Indeed, both Western and Eastern virtue ethicists agree that the pursuit of fame and fortune *interferes* with the cultivation of virtue.[65] MacIntyre observes, furthermore, that the institutions that administer practices like sport (i.e., the NCAA or FIFA) tend to be guided by external goods like wealth, power, and status rather than the pursuit of virtue.[66] So the solution to the problem of virtue in sport is to be found within the minds of practitioners and the values of the practice community itself. The beauty of virtue as the real prize of athletic competition is that it benefits not just the victor but also the community at large.

DISCUSSION QUESTIONS

1. Contrast self-called penalties in golf with the tendency in many sports to deceive officials. Do you think golfers would be less likely than other athletes to engage in deception outside of sports, such as understating income on one's tax return?

2. Have you ever been on a team that ran up the score against an inferior opponent? Have you ever been on the losing side of a blowout? How did your team react to the situation? Do you think that sports should have mercy rules to prevent the practice?

3. Overconfidence is the vice corresponding to courage on Aristotle's scheme. Can you think of an example—similar to the boxing example of Sugar Ray Leonard and Roberto Duran—that shows how sport penalizes overconfidence, thereby encouraging true courage?

4. Why do you think that schools and colleges tend to encourage excellence in either athletics or academics but make it difficult to achieve both? How do you think they could change to promote a more integrated idea of virtue?

Chapter Eleven

Ethical Spectacle

The first-century philosopher Lucius Annaeus Seneca was no stranger to the grandstands of Rome's Coliseum. What he saw there would be stomach turning even by modern horror film standards: the live slaughter of exotic animals, the live slaughter of human beings by exotic animals, and even the live slaughter of human beings by other human beings. Our ethical concerns about violence in boxing seem almost quaint by comparison. In fact, Seneca was known for his moral criticism of Roman spectacles even in ancient times. An inscription uncovered at Pompeii names him as "the only Roman writer to condemn the bloody games,"[1] and in letter 7, he warns against the corrupting effects of being a spectator at the arena:

> Nothing is as ruinous to the character as sitting away one's time at a show— for it is then, through the medium of entertainment, that vices creep into one with more than usual ease. What do you take me to mean? That I go home more selfish, more self-seeking and more self-indulgent? Yes, and what is more, a person crueler and less humane through having been in contact with human beings.[2]

As a Stoic philosopher, Seneca took virtue to be the highest good. Those concerned about virtue today might view his condemnation of the Roman arena as a warning about the morally corrosive potential of watching modern sports. Such warnings are not uncommon. Watching sports is blamed for a host of human ills, ranging from laziness to spousal abuse. On the other hand, sports' affinity with art, discussed in chapter 6, suggests that watching sports could be a source of social and moral edification. What is the connection between ethics and aesthetics in sport, and under what conditions might sports spectatorship be a morally constructive activity?

Our inquiry should start, as Seneca's does, with a critical attitude toward spectacles, but it needn't necessarily finish with a negative conclusion. Seneca's oft-quoted condemnation, cited above, is accompanied by expressions of his admiration for gladiators as paragons of Stoic virtue. The events that the philosopher found aesthetically repugnant and morally hazardous were staged public executions, especially those in which condemned criminals were armed and set to kill one another without skill, honor, or any hope of survival. Worse than this sad spectacle, in Seneca's eyes, was the blood-thirsty bleating of the crowds screaming, not unlike modern sports fans: "Kill him! Flog him! Burn him!"[3] The conduct of gladiators, in contrast, receives repeated praise from Seneca because they fight with valor in the face of death and are, by virtue of their enslavement, symbolically liberated from the vicious desires of mainstream society.[4] "The gladiator judges it ignominious to be set against an inferior," Seneca observes, "as he knows it is without glory to defeat one who can be defeated without danger."[5] After witnessing a barbarian plunge a knife into his own chest during a mock sea battle, Seneca calls the display "all the more striking because of the lesson men learn from it that dying is more honorable than killing."[6] Might the spectacle of modern sport be equally praised and condemned according to its moral value?

It certainly seems so. In 1977, Christopher Lasch lamented the "degradation" of modern American sport by the forces and values of the market and its understanding of sport as a form of entertainment.[7] Some thirty years later, William Morgan describes sport as a kind of moral wasteland in which

> winning trumps fair play; an assertive egoism triumphs over mutual moral respect; an anything-goes-as-long-as-I-don't-get caught attitude prevails over expressions of good will toward others; and a pervasive mistrust poisons most interactions and relations in sports, undercutting any sense of solidarity—of community—within them.[8]

On the positive side, Mike McNamee likens modern sport to medieval morality plays, which were performed to educate the illiterate about the value of virtue and the dangers of vice.[9] Graham McFee thinks that sport functions as a moral laboratory, in which virtues and vices are challenged and tested in artificial contests with relatively low stakes as preparation for more serious moral challenges outside the game.[10] And Stephen Mumford, utilizing an aesthetic ethics, describes sports as "contests of virtue" in which spectators observe real-life struggles between virtue and vice and draw meaningful moral lessons from the spectacle.[11] The term "contests of virtue" comes from my own book *Athletics and Philosophy in the Ancient World*, which recounts the use of athletics and athleticism to test publicly and demonstrate virtue since the time of Minoan kings and Egyptian pharaohs. Spectatorship, in short, has always been part of the moral evaluation of sport. In this chapter, we will explore the possibility of an ethical aesthetic for sport by revisiting sports' previously discussed affinities with art in a critical exploration of the conditions that make sport morally beautiful or repugnant.

FRAMING

Art and sport share the common play characteristic of being somehow separate from ordinary life. We observed in chapter 6 that this separation was marked by physical boundaries such as a tennis court's outline and rituals such as the postgame handshake but that it actually occurs in the mind of the spectator. The boundaries and rituals signal to spectators (and to athletes) to adopt a particular attitude—to create a mental frame that focuses our attention on what we see within it and diminishes our awareness of the outside world. In theater, the transition is called a "suspension of disbelief." Indeed, the beginning of a basketball game is not unlike the opening of a play, where the curtain opens up and invites us to focus on what will happen within that particular frame of space and time.

Although relaxation and entertainment are part of what we expect from such experiences, a true aesthetic attitude is one of *heightened* awareness. As Lasch observes, "[Games] obliterate awareness of everyday reality, but they do this not by diminishing awareness but by raising it to a new intensity of concentration."[12] This intensity of concentration is powerful enough to be felt by athletes, who often thrive on it because they find themselves performing at a higher level. Their reaction is in contrast to most workaday tasks, like teaching and gardening, where external observation might be dreaded and associated with poorer performance. Auto-repair technicians jokingly state that the labor rate doubles if a customer wants to watch. What seems different about sport and the performing arts is that spectators expect to witness excellence.[13] The players feed off this expectation and are moved to live up to it. In cases where the expected excellence has a moral connection, I would argue, the spectator's act of framing thereby becomes a kind of ethical act.

So one thing that gives sport and art aesthetic value is spectators' willingness to see them as extraordinary—to frame them off as spaces within which special things are expected to happen or where the *un*expected is expected to happen. Indeed, the space of art and sport, as we observed earlier, is characterized especially by the senses of freedom and possibility.[14] This not only makes art and sport welcome escapes from the stifling predictability of the "real world" but also reinforces a community's value for freedom and possibility—inspired not least by their ability to enable greatness. It is uncontroversial that the quality of genius is valued, and in comparing the concept of genius in art and sport, Teresa Lacerda and Stephen Mumford note its association with the aesthetic values of creativity and originality, which depend, in turn, upon an atmosphere of freedom and possibility.[13] If we understand sport in Bernard Suits's terms as "a voluntary effort to overcome unnecessary obstacles,"[16] the sporting genius or virtuoso can be understood as one who "can find new ways of overcoming . . . obstacles or can respond to their unpredictability through their creative acts."[17] An aesthetic morality of sport, then, simultaneously frames it as something separate from the ordinary world and elevates expectations of excellence by reaffirming such values as freedom and possibility within that frame.[18] Lasch observes that one of play's virtues is "its capacity to dramatize reality and to offer a convincing representation of the community's values."[19] In sport, likewise, an appreciation of freedom and the chances for excellence that it creates demand a certain kind of knowledge.

The ability to engage higher intellectual powers was a criterion expected by some to separate art from sport, but as I argued in chapter 6, sport is just as capable as art of engaging those powers if approached with the appropriate background knowledge. Even to see, much less appreciate, a brilliant play in basketball, a spectator needs a good understanding of the game. Because many modern sports spectators played popular games like football and basketball in their youth, such knowledge is not uncommon. But as the audience of spectators expands in response to mass marketing and especially to the rise of television, there emerges a need to "dumb things down." Morgan says that television "cannot but help to lower the level of understanding of fans,"[20] while Lasch observes that "as spectators become less knowledgeable about the games they watch, they become sensation minded and blood-thirsty."[21] Both critics point as evidence to increased tolerance of fighting in professional hockey as it expands into warm-weather markets where spectators lack experience playing the game. A similar correlation may be identified between the low rates of sports participation among ancient Romans (especially in contrast with the ancient Greeks) and the lurid violence of their spectacles.[22] The worry here is not so much about violence per se, which appears in a variety of cultures and epochs, including our own, but rather that violence appeals to raw emotions rather than understanding. That was also the basis for Plato's criticism of mimetic poetry and drama. By disengaging reason, he thought, we might disengage our ability to distinguish between art and reality.[23]

All of this brings us back to the question of framing: distinguishing sport from ordinary life and having the knowledge to appreciate the excellences displayed within that frame. If the aesthetic appreciation of sport is to function as a mode of moral education, it must involve the affirmation of common values, such as freedom, and it must also identify their link with excellence. This requires knowledgeable spectators who can distinguish aesthetically between performances that affirm those values and those that do not.

Indeed, the role of the spectator in ancient Greece was precisely to witness and affirm that the victory was awarded on merit to the person who earned it[24] —to affirm that the game was fair, a concept that, in many languages, carries both aesthetic and ethical connotations. Discerning fairness requires understanding the game and, to use the modern language of social practice theory, an appreciation of its "internal goods," which is most available to current and former practitioners.[25]

Reducing sport spectatorship to the dubious entertainment value associated with violence, sex, or greed not only removes it from the aesthetic sphere of engaging the higher intellect but also fails to separate sport from ordinary life as a place where excellence is expected. Indeed, Morgan links sport's failure to be extraordinary with a larger moral failure in society. Noting that professional sports no longer offer a welcome departure from regular life, he says that, "in both everyday life and sports these days, an instrumental regard for whatever people do is the rule rather than the exception, as is the concomitant rationalization of the unseemly dealings that are part and parcel of such a self-centered life."[26] The aesthetic framing of sport, in the end, is an ethical act, and spectators' failure to understand and expect excellence of athletes is ultimately a moral failure.

AUTOTELICITY

As Morgan suggests in the quotation above, instrumentalism—that is, viewing sport as a means to an end rather than an end in itself—is part of our failure to frame sport properly as something autotelic. Autotelicity was another of sport's important affinities with art, and indeed the value and experience of beauty seems antithetical to instrumentalism. Aristotle makes clear that what is *kalon* (good or noble) is done for its own sake.[27] As we observed in chapter 6, however, scholars like David Best take the intrinsic instrumentality of sport—that is, the need to play for ends of victory—as the key thing that *distinguishes* art from sport; in art, the ends and means are indistinguishable.[28] Even though the internal object of the game, the lusory goal in Suits's terms, is defined separately from the means, it does not mean that autotelic beauty has no value in sport.

Although deliberately playing to the crowd is discouraged and sometimes penalized, performing an action with grace and style is generally valued in sport. "Winning ugly" is never as good as winning beautifully. Not all sports award style points, but style still matters. Cesar Torres illustrates this point with the South American debate over soccer-playing styles, where "art football" is often preferred to "results football."[29] Soccer's nickname, of course, is "the beautiful game," and Torres argues, based on the rules and various critical interpretations of quality play, that its beauty is associated with "forward looking or creative" offense and virtuosity rather than defense and conservative, negative, play—even when the latter favors victory.[30] It is no coincidence that these qualities were associated with the aesthetic values of freedom and possibility, as well as the ethical value of excellence.

If the central importance of victory need not disrupt sport's aesthetic autotelicity, what about the quest for profits? The ethical-aesthetic values of freedom, possibility, creativity, and even genius are not reliably supported by the market. Lasch observes that the managerial apparatus of businesses work to reduce or even eliminate the risk and uncertainty at the center of sport's aesthetic value.

> When sports can no longer be played with appropriate abandon, they lose the capacity to raise the spirits of the players and the spectators, to transport them into a higher realm of existence. Prudence, caution, and calculation, so prominent in everyday life but so inimical to the spirit of games, come to shape sports as they shape everything else.[31]

Bradley Wiggins's victory in the 2012 Tour de France may be a case in point. Wasting little to no energy on individual attacks or solo breakaways and relying instead on his predicted superiority in the final time trial, Evans rode a hypercalculated race. It was a smart victory, but it wasn't really spectacular.

The vision of sport as a business whose purpose is to generate profit is instrumentalist in a way that focus on victory is not because the final goods in question are, to use Alasdair MacIntyre's term, external to the game. To play a sport to win is still fundamentally to play a sport, but to play a sport solely for the purpose of earning money brings the potential of selling out a sport's internal values—as a boxer or sumo wrestler does when he throws a fight for gambling interests. In fact, gambling illustrates an extreme form of spectator instrumentalism—one in which interest is detached not only from the quality of play but sometimes even from one team's victory as well. Gambling spectators' interest is limited strictly to the outcome of their bets. I visited a Keirin bicycle racetrack in Japan recently and was overwhelmed by the spectators' lack of engagement with the sport they were betting on. There was the same kind of pall in the place that one finds in a large casino; everyone was scribbling on paper and staring at screens displaying the odds—almost no one was watching the actual races. There was certainly no spectator framing of the sport as a place to affirm values like freedom. Playful possibility was transformed into idle chance. Excellence had no more to do with the spectators' expectations than it would if they were feeding slot machines.

The spectators' disengagement with sport at the Keirin track in Japan may also be a symptom of the market-driven self-centeredness that Morgan identifies as the central problem with modern sport. Following Lasch, he calls it "a thorough going narcissism . . . whose self-serving ways leave little if any room for others in sports or for the larger good of these practices themselves."[32] One might counter that a certain self-centeredness or individuality is part of sport's beauty: Dick Fosbury's unorthodox high-jump technique or Julius Erving's above-the-rim basketball play are examples that come to mind. Indeed, Víctor Durà-Vilà identifies such originality as having both aesthetic and ethical value. "[A] philosophy of football that promotes an aesthetically satisfying way of playing will, in turn, encourage the positive values of creativity, skill, technique, vision over discipline, improvisation over dullness, and individuality over uniformity."[33] But this is not the kind of individualism that Morgan has in mind. "The problem," he says, "is the kind of hyperindividualism to which markets give rise, wreaking havoc on sports because they turn them into crass exercises of self-promotion and self-assertion."[34] Instrumental individualism does not care for the goods of the game or even so much for victory; it is rather an attitude of doing whatever it takes to increase one's market value. In many cases, this entails not so much athletic or moral excellence but rather a flamboyant, obnoxious, or "bad boy" personality that appeals even to fans who know little about the game. Spectators' tendency to frame sports as nothing more than businesses, adds Morgan, contributes to our "abysmally low moral expectations" of them.[35] Spectators' acceptance of instrumentalism in sports is as morally problematic as the instrumentalism itself.

THE MORAL DIMENSION

It may be tempting to believe that the so-called moral degradation of sport has nothing to do with spectatorship and, more generally, that morality has nothing to do with aesthetics. Could we seriously blame moviegoers for depictions of moral depravity they passively witness on the silver screen? Probably not. But we should beware of making what Marcia Eaton calls the "separatist mistake," namely, the assumption that aesthetics and morality are separate.[36] As Torres explains, "Separating the aesthetic from the moral threatens the unitary aspect of experience and valuation in art, sport, and beyond."[37] Certainly, sport seems a particularly clear example of the connection between morality and aesthetics. Mumford argues that moral considerations inevitably intrude on the aesthetic appreciation of sport: ethically bad features detracting from its aesthetic value and ethically good features adding to it.[38] He points as evidence to our awareness of Ben Johnson's steroid abuse detracting from the aesthetic enjoyment of his 100-meter sprint victory in the Seoul Olympics, and to our awareness of Lance Armstrong's having overcome cancer as adding to our aesthetic enjoyment of his seven Tour de France wins.[39]

It is characteristic of sport that we want to know not just who won but also whether they *deserved* to win. The detection and punishment of cheaters is (at least presented as) a priority, and even immoral actions that have nothing to do with sport can tarnish an athlete's image and detract from his or her results. Swimmer Michael Phelps's eight gold medals at the Beijing Olympics were tarnished in many fans' eyes after he was photographed using illegal recreational drugs at a party. Revelations of golfer Tiger Woods's marital infidelities not only stained his image but also seemed to affect his game.[40]

Such moral scrutiny of athletes is evidence of a lingering conceptual connection between athletic and moral excellence. I say *lingering* because, as we saw in chapter 1, the link between athleticism and virtue goes at least as far back as the ancient Greek ideal of *kalokagathia*, a word that unites beauty and goodness and was explicitly associated with athletics and gymnasium life. The beauty of the Greek athletic form represented such moral virtues as self-control, such religious virtues as humility, and such civic virtues as liberty. In other words, it affirmed important community values. Just as an athlete's beautiful body produces beautiful actions, so moral virtue on Aristotle's account is the capacity to produce virtuous actions, which are not only beautiful in themselves but also are performed for the sake of beauty.[41]

Unfortunately, an ethical aesthetic like *kalokagathia* is probably *not* the motivation for the media's moral scrutiny of athletes in the modern world. As Morgan observes, sports commentators in the print and media "have long given up the mantle of moral criticism in favor of what can best be described as shrill carping: part of what some call the *outrage industry*."[42] In other words, rather than upholding high moral expectations for sport across the board and especially on the playing field, the media capitalizes on moral scandals that draw in viewers and bring in revenue. It's not unlike the gambler who bets that a team will lose. She is not interested in a quality game or in the values that underpin it; she is interested only in her personal profits. If the media could make as much money playing up moral virtue as they do in sensationalizing vice, they might actually contribute to the cause of ethical aesthetics. Likewise, if commentators educated audiences on the nuances of the games—praising, for example, good team play rather than individualistic sensationalism—aesthetic appreciation of virtue in sports might be more widespread.

It all comes back to the spectators, however, and their ability to appreciate the moral aspects of the game, which is based on their understanding of sport as a vehicle for promoting virtue and foundational values. Athletics, like art, in Christopher Cordner's words, "enact or realize life-values."[43] This ability is the foundation of art's value as moral education. It is said that art "shows" rather than "tells" us the morally relevant features of the world, by presenting us with complicated particular situations. Literature and drama in particular are thought to be a useful part of ethical education because they exercise our capacities for making good moral judgments.[44] Sport may actually be better than art in this respect because the contest of virtues acted out on a playing field is neither scripted nor contrived toward a particular outcome. Mumford suggests that spectators view sport not as a struggle between individuals for victory or a prize but rather as a battle between virtues—both athletic virtues like height or skill and moral virtues like courage and self-control.[45] This approach would allow us to appreciate more than simple outcomes in our spectatorship of sport. It may even allow sport to function as a "moral laboratory" through which we can reflect on the moral incidents we see in a relatively harmless and inconsequential environment.[46] Connecting ethics and aesthetics in sport may be key to its potential as a form of moral education for spectators.

"But I just want to *enjoy* watching sports," a fan may rejoin. The requirements that spectators frame sport properly, appreciate its autotelic elements, and adopt a morally critical eye might seem antithetical to the purely aesthetic enjoyment of sport. Pleasure, not morality, might seem to be a spectator's proper goal, and a morally critical attitude toward sport may seem as if it will rob all the pleasure from a spectator's experience. This is not the case, however, as it is obvious that knowledge of the game enables a spectator to engage more closely with the action and ultimately to enjoy it more. Many sports, like baseball, golf, curling, and cricket, have almost no spectator appeal to those unfamiliar with those games. Furthermore, having actually played a particular game increases spectators' aesthetic appreciation because they understand and value the sport's internal goods. Finally, there is a lingering link between virtue and athletics that affects our aesthetic experience of sport. People are much more likely to overlook the moral unscrupulousness of a musician, artist, or author than they are that of an athlete. Aesthetics and ethics are not independent in sport, and if Plato is right about beauty's ontological connection with the good,[47] we should not try to separate aesthetics and morality at all.

What we should try to do as spectators is to treat sport more like art—that is, to have high moral expectations for it and to try to learn from its moral lessons. There is, after all, an authenticity to the drama of sport that art and literature as mere representations of reality cannot claim. Returning to the example of ancient Rome, spectacles including public executions, exotic animal hunts, reenacted sea battles, and gladiatorial death matches were staged by political leaders to manipulate the populace. They were designed to demonstrate the state's intolerance of criminals, the scope of its empire, the strength of its military, and the authority of its rule—those great gladiatorial fighters, after all, executed their opponents only upon the highest official's explicit command.

By adopting a morally critical approach, however, Seneca was able to appreciate and find inspiration in the virtue of gladiators and other "lowly" performers without being sucked into the propaganda of the promoters. He did this, first, by framing the contests with an expectation of extraordinary virtue; second, by understanding the symbolic connection between the gladiator's predicament and the challenges of everyday life; and, third, by exercising the moral discernment needed to find beauty in displays of virtue and to express revulsion and disgust at gratuitous violence among unskilled fighters. In the end, the ability to appreciate sport ethically and aesthetically should result in spectators taking more pleasure in it and perhaps even in modern sport becoming more worthy of admiration. Any fan's most powerful weapon is the off button on his TV's remote control.

DISCUSSION QUESTIONS

1. Ugly athlete behavior, such as fighting in hockey, is caused partly by lack of knowledge and low moral expectations among spectators. How might audiences be educated to better appreciate games like hockey and to have higher moral expectations of athletes?
2. Identify an athlete who fits Morgan's definition of hyperindividualism—caring only for one's market share and not for the values and excellences of the sport. Now imagine that your child looked up to this athlete as a role model. What would be your response? Can you identify an example of positive individualism that you would encourage your child to emulate?
3. Do you think it is fair for the sporting press to subject athletes to moral scrutiny outside the game? Can you think of an example where such scrutiny crossed the line and became part of the sensationalist "outrage industry" rather than legitimate journalism?
4. Recently, a fan was ejected from a basketball game for loudly criticizing officials' calls from his seat behind the scorer's table. What does his ejection say about the sport's moral expectations of spectators? Do you think it was fair?

IV

Social and Political Issues in Sport

The metaphysics and the ethics of sport reveal its nature as a social activity, but they don't necessarily require us to think about sport from a community perspective. Just as a volleyball player should examine not only her individual performance but also the collective performance of her team, so too must sport itself be explored in social and political terms. The most common sociopolitical role of sport is its use in education. Chapter 12 shows that sport in education suffers from various forms of fragmentation. The mind-body split, familiar from metaphysics, results in the separation of physical education from intellectual endeavors. Meanwhile, moral education suffers from a theory-practice split where ethical concepts taught in the classroom are rarely tested or experienced in practice—as they might be through the medium of sport. Finally, intercollegiate athletics suffers from an academic-athletic split that fails to treat coaches as educators and tends to treat sports and athletes as means to financial ends—actions that can't help but have negative educational impacts.

Sport has a history of challenging social categories that goes back to ancient Greece. As chapter 13 shows, social categories are irrelevant from the pure perspective of sport, which measures only performance. Despite this, both the ancient and modern practice of sport have segregated and excluded people based on class, race, sex, and disability. Such practices may be intended to benefit the disadvantaged, but they also raise important questions about fairness—as does the use of prostheses like Oscar Pistorius's high-tech "cheetah legs," which may constitute a mechanical advantage over natural limbs. As with any social good, sport should be accessible to everyone, but questions of distributive justice abound.

Sport's connection with conventional politics is discussed in chapter 14. The Olympic Movement likes to dissociate sport from politics, but the Games are perhaps the most politically exploited event there is. What Olympic and other sports enthusiasts mean when they say sport should be kept separate from politics, however, is that political ideology (whether fascist, communist, capitalist, or whatever) should not affect sports' internal concerns (such as judgments about athletic excellence or eligibility to compete). We may observe conceptual connections between sports values such as freedom, and political values such as liberty, and we may try to put sports in the service of political ideals, like peace. But we should also recognize that sport has a politics of its own, derived from its metaphysical nature as a noninstrumentalist activity, which enables it to resist political exploitation.

Sport also plays a political role akin to a canary in a coal mine—as a kind of test case for larger social challenges to come. Chapter 15 discusses sport's relationship with globalization, the technology-driven shrinking of social existence. Globalization's tendency to favor those who already have power and privilege challenges both the values of sport and the political future of the planet. Sports like soccer are already enjoyed across the globe under a single set of rules, but there is risk in sport and in the world that cultural differences will be homogenized into a giant monolithic culture. Sports communities must therefore be vigilant to preserve diversity. What would soccer's World Cup be if the only difference between the teams were the color of their uniforms? A multicultural approach to sport does not entail uncritical acceptance of all cultural differences, no matter how repugnant. What sport needs is a common cause, such as environmental sustainability, to focus its values and efforts. The social and political potential of sport, on the international level as well as the local, is not automatic and should be intentionally pursued with at least as much enthusiasm as victory.

Chapter Twelve

Sport and Education

A philosopher walks into a gymnasium, frustrated with his regular students' unwillingness to learn, and is impressed by the masterful ball-playing skills of a certain young athlete. The youth seems poor and disadvantaged but clearly has the capacity to learn complex skills, so the philosopher comes up with a scheme to educate him. He offers to support the youth's athletic training, if he agrees to take lessons with the philosopher for a certain period every day. The athlete, eager for the financial support, takes up the philosopher's offer and begins his daily studies, earning a tidy sum for each lesson properly learned. After a time, the philosopher notices that the athlete's motivation to study has shifted from the money to intellectual honor, and so he cleverly announces that he will no longer be able to pay the student for completing the lessons. The athlete offers to continue studying for free. But the philosopher laments that the lessons are causing him to forgo more practical work and says he needs to end them so that he can find a regular job. The student, having developed a great passion for his studies, balks at this idea and offers to turn around and pay the philosopher for the lessons.

This is not the plot of a modern made-for-TV movie; it is the ancient origin of the ongoing saga that mixes sport and academics in education for youth. The gymnasium was in Samos, Greece; the year was around 535 bce; the lessons were in geometry; and the philosopher's name was Pythagoras.[1] The student's name apparently was Pythagoras as well, and it is said that he migrated with his soon-to-be-famous teacher to the Greek colony of Kroton in southern Italy where they again went to the gymnasium to recruit students, and eventually founded what may be the first academic-athletic institution in history. Even before Pythagoras's arrival, Kroton was famous for its athletes. In the Olympic Games of 576 bce, its citizens took the top seven places in the prestigious *stadion* race, inspiring the saying that "the last of the Krotoniates was the first among all other Greeks."[2] Pythagoras's school may be counted among the causes of Kroton's continued dominance, however. He was specifically linked with the city's most famous athlete, the wrestler Milo.[3] Graduates of the Pythagorean school excelled in nonathletic endeavors as well, especially medicine, mathematics, music, and politics.

When Plato travelled to Italy shortly after Socrates's death, he was greatly influenced by the Pythagoreans, and it is likely that he got the idea to found his school in the Academy gymnasium after visiting one of their schools there.[4] Indeed, Plato is the philosopher we most associate with the use of sport in education. His *Republic* declares gymnastics to be a tool for educating the soul,[5] and the *Laws* prescribes gymnastic education and games for both genders and all ages.[6] I believe that Plato saw philosophy itself as a reflection of athletic struggle.[7] He uses athletic metaphors constantly and depicts Socrates as competing with and defeating rival sophistic educators. Plato may even have inspired his less-athletic student, Aristotle, to see ethical virtues reflected in the beauty of the pentathlete's body.[8] The final goal of ancient Greek athletic-academic education was always *aretē* (virtue, excellence), a disposition expected to lead to success in any activity or profession.

Somewhere along the line, however, this holistic idea of education fragmented. Academics, though taking its name from Plato's gymnasium, became precisely those educational activities that take place *outside* the gymnasium. Gymnastics, meanwhile, came to be known as "physical education"—a name that reflects the mind-body split espoused by metaphysical dualism, discussed in chapter 7. The idea that sport is a form of character education, meanwhile, suffers from a theory-practice split, as we saw in chapter 10. Coaches, parents, and philosophers still propound the theory that sports can build character, but empirical studies of moral development in athletes suggest that it fails in practice and that sport may rather contribute to vice. Finally, the grand American experiment of intercollegiate athletics suffers from an academic/athletic split that has become part of institutional culture. In some ways, modern collegiate athletes resemble that ancient student of Pythagoras: seduced into studying by the promise of financial support for training. The difference is that Pythagoras made a scholar of his athlete while modern institutions seem more interested in making money from theirs. Regardless of the educational value sport has, it is not automatic or intrinsic. From the political perspective of communities, we must ask what can be done to make sport a more effective educational tool. The answer seems to be, first of all, to heal all of these splits.

PHYSICAL EDUCATION AND THE MIND-BODY SPLIT

The most profound contrast in the use of sport as education between ancient Greece and today is a different way of looking at the relationship between mind and body. As we saw in chapter 7, although most ancient Greeks were dualists—that is, they believed in the separation of mind and body—and they prized the soul (*psychē*) over the body, they understood human movement to originate in the *psychē*. Hence, athletic training was understood as a kind of spiritual training, and the beauty it produced in athletic bodies was understood as a reflection of virtue (*aretē*). The Greek idea was not much different from many Eastern philosophical perspectives, which avoid clear distinctions between mind and body and understand the movement involved in martial arts training specifically as a method of spiritual development. The Greek system, however, is expressly competitive and rule governed. In *Republic*, Plato stipulates that children's games be strictly governed by rules, so that they may grow up to be law-abiding adults,[9] and athletic competition is used in the education of the guardians to select students with the qualities, such as resoluteness and endurance, necessary for higher-level studies.[10] Plato's assumption, like Pythagoras before him, is that students who show character in the pursuit of athletic excellence have the potential to excel in academics.

Nowadays, by contrast, the prevailing assumption is that athletic excellence is a sign of low academic potential. People assume that there is an inverse relationship between muscularity and intelligence, a phenomenon popularly known as the "dumb-jock myth." The metaphysical causes behind this shift begin with Cartesian dualism, which not only posits the separation of mind and body but also asserts thinking to be our essential function. But there is also a problem with metaphysical physicalism—the belief that non-physical minds and souls don't exist and that human beings can be understood in entirely material terms. This view is inspired and endorsed by empirical science, which tends to limit its studies to phenomena that can be observed. The problem here is not so much metaphysical as cultural, in that this culture tends to view athletes in terms of their bodies and to leave the thinking part of their training up to others—especially scientists. A narrowly physiological approach to training is typical here. The focus is on physical parameters like body-fat percentage, oxygen uptake, and fast-twitch muscle fiber percentage; moral development is disregarded. Athletes are viewed as specimens, sites for experiments, but their own minds rarely contribute to the intellectual side of the endeavor. Of course, this is practical, to some degree, since the peak of athletic ability usually arrives decades before the peak of intellectual ability.

The social and political problem is that little to no effort is made in this culture to educate the athlete in the intellectual aspects of her performance.

Exercise physiology, nutrition, and even biomechanics are studied in separate departments, generally located in a different part of the campus from athletic facilities. What is more, the so-called sport sciences tend to marginalize and even exclude humanities and social science from their curricula. Not only are student athletes exempt from studying the empirical science behind their training and performance, but also students with sports-related majors such as exercise physiology are often left in the dark about the history, philosophy, sociology, and psychology of sport.[11]

On the other side of this same divide, many students and scholars in the sport sciences do not actively participate, and have not in the past participated, in competitive athletics. Even actively competing athletes are sometimes excluded from the intellectual aspects of their games, as when coaches call plays and make strategic decisions from the sidelines. The use of tiny radios to communicate during competition only further reduces athletes' intellection. Alasdair MacIntyre's social practice theory, which provides a framework for sport to function as a form of moral education, understands meaningful participation in a practice to include an understanding of the history, traditions, and fundamental nature of the activity—as we saw in chapter 5. To deprive athletes of access to the intellectual aspects of their sport is to deprive them of such meaningful participation and therefore to deprive sport of much of its educational potential.

Rather than reinforcing the mind-body split, sport in education should act intentionally to heal it. Even Eastern philosophy does not expect its doctrine of mind-body unity (or human-cosmos unity) to be understood naturally as metaphysical fact. Rather, as we saw in chapter 7, it regards such unity as an achievement—a form of wisdom that is, itself, cultivated and expressed through bodily movement. Some educators recognize an overemphasis on the intellectual in modern schools, but most have come to accept uncritically education as a purely intellectual endeavor. It is undeniable, however, that human beings have bodies and that we use our bodies to support and express our intellects. For instance, Paul Weiss thought athletic training could teach us to carry out our ideas in action, thereby "correcting the disequilibrium between mind and body."[12] Jim Parry notes, meanwhile, that the experience of moral concepts like trust are mediated through the body in sport, thereby transcending mere theoretical understanding. When we learn trust through participation in team sports, he says, "responsibility begins to emerge from the physical awareness of the other and the needs and concerns of the other in the context of risk."[13] Pierre de Coubertin believed that moral character was primarily formed in the body. In sport, he said, "the muscles are made to do the work of a moral educator."[14] Virtue is explicitly an embodied concept from the Eastern point of view; it is not merely a matter of abstract understanding.[15] Indeed, a plethora of subjects, including music and other performing arts, are taught using a holistic approach that combines physical practice with intellectual training. Sport's tendency to separate itself from the intellectual cannot help but hamper its educational potential.

MORAL EDUCATION AND THE THEORY-PRACTICE SPLIT

The evidence for sport as a form of moral education is almost entirely anecdotal. Perhaps the most famous testimonial comes from the existentialist philosopher Albert Camus, who once remarked that the context in which he really learned about ethics was that of sport.[16] The social science evidence, as we mentioned before, suggests the contrary: that sport does more harm than good.[17] Some attribute such findings to an overemphasis on competition, which they view as intrinsically immoral. Others point to the presence of money and the high-stakes game of college recruiting, which seems to affect children as early as junior high school. Additional studies may provide evidence for these theories. Meanwhile, from a philosophical point of view, the question of morality and its relationship to human practices like sport is extremely complex and controversial. For one thing, there are rival ethical theories, some of which might endorse traits conducive to competitive success, while others might condemn them. As David Carr points out, "One man's cooperation may be another's herd instinct."[18] The moral value of things like courage and self-discipline, furthermore, seem to ride on the nature and purpose of the activity. A courageous, disciplined murderer, for example, is not a public good.

This dichotomy between skills and virtue is recognized in virtue ethics by what Plato understood as the *technē-aretē* (skill-virtue) distinction. As we saw with the case of lying and deception, the moral value of a skill depends on the ends it serves. In sport, technical skills combined with competitive virtues like courage and self-discipline lead to victory and often reward. But the skills of most sports, such as shooting a ball into a goal using only one's feet, have little to no practical value independent of the sport. This *technē-aretē* distinction means that we cannot take victory in athletics as evidence for moral virtue, because the win may depend more on technical skill than character and, as MacIntyre points out, the moral virtues may actually hinder practical success in some practices. In basketball, for example, success depends partially upon the intentional strategic breaking of rules. An athlete who refuses to engage in that practice because she values rule adherence will find herself at a competitive disadvantage.

It is instructive to note, however, that the suggested use of athletic contests in Plato's *Republic* to reveal potentially gifted students and philosophers does not entail that the *winners* of the contests were those selected for advancement. It suggests rather that an athlete's performance in the contest reveals important facts about his character—including his lack of interest in fame and fortune as opposed to virtue.[19] An athlete's refusal to compromise his moral principles in the pursuit of victory is better evidence of character than victory itself. Insofar as sport in education focuses primarily or even exclusively on success in contests, it at best hampers and at worst is counter-productive to the cultivation of moral character.

On the other hand, sport has a great *advantage* over classroom-based methods of learning ethics and morality because, in sport, moral dilemmas are experienced firsthand. Moral behavior does not result from learning theories, rules, or principles; rather, it is learned through experience.[20] Philosophers have criticized the empirical studies that point to sport's failure as moral education on the basis that they tested knowledge of principles or levels of moral understanding, rather than moral behavior.[21] Sport's potential as moral education lies in its ability to offer people the chance to work with moral concepts like fairness in practice, to test the concepts themselves, to confront others who fail to act on them, and even to explore one's own failure to act on them. Since sports take place in a relatively contained and controlled environment, the morally relevant possibilities it presents can be tested and explored. This is why Graham McFee calls sport a *moral laboratory*.[22] He argues that even abstract moral rules, such as "thou shall not kill," must be made sense of in concrete contexts; we learn them by applying them to the situations in our lives.[23] In sport, we learn not only rules but more importantly how to play within rules and, most importantly, how to behave in accordance with the moral principles, such as fairness, that underpin those rules.[24] The ideas of fair play and the level playing field are not sports specific; rather, they are real moral concepts that need to be learned through experience; sport, understood as a moral laboratory, offers the opportunity to do that.

The problem is that sport is generally *not* understood as being potentially morally educative. In fact, its educational function is rarely questioned or defended at all. Coaches and physical educators are almost never trained as moral educators. Sometimes they aren't even considered teachers. They are pushed to win and evaluated on winning only. As Carr points out, coaches' function as moral educators derives from their particular professional relationship with young people, and their effectiveness at this function depends almost entirely upon their individual willingness to see their jobs "in the context of wider concerns about how to live and what to value in life."[25]

Parry proposes that sports and physical education activities in schools be seen intentionally as "practices which act as a context for the development of human excellences and virtues and the cultivation of those qualities of character which dispose one to act virtuously."[26] Such a proposal surely has implications for the training and treatment of coaches and physical educators, as well as the actual practice of sports in the schools. As McFee explains, "In teaching the rules of a game (for example, cricket), a teacher sensitive to the principles might inculcate those principles too. . . . Thus the model is of abstract principles learned from (and in) concrete instances in sport, then applied to concrete moral situations."[27] Perhaps sports education should strive to improve not just technical skills but also moral character. Perhaps its goal should be not just winning games but also playing them fairly—and discussing whether certain actions are fair rather than passively leaving those decisions to others.

COLLEGE SPORTS AND THE ACADEMIC-ATHLETIC SPLIT

Perhaps the grandest experiment in combining sport and education is the phenomenon of athletics in American colleges and universities. Intercollegiate sport is much in the public eye. In some disciplines, its championships command huge television audiences while its scandals spark endless political debate. The question of its educational role, however, is rarely raised and debated—even by the faculty of these very same institutions. High-profile cases of academic fraud, athlete and coach misbehavior, recruiting violations, and secret payoffs lead some critics to conclude that there is no justification for big-time college sports and the only solution is to abolish them.

Defenders of the educational value of intercollegiate sport, including philosophers Robert Simon and Drew Hyland, frequently restrict their praise to smaller, nonscholarship programs and prescribe a variety of reforms. Simon suggests restrictions on season length and travel time to keep athletics from dominating students' lives,[28] whereas Hyland encourages institutions to treat athletics as a serious part of the educational program, rather than as a business.[29] Significantly, both philosophers aim their criticisms at institutions— governing bodies like the National Collegiate Athletic Association (NCAA) and the colleges and universities themselves—rather than the student athletes. Student athlete misbehavior, though generally presented in the media as the result of individual vice, is very often a reflection of their institutions' values, which exhibit a familiar fragmentation.

The first split is clearly between athletics and academics, or perhaps more generally, between the academic mission of these institutions and the actual role that they envision and support for athletics. At the highest levels, there is a great potential for revenue from tickets and television, as well as from national exposure that leads indirectly to financial gain in the form of logo licensing, alumni donations, and the recruitment of tuition-paying students. The vast majority of college athletic programs—and few make a profit—can and do use sports to raise the profile and popularity of their schools. Arguably, the whole enterprise results in more potential students becoming interested in higher education and achieving college degrees. But these practical business benefits depend on winning games and championships, and as a result, athletic departments tend to be structured around that goal in a way that other educational programs are not. In the worst cases, athletic programs are run like miniature professional sports programs that just happen to be housed on university campuses. According to Hyland, the real casualty of this business-motivated overemphasis on winning is that it has "allowed us, no, led us, to forget what we recognized once to our credit, that athletics is a powerful educational force."[30] If the universities themselves don't regard sport as a means of education, why should coaches and athletes regard it as such?

Universities, as we have already observed, are hardly immune to the perceived incompatibility of intellectual and physical excellences. Not only are athletics kept separate from academics, but also, even in many sports-related fields, the academic demands on student athletes are frequently regarded as being at odds with their athletic performance—and vice versa. Professors and coaches sometimes perceive themselves to be competing for a student athlete's time and attention. Professors imagine that coaches disregard class commitments when scheduling practices and away games. Coaches imagine that professors are academically prejudiced against student athletes. Students, meanwhile, are not immune from taking advantage of the tension. Some are well practiced at playing one "parent" off the other. Recently, I noticed that one member of our baseball team was in a class from which his teammate had asked to be excused because of travel to a game. I asked the player in class whether he was going to the game, too. "Sure," he said, "but the bus doesn't leave until 12:15." Much of this tension between coaches and professors, like the disconnection between athletics and academics more generally, derives from a lack of communication and mutual understanding caused by the real and perceived division between the two programs. Perhaps coaches should be considered and evaluated as teachers, with emphasis on student learning outcomes rather than win and loss records.[31]

In addition, we might expand our idea of what counts as education beyond intellectual knowledge acquisition to the kinds of skills acquired in sport. Noting the importance of physical skills in performing arts such as music, dance, and drama, former NCAA president Myles Brand argues that this also justifies the presence of athletics in universities.[32] The opinion that performing arts are appropriate academic subjects though sports are not probably has its origins in social elitism. If sports performance were to become an academic major alongside the performing arts, however, a similar holistic approach incorporating history, philosophy, psychology, and the like would be called for. By the same token, a greater emphasis on skill development through practice and experiential learning might enhance other academic subjects. Foreign language is another traditional academic subject that demands practice, persistence, and interactive performance.[33]

Ethics, if the previous arguments are correct, also demands the kind of practice and experience characteristic of sport. Universities teach ethics most effectively, it turns out, through their ethical treatment (or mistreatment) of students.[34] When universities treat athletes as means to institutional ends, they are teaching athletes to treat others as means to ends, too—no matter how often Immanuel Kant's moral injunction against this behavior is repeated in the classroom. Likewise, if universities financially exploit athletes under the guise of amateurism, they are teaching everyone that such exploitation is morally permissible.[35] At its worst, it seems that intercollegiate athletics may not only fail to contribute to universities' stated missions but actually undermine them as well.

Happily, such cases seem to be relatively few, and college sports do make an important contribution to many students' educations. This is thanks to the individual efforts of thoughtful coaches, understanding professors, and of course the individual merits of the students themselves. The institutions can and should do more, however, to recognize and promote the educational potential of sport—especially its potential as a form of moral education. Robert Simon claims that athletic values can harmonize and reinforce academic values: "Participation in competitive athletics can require intellectual honesty and a concern for truth, including accuracy about one's own values and talents, in ways parallel to academic inquiry."[36] Hyland echoes Simon's reference to self-knowledge but adds to the list of educational benefits from sport the experience of "deep, passionate commitment" and sensitivity to social issues like racism.[37] His prescription for achieving such educational goals, including faculty-athletic team liaisons, is characterized by healing the aforementioned divide between the academic and the athletic programs. Indeed, healing divides has become the common theme of this chapter.

The educational value of sport, it seems, depends on a holistic approach. Pythagoras, the historical founder of sport in education, employed a superholistic approach that integrated not just athletic and academic endeavors but also every aspect of a student's life from diet to religion to sleeping and love. While there is no need to resurrect Pythagoras or even Plato's gymnasium to rehabilitate sport's educational potential, we should recognize the problem of fragmentation and seek to bridge the divides. First, we must question the mind-body split, which is not dangerous in itself—Pythagoras and Plato were ardent dualists—so much as subsequent assumptions about the incompatibility of intellectual and athletic ability and the resulting tendency to treat athletes as passive specimens upon which training experiments are performed and through which strategic theories are tested. Second, sport's potential as moral education is great, but it depends on healing a theory-practice split by taking an intentional approach to learning moral concepts through participation in sport and reflection about that participation. Sport, seen in this way, can function as a moral laboratory where one learns to apply ethical principles and to deal with their violation in a relatively low-stakes environment. Third, the phenomenon of intercollegiate athletics needs to be redirected toward specific educational goals by healing the academic-athletic split common on college and university campuses. Professors, coaches, and administrators can work to close this gap first by seeing students as whole persons and understanding their education to involve both theory and practice. This is the ancient Greek model that inspired the idea that sport can be educational, and it deserves to be revived.

DISCUSSION QUESTIONS

1. Fine arts activities such as music, theatre, and dance often have dedicated majors that combine performance with theoretical and technical study. Do you think sport should be treated more like these subjects in the university?
2. Have you ever learned a (positive or negative) moral lesson through sport? What were the factors that led you to reflect on the experience? Did it change your later behavior?
3. If college and university coaches were considered, above all, moral educators, how might the current system of coach education and evaluation change?
4. What can be done to bridge the athletic-academic divide in schools? What role should student athletes play?

Chapter Thirteen

Sport and Social Categories

The name of the backwater industrial college was Carlisle, but the inscription on the commemorative football reads "1911: Indians 18, Harvard 15." Carlisle was a school for Native Americans, and its upset of Harvard couldn't help but have overtones about race and social class. The victory was due largely to Carlisle's star player—a mixed-race athlete by the name of Jim Thorpe, who would go on to dominate the next year's Olympic Games. In Stockholm, Thorpe triumphed in both the pentathlon and decathlon, winning eight out of the fifteen individual events. The Swedish king Gustav V famously declared him the greatest athlete in the world, and he was welcomed home to the United States with a ticker-tape parade. But apparently not everyone was pleased by his victories. Late in 1913 some newspapers revealed that Thorpe—like many college athletes at the time—had been paid to play baseball over a couple of summers, which violated Amateur Athletic Union (AAU) rules. Although the official protest period had long since expired, AAU officials retroactively withdrew Thorpe's amateur status, and his Olympic medals and titles were stripped.

There is little doubt that racism and social elitism rather than sincere concern for the purity of sport motivated at least part of the condemnation. One of Thorpe's Olympic teammates, Avery Brundage, became a zealous promoter of the Olympic amateurism movement, which was eventually exposed as an effort to exclude the working classes—and not coincidentally many racial minorities—from athletic competition. This kind of social bias was not new to sport. The ancient Olympic Games had also been used by aristocrats to try to validate their supposedly innate superiority. In the long term, however, it didn't work. Lower-class athletes achieved success in both the ancient and modern Olympic Games, and myths about social superiority slowly eroded. By 1983, the Olympic medals and titles of the American Indian champion Jim Thorpe had been reinstated.

If sport is to function as a moral laboratory where principles of fairness and equal opportunity might be learned through experience, there seems to be a special reason to ensure that sport actually embodies those principles. Historically, however, and in the present day, sport has been a party to various forms of social exclusion and marginalization based on class, race, gender, and disability. The extent to which such marginalization reflects and reinforces social prejudices and the extent to which it might represent fair and respectful treatment needs to be examined from historical as well as contemporary perspectives. What does equal opportunity actually mean in sport, where abilities differ markedly? Although exclusion from sport based on race or ethnicity is no longer acceptable, segregation based on gender and disability are still the norm. Meanwhile, social class, understood economically, continues to affect athletes' ability to compete—especially when considered on a global scale. Amateur restrictions still apply to American college athletes, although most Olympic sports have eliminated them.

The use of classifications in sport can be justified, according to internal sport values, as an effort to improve competition by isolating variables for which the athlete is not responsible. As Sigmund Loland explains, "Competitors ought to be differentiated in classes only in cases in which inequalities in person-dependent matters that they cannot influence in any significant way and for which they cannot be held responsible have systematic and significant influence on athletic performance."[1] This justifies things like weight classes in wrestling and age classes in swimming, but what about sex and disability classes—especially in cases where female or disabled athletes outperform the athletes from which they are supposedly protected by their special category? Was it just to restrict Jackie Robinson to the Negro leagues when his baseball skills were superior to most of the players in Major League Baseball? The use of classes and categories and its connection to wider social issues is an important test of fairness principles in sport.

SPORT AND SOCIAL CLASS

The modern Olympic amateurism rules that tormented Jim Thorpe and many others were often defended as a reflection of athletics in ancient Greece. In fact, ancient Greek athletes were never amateurs in that modern sense,[2] although there was a distinction between less prestigious "money" games and more prestigious "crown" games, such as the Olympics, where nothing more valuable than a leafy wreath was (officially) awarded to the victors. What better resembled modern amateurism in the ancient world was rather the attempt by aristocrats to preserve an illusion of their innate athletic superiority as evidence of their superior virtue and worthiness to lead. As we saw in chapter 1, the link between athleticism and social entitlement is even older than sport, reaching as far back as the third millennium bce to the fabled athletic feats of ancient kings such as Gilgamesh, Shulgi, and the pharaohs of Egypt.[3] Like the mythological labors of Heracles, these feats were the result of neither training nor competition. Rather, they were real or imagined displays of a king's natural superiority and divine favor designed to impress and reassure his subjects. Even in Homer's epics, athletic competition is generally reserved for chieftains and other nobles.

It was not until the Olympic Games began around the eighth century bce that an interest in relatively fair and open competition appeared, and it did not take long from that moment for beliefs about the natural superiority of members of the aristocracy to begin to erode. We can find evidence for this in the increasing use of coaches and sponsors for promising young athletes, as well as in the rise of equestrian events, where success depended primarily upon wealth and the victory crowns went to the owners rather than the drivers, jockeys, or the horses themselves. The equestrian victory of the Spartan princess Kyniska has been touted as a triumph of feminism in a male-only milieu but was interpreted by some ancient authors as evidence that Olympic victory depended on wealth rather than virtue.[4] Meanwhile lower-class success in the nonequestrian events, by some accounts, led to the leveling down of class differences in ancient Greece and eventually to the emergence of democracy.[5]

Sport in the ancient world was transformed from a means of reinforcing social hierarchy to a method for promoting democracy by its truth-seeking logic. Since, at ancient Olympia, the race winner was symbolically sacrificed to Zeus, there was a common community interest in actually selecting the most worthy victor. Efforts were accordingly made to construct a fair contest and to open up access to plausible candidates who were not already at the top of the social hierarchy.[6] Eventually, this phenomenon offered an opportunity to demonstrate virtue even to those who were not expected to have it. In fact, the glory associated with Olympic victory motivated cities to recruit and support lower-class athletes. By Roman times, the upper classes had essentially removed themselves from competitive sport, not least to avoid doubts about the justice of their social entitlement. But Roman sport continued to function as a means of proving social worth, especially for gladiators who could earn freedom from slavery by demonstrating their virtue in the arena.[7]

If sports are valued today as a relatively accessible means to climb the social ladder, that function still depends on an equal opportunity to compete and the fair administration of the contest. Huge economic disparities still exist, of course, and they still affect individuals' access to and performance levels in sport. This is especially true on a global level, and it has motivated the International Olympic Committee (IOC) to fund a committee called Olympic Solidarity, which distributes a portion of the Games' television revenues to help needy athletes and national Olympic committees with funds for training facilities, coaching, and equipment.[8] On a national level, in many countries poor athletes are recruited and supported in their training. In some cases, this process involves removing children from their homes and requiring them to train in distant cities, all for the glory of the state. When such dedication is rewarded with financial perks and places in top universities, these young recruits' athletic progress can translate into social progress, but rarely does sport alone provide such benefits. Too often, furthermore, countries neglect to provide opportunities for widespread sports participation in favor of funding elite development programs.

In the American system, where athletes are recruited to play college sports, a free or discounted education is generally offered as part of the deal. On the face of it, this is an excellent chance for poor or socially marginalized youth to move up the social ladder, and many athletes certainly have benefitted from this opportunity. At the same time, however, the emphasis put on athletics in some programs undermines the value of the corresponding academic education, leaving professional athletics as the only plausible career option to lift some students out of poverty. But the chances of going pro are infinitesimal, even for top college players. According to the National Collegiate Athletic Association's (NCAA) own statistics,[9] the percentage of college athletes that go on to play professionally in the major men's sports of basketball, football, and soccer ranges from 1.0 to 1.7 percent—an abysmal placement rate if these sports are to be justified as preprofessional programs. Clearly, sport's enduring potential to level down differences of social class is not automatic. It requires understanding and vigilance.

SPORT AND RACE

Race remains an important social issue in sport, although it is no longer a criterion for segregation and exclusion, and it is no longer considered by many biologists to be a valid classificatory concept.[10] For people of African descent especially, but for ethnic minorities worldwide, sport in the modern world has provided a relatively unfettered opportunity for achieving and demonstrating excellence despite the lingering prejudice and stereotypes that continue to impede more conventional paths to success. In the United States, where blacks still lag behind whites in things like graduation rate and income, their athletic success is outstanding. Despite accounting for only about 12 percent of the population, African American players constitute more than a third of college and well over half of professional football and basketball players.[11] Commentators have suggested that black athletic success helped to lay the groundwork for the election of President Barack Obama by opening up American minds to what blacks were capable of doing.[12] Sport is seen by many as a powerful social tool for battling racial prejudice.

Sport generally does not reward racial stereotyping, and many learn to overcome racial prejudice by participating in sports. Observing that athletes are among the only students to socialize and eat together in mixed-race groups on campus, Drew Hyland questioned the basketball team at his college about the issue of voluntary segregation among other students on campus. The players explained that their commitment to the team enabled them to "put the question of race in its place." Hyland suggested to the team that they try to share their insight with the rest of the campus, and he reports that they "have come to understand that they should not, ethically cannot, regard their successful experience of integrated community as simply that they are 'the lucky few,' that instead the gift they had been granted conferred on them a *responsibility* to distribute that gift as best they could more widely."[13] Unfortunately, such positive, proactive stories are all too rare. The larger story is that black athletic success has led not so much to a greater sense of equality but rather to a revised stereotype of natural athletic superiority accompanied by intellectual inferiority.[14]

Ironically, sports leagues in America had originally been segregated by race because it was believed that blacks were physically inferior and *not good enough* to play with whites.[15] Now the risk is that whites are considered incapable of competing with blacks. Professional basketball player Bill Russell's career spanned the transformation. He was the only black player on his team as a rookie in 1957, and then as the coach of the Seattle Supersonics he had only two white players on the team. "In basketball, it took only twenty years to go from the outhouse to the in-crowd," Russell says.[16] There may or may not be some kind of biological explanation for black success in sports, but there are many plausible social explanations. As long as sports are run fairly and provide equal opportunity to all, the psychological barriers created by stereotypes can be broken through the experience of competition. A good example of this is Christophe Lemaitre, the first white sprinter to break the symbolic ten-second barrier in the 100 meters. According to sprinting expert Ato Boldon, "Lemaitre is important to sprinting for the same reason that the black quarterback is important in the N.F.L. It flies in the face of what *used* to be conventional wisdom."[17] Lemaitre himself thinks that psychological barriers may be holding other white sprinters back, and he hopes his performance can "make the statement that it has nothing to do with the color of your skin and is just a question of work and desire and ambition."[18] Race remains an issue in sport—especially beyond the playing field in coaching, officiating, and management. At the same time, sport's power to erode racial stereotypes is intact and has the potential to do even more good than it already has done.

SPORT AND GENDER

Given the educational benefits of racial integration in sports, one must question the justification of continued athletic sex segregation. On the one hand, there seem to be real biological differences between males and females that seriously affect sports performance and therefore justify separate categories. On the other hand, the biological concept of sex is not so cut and dried as it may at first seem. History tells us that allegedly scientific facts about the intrinsic nature of females are often based on social stereotypes and cultural constructions.[19] One need look no further for evidence than the objections to female participation in sport based on real or imagined threats to their reproductive capacities. Strikingly similar arguments were used to justify the exclusion of women from higher education. It was thought that these activities would cause too much blood to run to the brain and leave the womb to shrivel.[20] As a matter of fact, sports participation is linked with lower teen-pregnancy rates,[21] and more highly educated women do tend to produce less offspring, but it is not because of withering wombs.[22] Arguments based on sex differences between men and women in sport may have similar cultural biases, and even when they do not, they may turn out to be irrelevant. It may or may not be true that women are naturally less aggressive than men, but it is irrelevant to the question of their right to play sports.

What, then, *is* a good argument not just for female participation in sport but also for the elimination of sex categories—for desegregation? As we learned in the case of race, a primary reason is education—not just the education of participants but the education of onlookers as well. In *Republic*, Plato proposed the integration of males and females in gymnastic education because he envisioned full access to citizenship for women, including military service and government. Aristotle, by contrast, thought women incapable of governance and made no mention of gymnastic education for them.[23] In much of today's world, women compete with men in academia, business, government, and the military, so why shouldn't they compete together in sports as well?

Noting that sex is relevant to sport only in terms of certain statistical predispositions for particular characteristics such as height, strength, and speed, Torbjörn Tännsjö argues that they should. "If we should discriminate at all," he says, "we should discriminate in terms of this characteristic itself and not in terms of sex."[24] I have argued furthermore that the athletic contest itself is capable of measuring differences in strength, speed, and the like.

There is no need for us to prejudicially exclude people from contests based on assumptions about their inferiority.[25] It seems unfair that a small, spindly male is eligible to try out for the football team based on his sex while a tall, strong female is excluded because of hers. Shouldn't performance be what matters?

Some people suspect that the real motivation for sex segregation in sports is that males are afraid of losing their illusion of superiority.[26] They point to incidents like the resegregation of skeet shooting after a woman named Zhang Shan won the Olympic gold medal in integrated competition at the 1992 Games. Women skeet shooters were expelled completely from the Olympics for eight years after that, until a women-only competition was added to the program in 2000. In integrated high school wrestling, boys often forfeit to girls. The thought is that it is a no-win situation because, if the boy wins, he only beat a girl, and if he loses it is even worse. A top-ranked wrestler gave up a good shot at a state title in the 2010 high school championships of Iowa by forfeiting to a girl in the first round. His father explained it as a matter of faith. "Wrestling is a combat sport and they're out there and it gets violent at times, and my son doesn't believe that girls should be engaged in that way."[27] Neither athlete was pleased with the situation, and it is very hard to argue, based on ranking, that the boy was afraid of losing. The case shows that sport is not easily separated from culture. It can just as easily be used to support arguments against integration as arguments for it.

"The ideal of sex equality as sexual assimilation (sex blindness) seems inappropriate to the realm of sports," argues Robert Simon. "The operative principle should be equal concern and respect for all participants, and this may sometimes justify differences in actual treatment."[28] If the result of sex integration in sport is a drastic reduction in opportunities for women to participate competitively, it is hard to interpret it as an equalization of opportunity for men and women. Very few of today's female gold medalists would have had a chance at Olympic victory if their competitions had not been restricted to women. Heroes like Jackie Joyner-Kersee or Bonnie Blair would probably be virtual also-rans in integrated elite competition. "The recognition of sex differences in sports," says Simon, "frees women from traditional restrictions and makes it possible for them to engage in highly competitive forms of athletics in a variety of major, traditionally male, sports."[29] Angela Schneider agrees: "In a society where men's interests and strengths dominate . . . excluding women from elite sport (on whatever grounds) would have the morally disastrous consequences of further restricting the realm of what is possible for women."[30]

These are consequentialist rather than deontological arguments, of course, but they clearly support the idea of continued sex segregation in sports. Considering the wider educational consequences, furthermore, the desegregation stakes may be even higher. As Betsy Postow observed over thirty years ago, "Sports constitute a socially valued activity. Men's genuine physiological superiority to women in their capacity for achievement in sports can therefore confer a higher social value on men, thereby helping to perpetuate the image of female inferiority."[31] Would equality in sport, in the form of sex desegregation, only serve to undermine females' struggle for social equality? Given the enduring link between virtue and athleticism, perceived athletic inferiority might also encourage people to think that females are morally inferior. If sex integration in sport perpetuates a message of female inferiority, what educational value is it? If sex-segregated sport is already perpetuating such prejudices, for that matter, what educational value is it?

Let us return to the ideas of sports as moral laboratories and social practices that seek knowledge. Integration in sport may well teach us that males are, in general, athletically superior to females, as if that was something we had serious doubts about anyway. However, it might also teach us that athletic superiority does not equate with social superiority and is certainly not evidence of moral superiority.[32] As we observed earlier, the display of virtue in sport does not always result in victory. Athletes probably show more courage and self-control in the way they handle adversity and defeat than they do in easy victories. In fact, Tännsjö argues that, if typically feminine moral virtues were privileged in sport rather than typically masculine qualities like physical strength, the need for sex discrimination would eventually be eliminated.[33] It is hard to imagine just what such a change would entail, but sports like marathon and triathlon, where men and women compete simultaneously if not directly against one another, may offer women more equal opportunities to display their virtues. Gender-segregated sports teams that train together but compete separately seem to do the same. That was the model I experienced in cycling at the U.S. Olympic Training Center, and it is the model currently used by the men's and women's soccer teams at my college.

Some philosophers have argued that we need to change the nature of sports so that they better reward females' physical advantages in things like balance and endurance.[34] A possible example is the sport of pole vaulting, where the advent of pole technology has deemphasized sheer strength and focused more on gymnastic qualities like agility and technique. But if the problem with sex categories is that they perpetuate stereotypes by privileging statistically prevalent or merely presumed characteristics expected of certain groups rather than the real abilities of individual persons, a move to make sports more feminine does not solve it. It seems that fairness and equality, in the final analysis, demand that sport welcome people of all kinds, whether or not their personal characteristics line up the expectations or ideals of their gender. The 120-pound (55-kilogram) wrestler or bantamweight boxer may not be a paragon of masculine fighting ability, but is he so much less a champion than the heavyweight that he should be excluded from the sport?[35] If we imagined competition from the point of view of the ball, that is, from the perspective of sheer performance rather than the gender of the athlete, we might better support sport's intrinsic tendency to overcome human prejudice.[36] According to the logic of sport, athletes should not be excluded on the basis of their sex, and sex categories should be used to increase opportunities, not to deny them.

SPORT AND (DIS)ABILITY

In disability sports festivals such as the Special Olympics and Paralympic Games, the existence of relevant physical differences that justify categorization is not in question the way it was with race and, to a lesser extent, sex. Indeed, these games have invented a huge variety of categories in the attempt to group athletes in a way that fulfills the sporting value of close competition. Even then, the issue of fairness is complicated by the fact that grouping and regrouping athletes by performance may fail to reward individual athletes' progress within a particular class. On the other hand, trying to divide fairly the huge variety of physical and mental disabilities into a few simple groupings may lead to unbalanced and therefore unfulfilling competition.[37] From the larger perspective of social justice, meanwhile, there is the issue of the exclusion of these sports and athletes from "mainstream" activities. Perhaps the most famous example is Oscar Pistorius, a runner whose legs were amputated below the knee, yet he has been able to achieve world-class times by running on special prostheses known as "cheetah legs." If he runs as fast as other Olympians, should he be restricted to competing in the Paralympics? What about amputees who exceed the performance of nonamputees without the aid of prostheses? Are these cases of sporting justice or social prejudice infecting sport?

Sport for the disabled is rarely discussed in the academic literature, perhaps because it is considered something other than "real sport" and certainly because it enjoys little to no exposure in the media. Of course, the same could be said about some people's attitude toward women's sports. However much practical sense it makes to keep disability sports separate from nondisability sports, the separation immediately sends an educational message about the "place" of people with disabilities in society, and even in schools themselves. We must ask what sport is teaching when it unconsciously discriminates against disabled students.[38] As in the case of females, the educational message of separation can have troubling consequences. In fact, separation of males and females in elementary school sports cannot be justified on the basis of feminine weakness, since girls are often stronger at that age. If we are instead protecting boys from losing their illusions of superiority, is segregation any more justified? What are we to say, then, about the separation of children with disabilities? Who exactly is being protected and from what?

Obviously there are very sophisticated pedagogical rationales for the separation and mainstreaming of disabled students in school sports, but they don't always consider the deeper question of what actually constitutes disability in a sporting context. "There is no medical categorization of disabilities that fits smoothly and logically into the context of sport," explain Ivo van Hilvoorde and Laurens Landerweerd. "What is considered a disability in 'regular life' may even become an advantage in the context of elite sports."[39] Take the case of wrestlers like one-legged NCAA champion Anthony Robles, double amputee Rohan Murphy, or quadruple amputee Kyle Maynard. They have been successful competing in the mainstream version of their sport, partly because the weight classes and emphasis on core strength in wrestling make their *lack* of limbs a slight advantage. Says Murphy, "I always viewed my disability before I started to wrestle as a negative, but once I started to wrestle, it became a positive."[40] Amputee weightlifters in events such as the bench press have likewise been able to outperform able-bodied athletes in the same weight class, sometimes by a wide margin.[41] We might be tempted to say that these athletes' disabilities constitute an unfair advantage in these sports. But how is their extraordinary physical situation different from that of a basketball player who is uncommonly tall or a gymnast who is uncommonly light?

In addition to the fairness questions provoked by disabilities and superabilities, there is a further issue involving reasonable compensation for disabilities. The idea of a handicap is an old one in sport. It is a compensation for advantage or disadvantage given to certain competitors in the interest of making a closer competition. In horse racing, the faster animals are made to carry more weight. In golf, a numerical handicap is calculated into each player's score. In running and cycling races, slower competitors may be allowed a head start. When it comes to disabilities, however, compensatory measures usually result in new classifications. For example, a legless athlete who competes in a marathon using a wheelchair is in a different class from those competing on foot. If he weren't, he would almost certainly beat most of the traditional marathoners. But at what point does compensation for a disability become an unfair advantage? South African sprinter Oscar Pistorius is pressing that question with his battle to compete in the Olympic Games running on high-tech carbon-fiber prostheses designed to maximize speed.

Pistorius, also known as the "blade runner" or "the fastest man on no legs," was banned from competing against able-bodied athletes in 2007 when a scientist declared that his prostheses gave him an unfair advantage by returning more energy than a natural human leg. The ruling was overturned in 2008 by the Court of Arbitration for Sport based on more scientific evidence that challenged the energy-return theory. In the end, the question of whether and how the prostheses constitute an unfair advantage over normal legs is very difficult since the whole biomechanical process of running is different for Pistorius than for conventional athletes.[42]

The ambiguity surrounding the issue of the prostheses' fairness, meanwhile, raises a further question about the motivations for trying to keep Pistorius separated from the other athletes. "There seems to be a fear that running on prosthetics might become faster than 'normal' running," say van Hilvoorde and Landerweerd.[43] Are we afraid that superior amputee runners will make able-bodied runners look bad? Is it different than being afraid of females outperforming males? We may say that the prostheses aren't natural, but then the able-bodied runners have high-tech artificial things called shoes attached to the ends of their lower limbs. It seems that Pistorius wants nothing different than other athletes, namely, a good challenging race. He has never lost a Paralympic race and needs to race with (world-class) able-bodied athletes to best test his skills. The advantage provided by his prostheses, like any piece of sporting equipment, needs to be regulated, but using disability as a reason to deny access to the most prestigious competitions runs counter to the logic and spirit of sport.

Human beings are natural organisms with all the lack of uniformity and untidiness that that implies. They defy orderly biological classification, and yet they cling to social categories and allow their judgments to be swayed by stereotypes. Sports, on the other hand, are artificial human creations capable of reflecting either our highest ideals of justice or our lowest impulses toward prejudice. Historically, sport has functioned both to reinforce and to challenge social categorizations such as class, race, gender, and disability. Exclusion and marginalization in sport generally derive from the social forces and not from the logic of sport itself. Clearly, sport best reflects the ideal of justice when it provides opportunities to people of all kinds to discover what they are capable of, rather than restricting opportunities on the basis of assumptions about what they are not capable of.

But providing equal opportunity in sport is not as simple as removing all classes and categories and opening up all contests to all-comers. We need to create sporting opportunities for different abilities and interests, including large, aggressive women as well as small, graceful men. We should ask what we are teaching through sport when we apply elite level categories even to young children's activities. What we should be teaching through sport is that different people can perform in different activities—just as in academia or business. The blues may historically be a form of African American music, but does the race of the musician affect how it sounds on the radio? Let sport be played by different people with different styles, and let the game decide who is excellent, not the presumptions of society.

DISCUSSION QUESTIONS

1. Do you think college sports do an effective job of helping low-income students to gain a higher education, or do they motivate them to sacrifice their education for the high-risk pursuit of a professional contract?
2. If scientific studies were to prove racial differences between whites and blacks that affect athletic performance, would separate athletic classes for the races therefore be justified?
3. Do you think that removing sex categories from sport would help females' struggle for social equality or undermine it?
4. Should amputee wrestlers be forced to compete in higher weight classes to compensate for the advantage gained by their missing limbs? Does the same go for powerlifters in events like the bench press?

Chapter Fourteen

Sport and Political Ideals

The most notorious example of sport serving political ideals has to be the 1936 Olympic Games in Berlin, Germany—referred to these days simply as the "Nazi Olympics." Videos from these Games juxtapose images of Hitler and swastika-adorned pageantry with those of smiling African American sprinter Jesse Owens. It was the year of the first Olympic torch relay—a spectacle that symbolically connected ancient Greece with Nazi Germany. These Games were also the subject of Leni Riefenstahl's film *Olympia*, famed for its aesthetic grandeur and groundbreaking sports photography techniques. We can look back at the pictures and choose the interpretation we like: the dark foreshadowing of a twisted regime's evil ambition or the triumph of pure athletic achievement over racist propaganda. One of the International Olympic Committee's (IOC) favorite images is that of Owens with friend and rival Luz Long of Germany, who generously helped his opponent to avoid fouling out of the long-jump qualifications. The story is meant to show how sport can succeed where politics fails. [1]

But in a way, the IOC's telling of this (true) story of athletic friendship is just as political as the (false) story that Hitler refused to shake Jesse Owens's hand. The stories simply support different political ideals. The Olympic Movement may strive to keep itself free from political influence, [2] and Avery Brundage may have declared that "sport transcends all political and racial situations," [3] but sport is, always has been, and perhaps always will be at some level political. As we saw in chapter 1, athletic rituals and displays were put to political use as far back as the third millennium bce. [4] The ancient Romans were masters in the political use of sport—gladiator fights (*munera*), exotic beast hunts (*venationes*), and staged naval battles (*naumachia*) demonstrated to the masses the strength and scope of the empire as well as the emperor's ability to rule it while keeping them safe. [5] Imperial triumphs served purposes—such as the public exhibition of virtue and justice—analogous to those of traditional Greek sport. Meanwhile, the wildly popular chariot races allowed a diverse population to root for four color-coded teams and symbolically gathered all of Rome into one universe with the emperor at its center.[6]

To say that sport has a political dimension is not necessarily to condemn it. There is an identifiable link between sport and democracy that goes back to ancient Greece. There is also a connection between sport and fascism that may have endured beyond the Nazis' Games. During the Cold War, sport was used to demonstrate the validity of communism. More recently, sport has been linked with the ideals and processes of capitalism. Whatever political ideal sport gets linked with, however, it also seems to contain its own political power—a power borne of its playful, gratuitous, noninstrumental nature. As our study of sports metaphysics showed, sport's value derives ultimately from its *lack* of external purpose—its autotelicity. It is this sport-specific value that *resists* political exploitation. There's no question that the 1936 Olympics were of great political value to the Nazi Party. Through sport, the Germans outperformed the previously dominant Americans, suggesting to the world that totalitarianism was better than democracy.[7] But sport also enabled Jesse Owens to refute Nazi race theories and to temper national rivalry through his friendship with Luz Long. As historian Richard Mandell observes, "The portrayal of the Berlin Olympics to the world as a nonpolitical festival was itself a political act, as well as a lie."[8] Portraying sport as nonpolitical would equally be a lie, but that is not to say that sport lacks political power of its own.

SPORT AND DEMOCRACY

Perhaps the first political ideal said to be derived from sport is democracy. Ancient Greek athletics predated the birth of democracy by centuries, and many of the foundational ideas of democracy appeared in sport long before they became ideals of governance. Archaeologist Stephen Miller argues that the concept of *isonomia*, equality before the law, is a creation of sport and constitutes its most important contribution to society.[9] To this we may add freedom from tyranny, rule of law, equal treatment, and public scrutiny to the list of characteristics common in both ancient sport and democracy.[10] The inclusion and success of nonaristocrats in ancient Greek athletic competition, as we discussed earlier, eroded the belief that excellence and worthiness to lead were a matter of noble birth. Insofar as democracy is understood as rule of the people, by the people, and for the people, it depends upon the once revolutionary idea that common people are actually capable of leadership.

Since sport was one of the only arenas in which relative commoners could demonstrate their *aretē* (virtue) in competition with aristocrats, it provided a place for democratic ideas to take root. In modern times, sport still provides an opportunity for lower classes to demonstrate publicly their worth. Indeed, in his 1989 presidential address to the International Association for the Philosophy of Sport, Peter Arnold argued that sport was an ideal means for teaching democratic values. [11]

Freedom is usually the first democratic value to be associated with sport, and it is connected specifically with the idea that sports participation is always voluntary and never forced. Miller marvels at the willingness of free-born, possibly noble men to subject themselves voluntarily to the rules of sport and risk being flogged in public if they transgressed them. [12] Since public flogging was a punishment otherwise associated exclusively with slaves and animals, participation in sport effectively entailed the renunciation of certain privileges associated with social status. In ancient Rome, citizens and even senators who wanted to compete as gladiators had to formally renounce their civil rights by swearing to be "burned by fire, bound in chains, to be beaten, to die by the sword." [13] Lest all this make democracy sound like some swashbuckling adventure, the point is that the freedom within both sport and democracy depends upon participants' willingness to give up some portion of their liberty by subjecting themselves to the rules of the game. As Arnold puts it, "In so far as sport demands of its participants freedom with responsibility and involves benefits as well as burdens, it is in accord with the democratic process." [14] It is the public's voluntary acceptance of and adherence to law that makes democracy possible, not least by subjecting everyone equally to punishment under those laws.

So the freedom in democracy isn't just pure freedom, as in the absence of constraints (i.e., negative freedom). It is also freedom from imposed tyranny by virtue of voluntary subjection to the law (positive freedom). Likewise in sport, it is the athletes' understanding of and voluntary subjection to contest rules that make the freedom experienced within the game possible. Importantly, this voluntary subjection is undertaken collectively—that is, we agree to follow rules or laws on the understanding that everyone else will follow the rules, too. As Arnold explains, "When an individual voluntarily chooses to enter a sport he or she can be regarded as tacitly accepting an agreement with others to participate in a way that the rules lay down." [15] Neither political leaders nor elite athletes, furthermore, can expect to be "above the law" in sport or democracy. In fact, the rule of law in sport is often enforced indirectly by the spectators. In general, they are aware of the rules, and if an official fails to call some transgression, the crowd is expected to protest. These days, slow-motion replays are often displayed on giant television screens in the arenas, making it easier for spectators to see infractions. This creates the kind of collective responsibility and collective authority that one expects in a democracy.[16] So freedom in sport and democracy depend on voluntary subjection to rules that depend for their enforcement on officials empowered and scrutinized by the public. Democracy is a community effort for which each member bears responsibility.

Equality in sport or democracy is likewise bound up with rules or law. In the ancient context, where social equality was all but unknown, athletes were equal before the absolute standards of sport, such as distance, speed, and strength, as measured by the performances of other competitors rather than the subjective interpretation of any human being.[17] We can compare it with the difference between winning a race and winning a job. The interview process in the latter depends upon the subjective judgment of one or more powerful officials, and the reasons for their choice are seldom obvious and almost never made public. Candidates rarely even know who their competitors are. A running race, by contrast, takes place out in the open where everyone can see the process and judge its fairness for themselves. Democratic elections, likewise, should be transparent processes that depend on not special judges but rather objective results. Equality in democracy is expressed in equality of opportunity. It must allow for reward according to merit. Said the ancient Greek statesman Pericles in describing Athenian democracy, "But while the law secures equal justice to all alike in their private disputes, the claim of excellence (*aretē*) is also recognized; and when a citizen is in any way distinguished he is preferred to the public service, not as a matter of privilege, but as the reward of merit."[18] Sport, too, treats competitors equally as a precondition for rewarding worthy victors.

"Democracy," says Arnold, "is based on the belief that each human being is of value."[19] Sport also strives to value each of its participants, although like democracy, many worthy participants have been excluded historically because of their sex, race, or social class. On the other hand, sport seems to have taught us something about the value of democratic ideals: freedom in the form of voluntary participation, equality before the law, and collective responsibility for the enforcement of the law. Democratic thinking is community based, as were athletics in ancient Greece as they performed their religious function of propitiating powerful gods. In the nudity of ancient athletes, Miller sees the roots of democratic equality—once we take our clothes off, social differences are harder to spot.[20] And once we witness the excellence of our fellow competitors, the pretense of hierarchies is harder to sustain. It is our willingness to subject ourselves equally to the law that makes sport and democracy function as just systems of governance. As Arnold observes, sport teaches athletes not only to abide by common rules but also to "understand that it is only by following them that the aspirations and interests of others as well as themselves . . . can be realized."[21] Democracy values not only individuals but also the community as a whole.

SPORT AND FASCISM

Given the historical and conceptual connections between sport and democracy, it may be surprising that the Nazis found the Olympic Games to be an effective means for promoting fascism. Whereas democracy prizes individual freedom, fascism promotes nationalistic devotion. Whereas democracy is based on equality before the law, fascism is authoritarian, controlled, and regulated. Whereas democracy is based on universal human value, fascism posits the superiority of a particular race and seeks to eliminate those who weaken or degrade the state. According to philosopher Torbjörn Tännsjö, contempt for weakness is the core of fascist ideology, and it is also intrinsic in competitive sport.[22] In his view, sport, and especially our admiration for athletic victors, is more closely aligned with the ideals of fascism than democracy. Tännsjö gives ideological and pragmatic justifications for this claim. It is simply a matter of fact that team sports have been used by nationalist leaders to create a chauvinist zeal in their own populations, which favors the formation of totalitarian governments, the oppression of minorities, and military expansion.[23] The Nazis are an obvious example here, but it would be naive to think that sport's fascist potential died along with their regime. Even democratic governments and educational institutions openly use sport to promote community spirit and garner popular support for their projects. Could all those rabid sports fans who paint their faces in team colors and chant against opposing teams be a fascist force in modern sport?

On the face of it, sport's ability to generate community spirit in schools, cities, states, and even nations seems like a positive force. It is sobering, however, to read the words of Joseph Goebbels, Adolf Hitler's minister of propaganda and one of history's most notorious anti-Semites. Said Goebbels on April 23, 1933, "German sport has only one task: to strengthen the character of the German people, imbuing it with the fighting spirit and steadfast camaraderie necessary in the struggle for its existence."[24] In fact, Baron Pierre de Coubertin had been motivated by similar concerns to revive the Olympic Games. He saw it as a chance to strengthen French youth and prevent further military defeat.[25]

Perhaps the positive or negative value of sport's spirit-building power depends upon the end goals of the relevant community. Endemic in any nationalistic or community-spirit promotion, however, is the risk of denigrating outsiders. The Nazi promotion of a pure Aryan race excluded not only Jews but also blacks and other minorities. Attempts were made, with varying success, to ban Jews from the German team and blacks from the 1936 Games more generally. It was claimed by one Nazi newspaper that the ancient Greeks would "turn in their graves" if blacks were allowed to compete.[26] As we observed in the previous chapter, racial exclusion from sport seems to be a thing of the past, but exclusions and marginalization based on criteria like sex and disability endure. The point is that team and nationalistic spirit can have an ugly side. Tännsjö cautions that "there is only a small step from being a soccer hooligan to joining a fascist organization modeled on the Hitler Jugend."[27]

Nationalism becomes an especially dangerous force when it is used to manipulate individuals to act against their own interests for the benefit of very abstract and perhaps merely symbolic values. When American gymnast Kerri Strug vaulted and landed on an injured ankle at great personal risk in the team competition at the 1996 Olympic Games, she was lauded as a national hero. But it is not at all clear how her sacrifice actually benefitted the nation. It did not even benefit the team, which would have won the gold medal even without her final vault. An athlete who risks injury for the sake of his team is a clear reflection of a soldier who risks injury and even death for the sake of his country. But in the soldier's case, especially when the battle is for the defense of one's own homeland, there really may be an alignment of personal and national interests. The athlete's case is not so clear. Instead, praise of this kind of athletic devotion may be seen as a way to train youth to sacrifice their interests for the state and to blindly obey its commands. According to Tännsjö, "This kind of sacrifice is the rule rather than the exception when a nationalistic ideology gets a firm hold on the members of a nation—in particular if the nation in question does not face the least *threat* from any other nation."[28] The *Olympic Charter* states clearly that the competition is between athletes and not countries,[29] but the ideology of athletes competing for the benefit of their national teams is such a part of international sport that it is hard to imagine sport without it.

For his part, Tännsjö believes that nationalism in sport is dying and will soon be overtaken by corporate identifications. In fact, athletes are often torn between commitments to their professional and national teams. Meanwhile, teams that represent cities and state universities routinely include athletes from outside the area—often from outside the country. It is common for teams like English football's Manchester City not to have a single player who was actually born in that city. This fact does not eliminate sport's fascistic tendencies, however. According to Tännsjö, it makes them worse, because it shows that our admiration for sports heroes springs not from nationalism but from contempt for weakness, the idea at the very core of Nazism.[30] Fascism, like sport, celebrates youth and strength (not to mention masculinity). It encourages us to imagine those who are stronger as superior, not merely in terms of athletics, but in general as well. The strong are also considered morally superior. Because such an attitude leads to neglect and even contempt for those who are weaker, Tännsjö argues that we have a moral obligation to resist it—indeed to resist sport altogether.[31] If the fascistic danger of sport really derives from sport's selection and celebration of winners, it seems that the danger cannot be removed without changing sport fundamentally.

But is sport really intrinsically fascist? Philosophers Claudio Tamburrini and M. Andrew Holowchak resist Tännsjö's argument. Tamburrini replies, first of all, that nations, at least in the sporting context, are not abstract symbols but rather groups of people.[32] On that view, Kerri Strug was risking injury not for the benefit of some hollow abstraction but rather for the real emotional benefit of a group of real people who were watching and perhaps receiving valuable inspiration from her display of courage. Furthermore, says Tamburrini, it is an overstatement to characterize the public's attitude toward losers as one of scorn or contempt.[33] Finally, it is too narrow in Tamburrini's view to interpret our admiration for athletic excellence as simply based on strength.[34]

Holowchak takes this last point a step further, pointing out that Nazi ideals of strength certainly surpass athletic superiority. "At the core of Nazism are brutality, single-purpose focus, and a crush-at-all-costs attitude," says Holowchak. "With strength comes desert: Because one is 'better' (i.e., outperforms others) at some physical task, one is thereby 'better' (i.e., morally superior) and deserving of more of the good things in life (whereas losers deserve contempt)."[35] But this kind of attitude is certainly not entailed by sport, Holowchak argues, adding that it constitutes a violation of Immanuel Kant's ethical imperative to treat others as ends and never as means.[36] Whatever fascist tendencies it may have, sport can undermine them by keeping winning in perspective and showing respect for nonwinners. That sincere end-of-the-game handshake may be politically more important than it first appears.

SPORT AND COMMUNISM

In the second half of the twentieth century, international sport was more often associated with communism than fascism. At first glance, it seems odd that competitive sport should be embraced by a political system that focuses on cooperation and sharing. The philosophical founder of communism, Karl Marx, said almost nothing about sport. He, along with his more practical successor, Vladimir Lenin, envisaged physical education and sport as a routine part of school and of working life—a vision not dissimilar from that of most societies around the world.[37] In 1920, Lenin declared, "The physical culture of the younger generation is an essential element in the overall system of communist upbringing of young people, aimed at creating harmoniously developed human beings, creative citizens of communist society."[38] If anything was radical about the early communist view of sport, it was that they expected all members of the society, including women, to partake. The goals of communist sport were originally modest. It was not until the 1940s that competitive sport was envisioned as a kind of propaganda for communist ideals. Said N. N. Romanov, head of the Soviet Sport Committee in 1947, "Sport [is] a mass, popular movement with the goal of establishing the capacity of Soviet athletes to struggle for national and world records for the glory of our homeland."[39]

As we have seen, by this time it was not particularly original to use sport as political propaganda. What was odd about communists doing it was the apparent conflict between athletic values and their own political ideals. On the other hand, sport's ability to level class differences and to discount social differences goes well with communist goals. Perhaps the most notable impact of communism in sport was nearly equal training and funding for men and women, which effectively gave communist women an advantage over female athletes from countries where resources were distributed disproportionately to men. Susan Brownell notes that in China equal athletic opportunities for women appeared around 1955 (nearly twenty years before the passage of Title IX gender equity legislation in the United States), and the results were immediate: only two years later, a Chinese woman bettered the high-jump world record.[40] East German and Soviet women also had great success in international sports during the Cold War era. It is plausible, moreover, that funding and attention for women's sports in the rest of the world was motivated at least partly by an effort to keep up with communist women's success. In fact, Lenin himself had envisioned sports as a tool of female emancipation, calling it an "urgent task to draw working women into sport."[41]

But not every marginalized group benefitted from the communist approach to sport. Communist countries largely rejected disability sports, which may betray their interest in propaganda at the expense of political ideals. Huge government resources were committed not so much to increasing lifelong participation for the masses but rather to the early selection, development, and performance of elite athletes. Those elite athletes, whose success was supposed to prove the superiority of the communist way of life, in fact lived lives radically different and largely separate from the common people. Resentment was accordingly expressed at the special privileges given to athletes, and much of the populace came to perceive athletics as nothing more than a diversion from the harsh reality of life in a communist system.[42] The unbridled zeal to "prove" communism's superiority through sport eventually led in East Germany to experimentation with performance-enhancing drugs on athletes as young as fourteen years of age, often without their knowledge or consent.[43] In these cases, sport not only fails to demonstrate the superiority of a regime's ideals but also runs counter to them and undermines the legitimacy of both the government and the political system it is trying to promote.

SPORT AND CAPITALISM

Since the fall of communism in Eastern Europe, sport has been more closely aligned with its opposing political ideal: capitalism. Countries like China, without a history of capitalism, may even be looking to sport to teach their citizens the values they will need to compete in a global market. Philosopher Ann E. Cudd argues that widespread use of athletic metaphors such as "a level playing field" in capitalistic discourse actually betrays important similarities between sport and capitalism—some of which should be taken more seriously. "Skills associated with good athletes such as strategic decision making and team play," she observes, "are valued in business executives, managers, and investors."[44] Capitalism, in opposition to communism, allows private ownership of the means of production as a way to create markets for almost everything, including labor. Cudd notes that both sport and capitalism are voluntary, rule governed, and competitively challenging.[45] She also warns that both sport and capitalism exhibit a competitive culture that can "breed a psychology of intensity, greed, and egotism."[46] Although competition, or at least play, is thought to have intrinsic value in sport, Cudd believes that competition in capitalism is valued only for its results.[47] Such instrumentalism is a cause for concern.

As in sport, competition in capitalism needs to be directed toward noble goals. Just as lopsided victories fail to achieve the internal goods of sport, a capitalistic competition that results in one party having control of most or all the wealth would fail to achieve the internal goods of capitalism by unbalancing and then effectively terminating market action. So winning is not and cannot be everything in any enlightened view of sport or capitalism. Cudd prefers a model of competition more reflective of Robert Simon's ideal of a "mutual quest for excellence,"[48] that is, a model of economic competition that is at the same time a form of cooperative interaction that has the effect of increasing the overall level of welfare in the society.[49] In sport, the model evokes a noble rivalry between two or more athletes who inspire each other as well as other athletes in their sport to achieve at higher levels. The tennis rivalry between Chris Evert and Martina Navratilova is a good example. Not only did these two women push each other to ever higher levels of play, but also they brought the quality and visibility of women's professional tennis to unprecedented levels, thereby benefitting the larger community. One might compare this with the business rivalry between computer giants Apple and

Microsoft; it has resulted not only in great success for the rivals but also in better products for the industry and all of the consumers who use them.

As in sport, however, healthy competition depends on the existence of a level playing field and a willingness to play by the rules. A successful capitalist economy, Cudd argues, depends on a balance between firms, consumers, and workers, which in turn depends on fair competition.[50] The understanding of competition as the alienated and unbridled pursuit of victory is harmful both to sport and to capitalism, not least because it ignores the importance of cooperation and respect within healthy competition.[51] Unfortunately, according to many commentators, an unhealthy and sometimes brutish win-at-all-costs attitude prevails in both sport and capitalism today— to the point where one seems inseparable from the other. Competitive sport in education is sometimes justified as a way of preparing youth for the cutthroat world of business, but this may amount more to a rationalization of people's brutish impulses than an explanation of sport's educational value.[52] If Cudd is right about the need for a model of cooperative pursuit of excellence in capitalism, however, sport may indeed be good preparation—but only as long as the principles of fair play are emphasized, rather than the end goal of victory.

In *Leftist Theories of Sport: A Critique and Reconstruction*, William Morgan rejects as too simple those theories that equate the logic and ethos of capitalism with the logic and ethos of sport.[53] Morgan is hardly apologizing for capitalism here—as we have already seen, he is harshly critical of it. In his most recent book, *Why Sports Morally Matter*, Morgan identifies "capitalism run amok" as our greatest social threat.[54] "The result," he says, "is that sports are treated more as means than ends, as pursuits with a value to be instrumentally calculated in the same fashion as any other commodity: by the money they fetch."[55] This hyperinstrumentalist capitalism is equally damaging to American business in Morgan's view. However, sports are importantly *unlike* business, *unlike* capitalism, and even *unlike* politics in that they are fundamentally noninstrumental, gratuitous ends in themselves. Moreover, to really experience what makes sport great, you need to practice it under those gratuitous conditions.[56] From the outside, it may be hard to see sport as anything other than a capitalistic endeavor. Why does it exist, if not to make money? But from the inside, as a player, and even from the perspective of an experienced and informed spectator, sport's unique and intrinsic value can be appreciated.

The point here is not that sport cannot be used as a means to market ends. It certainly has been instrumentalized in the modern world. The point rather is that it contains within itself the power to *resist* such instrumentalization. Morgan uses Alasdair MacIntyre's notion of a social practice (detailed in chapter 5) to distinguish between production and culture. Sport's status as a social and cultural practice means that it is more than just another means of production. Specifically, Morgan identifies sport's gratuitous logic—its contrivance of unnecessary obstacles—as the feature that most distinguishes it from everyday life and gives it its emancipatory potential, even while it is harnessed to capitalist goals.[57] That is to say, sport has the power, by virtue of its noninstrumental character, to liberate us from the pervasive instrumentalism of late capitalist society. Just as MacIntyre identified the power of social practices to resist the instrumental logic of the very institutions that govern them, Morgan identifies the power of sport to resist capitalistic forces.[58] More generally, sport's intrinsic gratuity may empower it to resist all kinds of exploitation—including political exploitation by any regime or ideologue.

The resistance is not automatic, however. Sport practitioners, as we discussed in chapter 10, must first of all *choose* to view sport as something more than merely a means to external ends. This would seem to require a change of culture, especially when athletes themselves are exploited as means to institutional or financial ends by their teams. Morgan argues that sport, like religion and academia, should be kept separate from forces like capitalism in order to protect its integrity.[59] Sports should be managed by communities of practitioners, past as well as present, who derive their authority from a shared understanding of the sport itself rather than wealth or bureaucratic power.[60] This is not such a far-fetched prospect, especially in Olympic sports governed by international federations. The key is that those who manage sport recognize its intrinsic value and resist its instrumentalist abuse. The relationship between sport and political ideals whether democracy, fascism, communism, or capitalism—is too often one of exploitation and even abuse. But sport has a politics of its own that resists such exploitation. Jesse Owens's athletic triumph at the 1936 Berlin Olympic Games was not a triumph of democracy over fascism—after all, he faced serious discrimination in his home country. Instead, it was a triumph of an expression of the intrinsic values of sport over exploitative political forces.

DISCUSSION QUESTIONS

1. Give a specific example from sport that illustrates the following features of democracy: voluntary participation, equality before the law, and collective responsibility for the enforcement of the law.
2. When athletes like Kerri Strug take great personal risks for their national teams, do you view them as victims of fascist exploitation (i.e., sacrificing their rational self-interest for the good of the state) or as

courageous leaders inspiring their communities? Does it matter whether the athlete is from a democratic country or not?

3. The Cold War rivalry between communist and democratic countries has been praised for improving support for women in sport and blamed for motivating the use of performance-enhancing drugs. How would sport be different without political rivalry?

4. In the famous "Black Sox" scandal surrounding baseball's 1919 World Series, several players were banned for life from the sport after they intentionally lost games in order to make money. Does this example show that sport and capitalism are at odds? Why or why not?

Chapter Fifteen

Sport and Globalization

The ideal expression of harmoniously globalized sport may be the closing ceremony of the Olympic Games. Instead of marching into the stadium as orderly, uniformed regiments lined up behind their countries' flags, the athletes abandon national ranks and burst into the stadium in a colorful, cacophonous, joyful swarm. Gymnasts perch on the shoulders of weightlifters; victors offer an up-close look at their newly won medals; and Korean swimmers pose to have their pictures taken with American basketball stars. It is a welcome image of a globalized world, but it wasn't part of the original Olympic plan. Rather, it was the suggestion of a seventeen-year-old local boy named John Ian Wing during the 1956 Melbourne Games. "The march I have in mind is different than the one during the Opening Ceremony and will make these games even greater," stated Wing in a letter to Games' officials. "During the march there will only be 1 NATION. War, politics and nationality will be all forgotten, what more could anybody want, if the whole world could be made as one nation."[1] In fact, the world in 1956 and even athletes' behavior at the Games had been characterized less by harmony and more by simmering political tension and bitter national rivalry. Infamously, a violent water polo match between Russia and Hungary had to be cancelled because of fighting that tinged the pool water with blood. Sport may seek to promote international harmony, but the reality often falls far short of the ideal.

The relationship between sport and globalization is simultaneously ancient, modern, and futuristic. It derives from the phenomenon of the ancient Olympic Games, the religious purpose of which had the (probably unintended) effect of pacifying and unifying diverse and often warring tribes in the ancient Mediterranean. It is replicated in the philosophical underpinnings of the modern Olympic Games, which were inspired by the ideals of the European enlightenment. And it is futuristic in that international and especially Olympic sport functions as a kind of trailblazer for the political future of a globalized world. The term "globalization" refers primarily to "fundamental changes in the spatial and temporal contours of social existence."[2] Advances in travel and communication technology have been "shrinking the world" and increasing contact between people despite geographical and cultural distance for some time. Olympic-style sport has long been at the forefront of this process. Increased intercultural contact through trade and shipping even had a hand in the development of the ancient Olympic Games,[3] and developments in telegraph and train technology helped to motivate the first modern Olympic Games in 1896.[4] In recent years, we have experienced an acceleration of the globalization process, and predictably, international sport and the Olympic Games in particular seem to have embraced the phenomenon.

Spectators in every corner of the world can experience and discuss sporting events live through television and Internet technology. Roughly 70 percent of the world's population, 4.7 billion viewers in all, watched the 2008 Beijing Olympics on television.[5] Relatively cheap and increasingly quick transportation makes it easier for athletes at almost every level to play with competitors from different cultures and backgrounds. It has also made professional sports an exportable product. America's National Football League plays annually in Europe. The Tour de France routinely starts in foreign countries. Its rival, the Giro d'Italia, has even considered a start in Washington, D.C. Formula One car racing, once a strictly European affair, loads its cars and equipment on planes and flies off to compete at tracks as far flung as Bahrain, India, and Malaysia. Even when leagues don't travel, their athletes do. European football, American basketball, and even Japanese sumo include athletes from outside the geographical region, often from the other side of the globe. Indeed, sport may involve more interaction among culturally diverse people than any other human activity. In that sense, it can teach us something about globalization—but the lesson isn't always positive. What can we learn about globalization from sport, and how can sport's values be protected from its dangers?

GLOBALIZATION: THE REALITY

For all its potential benefits, globalization brings with it some serious problems, not least of which is its tendency to benefit the wealthy and powerful, who in turn often try to impose their cultural paradigm upon the rest of the world. As far back as 1950, the philosopher Martin Heidegger worried that the removal of distance between people, rather than increasing possibilities for richer interaction, would homogenize our differences into one bland experiential mass.[6] What would the Olympic Games be if the cultural diversity of the athletes was eliminated and the only difference that remained was the color of their uniforms? The philosophical vision behind the Olympic Games is cosmopolitan, based on a vision of global community. Its stated goal is "to place sport at the service of the harmonious development of man, with a view to promoting a peaceful society concerned with the preservation of human dignity."[7]

In practice, however, the global playing field of sport seems tilted toward the West and toward wealth. It is a mechanism well adapted for reinforcing existing power structures and promulgating the cultural values of the elite. The Olympic Movement, like most of international sport, is dominated by Western cultures, especially North America, Great Britain, and Western Europe. This is seen not only in the selection of host cities (including Beijing, the Summer Games have ventured just three times outside the West) but also in the cultural origin of the Olympic sports and, perhaps most visibly, in the ethnic makeup and political ideals of the International Olympic Committee (IOC) itself.

The Olympic Movement is sometimes accused of being Eurocentric, despite its universalistic ideals. This is not to say that the organization self-consciously privileges Europe or the West but rather that its perspective is conditioned by a European heritage and set of assumptions that are not always shared by the rest of the world. Indeed, the very *understanding* of what universalism is differs around the world. In the philosophical heritage of Europe, for example, following figures such as René Descartes and Immanuel Kant, there is a one-size-fits-all understanding of universal truth. Even complex ethical concepts are thought reducible to purely rational formulas that can be communicated to and applied by everyone.[8] The philosophical heritage of China and most of Asia, by contrast, tends to think of universal truth as something inexpressible and able to accommodate multiple diverse expressions.[9] The problem is not that the world contains different and sometimes incompatible viewpoints. The problem is failing to acknowledge this. In the current era of globalization, where the wealthier and more powerful countries of North America and Europe tend to dominate economics and politics, it is easy for the West to think of their own heritage and values as the universal standard.

This phenomenon can be especially frustrating as it extends to political ideals. In the West, liberal democracy—in particular the rule of law—is often seen as the only acceptable form of government. Jim Parry observes that Western liberals who insist on individual autonomy (i.e., autonomy-based liberalism) cannot tolerate illiberal cultures (i.e., those who do not allow individual autonomy). Rights-based liberalism, by contrast, "protects all cultures that provide their members with a decent environment and life chances."[10] Even so, it is hard to know the appropriate limits of tolerance across cultural boundaries. Democratic politics presuppose feelings of trust, commitment, and belonging that are hard to find at an international level. [11]

At the same time, it can be difficult to sort out how much of one's resistance to foreign politics is merely cultural and how much is moral. Many believe morality itself is conditioned by cultural differences or that ethics is completely relative. But uncritical acceptance of all cultures (however abhorrent their practices) is not politically responsible. Parry sees it as a kind of concealed ethnocentrism. "It is not true that to respect other cultures is to abstain from criticizing them," he explains. "Rather relativism is a kind of disrespect—failing to apply to others (denying to others) the standards of justification and argument we apply to ourselves." [12] Tolerance of cultural difference, then, is only respectful up to a point. A community with no moral standards is not a community at all. What we need is a community that respects cultural difference while upholding some mutually acceptable standards of morality.

Sport may provide a model for this insofar as it promotes general principles of justice such as equal opportunity and fair play, while making room for diverse styles of play. But even as individual athletic contests offer level playing fields and common starting lines, equal opportunity is far from reality in the global village. Huge economic disparities between countries and within countries challenge the ideals of distributive justice. National teams are far from equal in terms of facilities, coaching, medical support, and even funding for travel. The IOC commission on Olympic Solidarity tries to overcome these international disparities by distributing a portion of the Games' television revenue to the national Olympic committees most in need, but the demand is huge and the resources are limited. [13]

The euphoric spectacle of the Olympic Games should not lull us into thinking that global athletic competition is really fair. The tables that rank countries according to medals won, for example, embody none of the principles of fairness expected in sport. The teams do not have the same number of athletes, and they do not compete in all the same events. Olympic medal table rankings, furthermore, correlate more reliably with gross domestic product (an indicator of size and wealth) than with any other variable. [14] Countries may proudly outperform their predicted rankings, and athletes from relatively small and poor countries, like Jamaica, may come to dominate competitors from larger and wealthier neighbors—but this neither rectifies nor justifies globalization's tendency to favor those who, to use a popular sports metaphor, were born on third base but thought they hit a triple.

It is also worth remembering, from a cultural point of view, that the traditions and ideals of the West, particularly Europe and the United States, continue to dominate Olympic sport. The image of women in skimpy bikinis playing beach volleyball in a stadium as a mixed crowd of males and females looks on may seem emblematic of a laid-back California attitude toward sports. In many cultures, however, such a spectacle is at best immodest and at worst grounds for serious punishment. It may be tempting to declare that such cultures repress women, deny human liberty, and need to rise to the standards of the international community. But there is a real risk that such sentiments are ultimately cultural hegemony—the imposition of the values of the dominant class upon all others. Cultural hegemonists, furthermore, need to be careful of what they wish for because the dominance of one particular culture—no matter how rich and valid it is—may cause the demise of other local cultures and of cultural diversity in general. It is hard to imagine *any* single culture being so great that no other cultures are needed or desired. I really love Italian cuisine, but I would never wish that all other cuisines should disappear, leaving me with only one choice. Just as we value a variety of culinary styles and traditions, we may value variety in other cultural products such as art, music, literature, and even sport.

MULTICULTURALISM: THE METHOD

Multiculturalism is a response to the phenomenon of globalization that emphasizes the appreciation of cultural diversity and seeks to preserve it, even while working toward common principles like justice and fairness. Sport provides some good examples of this. In World Cup soccer, for example, teams from around the globe play according to a common set of rules while exhibiting a variety of culturally specific styles. As we saw in chapter 11, aesthetic rather than pragmatic values are often demonstrated in the play of teams from South America. Meanwhile, teams from Northern Europe are expected to play more conservatively and defensively. Part of the beauty of the tournament comes from the diversity of playing styles, and it would be a shame if pressure to win dictated a single successful style of play.

Globalization, like sport, carries this risk of homogenization not least because it diminishes the isolation of communities. Words and images from outside a community inevitably arrive inside, while words and images from inside a community inevitably make their way outside. The development of social media has accelerated this phenomenon and helped to attract international attention to previously ignored oppression in countries around the world. Sports, however, are also communities in themselves—practice communities—as we learned in chapter 5, and that means they can value diversity within their community even as its boundaries remain porous. In other words, the soccer community can value and preserve diverse styles of play even while promoting one common game.

It is important to distinguish between strangeness and difference. Declaring something strange is not just to say that it is different but also to express an emotional reaction of puzzlement or even repulsion. Valuing diversity, by contrast, involves expressing a reaction of acceptance and curiosity toward new and different ways. Within sport this means, first of all, the acceptance of multiple interpretations of a game. Let the South Americans play "beautiful" soccer, while the Northern Europeans play conservative soccer, and try to ensure that diverse styles are encouraged by the rules. Let us not call one style of soccer strange—even if it turns out to lead to fewer victories. Let us try to appreciate the different values and objectives that different people bring to the game.

Multiculturalism may also mean temporarily setting aside intercultural debates to make athletic interaction possible. For example, some people regard the Muslim requirement of head coverings for women as a form of unjust oppression. The Iranian women's soccer team was forced to forfeit a qualifying match and give up its chance of competing in the 2012 Olympics because they insisted on wearing headscarves, which go against the international soccer federation's rules.[15] It is certain that the wearing of headscarves is not a violation of human rights, and the rule prohibiting them is not fundamental to the game of soccer. Why not make an exception to the rule, or rewrite it in such a way that allows Muslim women to play soccer and observe their religious beliefs? If the motivation for the rule is safety, work to develop a safe headscarf. A multicultural sporting community that values diversity must make an effort to encourage it.

The Olympic Movement certainly seems to value diversity, but it must not become so narrow in its interpretation of its own ideals that they become an obstacle. Jim Parry maintains that the *concept* of Olympism, understood at a high level of generality, may admit of diverse interpretations or *conceptions* that bring the concept to life in particular contexts.[16] Multiculturalism in the Olympic Movement must be a concerted effort. Not only should athletes, officials, and IOC members represent a variety of cultural backgrounds and perspectives, but also the program of sports itself should show more cultural variety. Judo and taekwondo are the only two sports on the current Olympic program with a non-Western origin, and even they had to be adapted to a Western-style scoring system that chooses clear winners and losers.

New sports are considered for the Olympic program based on such criteria as history and tradition, universality, and popularity. This system seems to set the cart before the horse in multicultural terms since sports tend to become popular and universal *after* they are accepted into the Olympics. Parry suggests a compensatory policy according to which one popular sport from each continent would be included in the official program.[17] This would combat globalization's tendency to homogenize sport while serving the Olympic Movement's cultural education goals. It is a multicultural solution to one of globalization's problems.

SUSTAINABILITY: THE COMMON CAUSE

One thing that underpinned the ancient Olympic Games' success at unifying and pacifying diverse Hellenic tribes was the sense that they were working toward a common cause. In their case, the cause was religious. As we saw in chapter 1, the ancient games were a form of worship designed to propitiate common gods and therefore receive such collective benefits as abundant harvests and healing from illness. This worthwhile religious purpose inspired a ban on attacking worshippers in transit to the site, known as the *ekecheiria*. In some years, the *ekecheiria* was extended to a temporary suspension of military hostilities.[18] Even when wars continued, however, delegations from the tribes could meet safely at Olympia, and for that reason it was a good place to negotiate peace treaties.

In fact, all kinds of intellectuals and politicians met and debated common issues at the ancient Olympic Games. Many of the most famous orations dealt precisely with Panhellenic unity and the importance of working together rather than against one another.[19] An Olympic Truce is still called every four years, and the United Nations passes a resolution endorsing it, but its success in stopping wars is—at best—limited. The Olympic Games would benefit from a common global project akin to the religious cause that united the ancient Greeks. The issue of environmental sustainability seems perfect, and indeed, it has been adopted by the movement as a third objective alongside sport and culture.

Sustainable development can be defined as a strategy that "meets the needs of the present without compromising the ability of future generations to meet their own needs."[20] Given the global effect of environmental degradation, sustainability requires a global response. In the words of William Scheuerman, "A dogmatic insistence on the sanctity of national sovereignty risks constituting a cynical fig leaf for irresponsible activities whose impact extends well beyond the borders of those countries most directly responsible."[21] Common ground among nations, including some agreement about the nature of moral responsibility, must be found if the world is to find an effective solution to its environmental challenges.

A system of liberal democracy confined to nation-states is not well placed to deal with this problem. Indeed, continued environmental degradation potentially erodes democracy by undermining its legitimacy and perceived effectiveness.[22] This may seem an issue far removed from sport and Olympism, but after the United Nations, the Olympic Games may provide one of the best forums for international discussion and debate. The IOC's Sport and Environment Commission seeks to make the Olympic Games a model of sustainability, not least by including environmental concerns as part of the process for selecting host cities and subjecting the Games to scrutiny from nongovernmental organizations (NGOs) and the media. [23]

Of course, modeling is a form of education, and the practice of sport can itself better model an ideal of sustainability. Observing that the Olympic motto *citius, altius, fortius* (faster, higher, stronger) suggests unlimited growth in human performance, despite the limited nature of human biomotor abilities, Sigmund Loland sees a reflection of the ecological crisis, which is caused by the pursuit of unlimited growth of wealth and population on a planet with limited natural resources. [24] Sports that focus on absolute records, like the 100-meter dash, the 50-meter freestyle swim, or the kilometer time trial in cycling, are the least sustainable because they are the least complex. They try and replicate identical testing conditions and leave pure performance as the only variable. It is no coincidence that these sports also have an increased incidence of drug use and other performance-enhancing techniques. Sports like basketball, where a variety of skills and techniques are demanded, are more sustainable.

Loland sees a solution to this problem in increasing the diversity and complexity of less-sustainable sports. [25] For example, why not vary the surface and other external conditions faced by sprinters? Why not test the swimmers not only in pools but also in open water? Rather than ranking athletes by single record performances, why not keep track of their consistency over a season under different conditions? Rethinking sport would in this way give us a chance not only to improve sustainability but also to address collateral issues such as economic disparity. Why not privilege sports that require less equipment and facilities, eliminating those, such as equestrian sports, accessible only to the wealthy? The guiding principle for reforming sport need not be original. It can be intrinsic sporting values such as fairness; they just need to be rethought globally.

The values required to implement environmental sustainability integrate well with the internal virtues and values of sport. In his foreword to the Olympic Movement's *Agenda 21* statement on sport for sustainable development, Klaus Topfer of the United Nations Environment Program (UNEP) points out that environment is like sport in that it knows no borders, transcends ideological cleavages, and does not recognize artificial distinctions between North and South or East and West, but is one and indivisible. [26] It is not enough to say that sport, like the environment, needs to be open to everyone. Foundational sports principles such as equal opportunity and the level playing field need to be reconceived globally. This entails an effort to overcome social inequities by working to improve the socioeconomic condition of the least advantaged.

The first objective of *Agenda 21* states that "sustainable development is only conceivable if accompanied by the satisfaction of those cultural and material needs that are essential for all individuals to live with dignity and play a positive role in the society to which they belong."[27] Likewise, *Agenda 21* asks sport to battle social exclusion by "promoting sports activities by groups of individuals who are excluded from them for reasons of economic resources, sex, race or caste."[28] Not only is inclusion part of the logic of sport—because the most able victor can only be found if all candidates compete—but also it is fundamental to sustainability, which demands that resources are managed in a way that all persons are able to live with dignity. Sport's international visibility puts it in an ideal position to model sustainable values—values that in any case are characteristic of sport.

PEACE: THE GOAL

The political goal of the Olympic Movement and, ultimately, all international sport is peace. This goal is viewed as an inheritance from the ancient Olympic Games that, as we have already seen, declared an effective truce to protect travelers and played an important role in the unification and internal pacification of the Hellenes. I have argued that this association between the Olympic Games and peace was probably more a by-product of the social dynamics of sport and human contact than a conscious goal of the ancient festival.[29] Specifically, the athletic festival required people to set aside their conflicts, at least for a limited period of time. It required them to treat strangers and rivals as equals—at least with respect to the rules of a particular contest. And it encouraged them to tolerate their differences, at least well enough to inhabit a small river valley at close quarters during the summer heat. In short, the ancient Olympic Games used sport to motivate people to make a special effort to live together in a small space. Insofar as globalization represents the virtual shrinking of social space, the values of Olympic sport may help us to deal with this challenge. But what does this really mean in a practical sense?

The first element is the demarcation of a common space within which political conflicts are put aside. As we saw in the comparison of sport and art in chapter 6, such extraordinary spaces are part and parcel of play activities—that is, they are set off from the ordinary workaday world. In ancient Olympia, the relevant space was religious, a sanctuary bounded by a wall known as the Altis. The modern Games use decoration and pageantry—in particular, the opening and closing ceremonies along with the burning of the Olympic flame—to transform whole cities, at least temporarily, into special kinds of places. Anyone who has ever attended an Olympic Games can attest to this change. In the future, the relevant space may be virtual rather than physical. The important thing, however, is that it is recognized as a place where worldly conflicts are temporarily set aside and a special effort is made to interact both competitively and cooperatively despite human differences. Hopefully, we will come to appreciate these differences, or at least to learn from them, as we occupy this intercultural space. Most important, as on the field of sport, we must treat others as equals under the rules no matter our personal feelings of like and dislike.

It must be said that international athletics, as practiced, could do a much better job of engaging athletes, coaches, officials, and even spectators in these peace-promoting aspects of sport. As Bruce Kidd observes, very few athletes are encouraged to take part in the extraordinarily rich opportunities the Olympic Movement provides for cultural education and exchange.[30] Athletes with early events routinely skip the opening ceremony and often leave town before the closing ritual. Many refuse to live in the Olympic Village, which itself could be better integrated by having athletes of different countries actually room together. Some are even advised by medical staff to avoid shaking hands with competitors for fear of contracting illness.[31]

The obvious obstacle is that many athletes are so focused on their performance that they eschew anything that might interfere with it, no matter how culturally valuable. Ironically, some of the star professional athletes for whom the Olympics is not a primary athletic objective seem to take best advantage of the cultural opportunities of the Games. It is not all the athletes' fault, however. As Kidd points out, "Relatively little effort is made to use the common language and experience of Olympic sports as a first step toward helping participants consciously navigate the divides of culture, be they structured by religion, ethnicity, class, or gender."[32] The educational potential of sport, on the international level as well as the local, is not automatic and must be intentionally pursued with at least as much enthusiasm as victory is pursued.

As a solution, Kidd proposes an "Olympic Curriculum" that would focus not just on competition but also on education, emphasizing intrinsic sport values like fair play; including competitors from different backgrounds; instructing athletes on the health risks of intensive training; cultivating an awareness of the history, geography, and environmental influence of their sports; and developing the skills of intercultural communication, including foreign language. The curriculum would include community service, and honors and ranks would be based on overall achievement rather than mere athletic performance.[33] Those who find such a transformation of sport implausible should ask themselves why, given the curricular demands already placed upon athletes in universities. The obvious objection is, again, that elite athletes are too focused on performance to take advantage of the intercultural opportunities provided by international sports. This, of course, begs the question of the *purpose* of international sport. If its goal is peace and if its peace-promoting ability depends on intercultural communication, why are we neglecting that in order to achieve ever greater performances? What good does adding another centimeter to the pole vault record really do for society? If it is indeed too much to ask of elite athletes to focus on high-level sport and peace politics, too, perhaps the Olympic Movement is to some degree wasted on them.

A very successful form of peace-promoting education is offered by the International Olympic Academy (IOA). This organization, housed in ancient Olympia, Greece, brings together students from all over the world to live and play together for extended periods each summer. I have participated in the academy's session for postgraduates on three separate occasions, and I can say from experience that the peace-promoting ideals of international sport are ably disseminated there. First of all, the academy is an extraordinarily beautiful campus set apart from ordinary life at the foot of the ancient Mount Chronion. Students know to put aside their differences while they are there. Roommates often come from countries with a history of conflict and rivalry. Mornings are generally spent in the classroom, while afternoons involve various sports activities. Students treat each other as equals in these activities, regardless of their differences in academic preparation or language capacity and their level of athletic ability. At the IOA, unlike the Olympic Games, males and females compete together. The evenings are devoted to cultural exchange, with students presenting their home countries' history, traditions, food, and drink. They don't always like one another, but they learn to live together and even appreciate their differences, often forming close bonds that last well beyond their time at the academy.

The point here is that sport's response to globalization need not be limited to the utopian image of the Olympic closing ceremony. More specific things can be done. Globalization provides not just great opportunities for sport but also serious challenges. A key sport value is equal opportunity, but globalization has historically favored the rich and powerful. Sport needs to be intentional about countering this tendency by providing opportunities for those less fortunate and by including those conventionally excluded. Another key risk of globalization is the loss of diversity, the homogenization of sport and culture more generally. Sports can be understood metaphysically as communities, and as communities, sports are capable of valuing and promoting diversity. Soccer should continue to celebrate different styles of play, and multisport festivals like the Olympic Games should seek to promote nontraditional sports. Furthermore, cultural differences, such as wearing appropriate headscarves by Muslim women, should be tolerated so long as these differences do not interfere with the fundamental principles of sport.

Sport should be a partner and a model for global projects such as sustainable development. This entails less emphasis on records at the narrow end of the sport-selection cone and more emphasis on inclusive participation at the wide end of the cone. Finally, sport should work toward peace by providing an appropriate space where people can meet as equals, setting aside conflicts and tolerating or maybe even celebrating their differences. Athletes should be encouraged to take advantage of these opportunities for cultural exchange; and at the same time, these opportunities should not be limited to athletes. As the example of the International Olympic Academy shows, the international political potential of sport may be best expressed through the play and interaction of nonelite athletes or even nonathletes who nevertheless can take part in the Olympic dream.

DISCUSSION QUESTIONS

1. For the 2012 London Olympics, beach volleyball relaxed its requirement that women compete in bikinis. This shows concern for cultural diversity, in particular, the more modest standards of dress found in many Muslim countries. Does this change reflect or resist the forces of globalization? Do you think it is good for the sport? For women?

2. Multiculturalism in sport means valuing diversity, not only in styles of play but also in the variety of sports offered—but space and funding are always limited. Looking at the list of sports offered by your school or those on the Olympic program, identify one sport to remove and one to add in order to increase diversity.

3. Making global sport more sustainable means making it more complex and less expensive. Soccer is a great example of a complex and inexpensive sport. How could other sports change to become more sustainable? Are some sports simply unsustainable?

4. The examples of competitors being discouraged from shaking hands or living in the athletes' village at the Olympics shows how the peace-promoting potential of the Olympic Games can be compromised by athletes' overemphasizing performance. What should Olympic committees do to resolve this problem? Should Olympians be trained and selected for their ability as ambassadors as well as athletes?

Conclusion

Ten Intrinsic Values of Sport

When I teach courses in the philosophy of sport, I usually ask students to introduce themselves by describing their sports experience. At the beginning, it seems to them as though the differences between their sports will yield big differences in their philosophies of sport, but by the end even the football players and dance team members have discovered how much they have in common. Despite the metaphysical difficulties in defining sport, despite the ethical ambiguity of concepts like fair play, and despite the diversity of political beliefs that link themselves with sport, the philosophy of sport does lead us toward some unifying ideas. Although it might be incorrect to say that "sport" has certain values, I think we can say that people who value sport and understand it philosophically should also value certain things because they are somehow intrinsic to sport. As a conclusion to this exploration of the philosophy of sport, let me attempt to gather a variety of ideas from the text and assemble them into a list of ten intrinsic values of sport.

AUTOTELICITY

We begin, as Plato and Aristotle did, with an appreciation of sport's autotelicity—the notion that it is (at least ideally) an end in itself, done for its own sake, without the need of external purpose or justification. In sport, we invent unnecessary obstacles and try to overcome them just because it makes the activity possible. This internal purposelessness of sport—what scholars sometimes call its "gratuitous nature"—resists attempts to reduce it to noth-

ing more than a means toward such external goods as power, fame, or fortune. Match-fixing scandals like the one we discussed in sumo, as well as
similar cases in soccer and cricket, are condemned not because players profit;
they are *already* professionals. The problem is that such scandals bring profit
making inside the game, selling out its internal principles for the sake of
external goods. A true professional, one who values and identifies with a
particular activity, will not reduce that activity to mere means toward other
ends. Like art, poetry, and staring at sunsets, sport is an activity that should
be valued primarily for its own sake.

BOUNDARIES

The match-fixing scandals' violation of autotelicity can also be understood as
a violation of sport's boundaries—a transgression of the limits that mark it
off from everyday practicalities and of the rule-based constraints that carve
out a space dedicated to open responsiveness. When the referee blows his
whistle three times to mark the end of a soccer game, we know that a special
piece of time has come to a close and, with it, the extraordinary sense of
freedom and possibility that characterize sport. Real boundaries, like whistles
and court outlines, act like theater curtains or temple doors, as signals to
adopt a particular attitude or to "frame" the upcoming experience—whether
as an athlete, an official, or a spectator—in a special way. By keeping sport
conceptually separate from the ordinary activities of life, we can temporarily
relieve ourselves from workaday concerns and carve out a space within
which to test and transcend our normal limitations, to explore the best of
ourselves.

FREEDOM

Within the boundaries of sport we also discover a paradoxical sense of freedom. This freedom derives not from the absence of constraints; to play a
sport we must subject ourselves to an intricate network of rules. Because we
voluntarily accept these rules, however, we gain the psychological feeling of
freedom. Because we collectively accept these rules, furthermore, the community of sport achieves the liberty identified by John Stuart Mill as foundational to creativity and thriving. We discovered that the absence of constraints in sport—such as the repeal or lax enforcement of doping regulations—can actually diminish athletes' sense of freedom, in that case by making them feel coerced to dope. Meanwhile, the rules' definition of simple
tasks, like running 100 meters, gives us the freedom to go all out within that

task—setting the stage for the perfect alignment of skill and ability that causes the extraordinary experience of freedom known as "flow" or being in "the zone."

CHALLENGE

Many of sport's internal benefits derive from the challenges it presents. Sport challenges are characteristically unnecessary and contrived (to get from the start to the finish line of a 400-meter race, it is hardly necessary to run around the track). But it is precisely sport's prescription of artificial inefficiencies that creates the challenges that produce such goods as enjoyable absorption in the game and the cultivation of virtues. Valuing challenge in sport entails a sincere effort to win because competitors provide much of the challenge for their opponents. But victory should not be sought through technological efficiencies. As the saga of the hydrodynamic swimsuits showed, efficiencies that undermine the inherent challenges of a sport potentially erode its value. It is the process of training and hard work that gives the faster swimming time its worth—gaining the same thing instantly by a magic suit or any other trick ultimately robs the performance of its value (and, once the trick is widely used, of its exclusivity) by undermining the challenge inherent in the sport.

FAIRNESS

We observed, in fact, that it was illogical to seek equipment advantages in sport because, once such an action is willed universally, according to Immanuel Kant's categorical imperative, any advantage gained is neutralized immediately. Equal opportunity and reward according to merit—the basic principles of fairness—are inscribed into sport's rules and logic. Winning can only imply athletic superiority if the contest itself was fair and no potentially superior athlete was excluded from it. It is for this reason that competition classifications according to social categories like race, gender, and disability can challenge sports' fairness. Such categories are not essential to sport, which reminds us that fairness is also a property of human beings and communities. In golf, we found players calling penalties on themselves to safeguard the game's fairness—a tradition that derives from community expectations as much as individual virtue. Other sports communities tolerate or even encourage intentional fouls, deception of referees, or deliberately mismatched contests that risk humiliating the losers. As baseball's "pine-tar incident" showed, fairness is an ethos that must go beyond written rules in order to express a human appreciation of the nature of a good contest.

UNCERTAINTY

Uncertainty of outcome is a primary quality of good contests. Mismatched competition was condemned in activities as diverse as Roman gladiatorial fights, martial arts matchups, and high school basketball. We saw that sincere doubt about the outcome was a key innovation of Olympic-style sport in ancient Greece—one that might have inspired the advent of philosophy. Uncertainty, furthermore, is what absorbs us in sport and makes it a welcome relief from everyday predictability. College football teams often schedule much weaker opponents for the first game of the season for strategic reasons, but these games are rarely good experiences for the teams or the spectators. Crowds often leave stadiums once the outcome of a game seems decided; insofar as the aesthetic value of the event depends on a sense of possibility, that value diminishes as the predictability of outcome increases. That 2006 Rose Bowl where my father had hoped for a blowout turned out to be a closely fought game that wasn't decided until inside the final minute. We got the "good game" he didn't want (and the result he didn't want), but the enduring uncertainty made it a great contest.

LEARNING

Uncertainty is also the foundation of learning, as Socrates's famous insistence on his ignorance so ably shows. Philosophy begins in wonder and uncertainty and, like sport, it seeks truth and knowledge. Just as scholars test theories through questioning and scientists test drugs using double-blind trials, sport tests athletic performance using the open and impartial mechanism of contest. So sport itself is a kind of truth-seeking process, but we also learn things through the experience of sport. They say you can learn a lot about people from the way they play games—we can also learn about ourselves. In sport, we learn experientially, in a holistic way that integrates mind and body. Ethical concepts are manifest in behavior, giving sport the educational potential to function as a moral laboratory. The world is even learning from sport about globalization. But learning from sport is not automatic, and its lessons are not always positive. Education through sport can transcend the theoretical, but it has to be intentional. We need to make learning a primary goal of sport—one not so easily sacrificed in the name of increased performance.

EXCELLENCE

The difference between performance and excellence is important to understand. As Plato's distinction between *technē* (skill) and *aretē* (virtue) showed, the former derives its value from the latter. In other words, the tennis player's ability to hit high a speed serve is less humanly valuable than the humility, courage, self-control, and persistence that were required to achieve that skill. Excellence in sport demands virtue; in fact, virtue and excellence are both translations of *aretē*, the Greek ideal prized in athletics and education. *Aretē* is a disposition for good actions that must, on Aristotle's terms, be actualized through their performance. Being the best and outperforming all others, what Homer called *aristeia*, is valued in sport not because sport-specific skills are worthwhile but rather because the virtues that contribute to that performance can be transferred to other human endeavors. As my student athlete example showed, positive qualities exhibited in sport such as focus and endurance are not virtues at all if the athlete is incapable of exercising them in other activities. When athletes strive for Olympic gold medals, what they really should seek is to become the kind of person who deserves the gold medal—one with virtues that can produce good in many activities and not merely sport.

COMMUNITY

The cultivation of virtue through sport was shown, furthermore, to be a community activity. Alasdair MacIntyre's theory of social practices reveals the important sense in which sports are ultimately communities. We acquire virtue through sport not so much by training and improving our individual performances but rather by participating actively and thoughtfully in sports communities with histories, traditions, and shared standards of excellence. Becoming a great cyclist involves more than pedaling a bike: you must enter into a community and learn its history and standards of excellence; you must humbly subject yourself to coaching from recognized experts; and you must take responsibility for the effect your own actions have upon that community. This community aspect of sport contrasts with what William Morgan identified as the hyperindividualism exhibited by some athletes with the encouragement of the market. Pretensions of athletic autonomy are quickly unmasked. What would a hot-shot sports star be without his team? Without his youth league coaches? Without the great players of the past who brought his sport into the public eye? Understanding sports as communities with sport-specific values allows them to resist the instrumentalizing tendencies of institutions and also to exhibit such values as diversity, equality opportunity, and collectively enjoyed internal goods.

BEAUTY

It is notoriously difficult to articulate the internal goods of sport because their appreciation depends upon a sport-specific understanding that is acquired primarily through the experience of participation. In this sense, they are not unlike beauty—indeed, beauty may be an appropriately amorphous description of an intrinsic value with diverse expressions. We have discussed a variety of examples, from the record flight of the Olympic ski jumper, to Roger Bannister's four-minute mile, to Rulon Gardner's retirement gesture in Athens, and to the simple sense of achievement gained through perfecting a spike move in volleyball. We have also discussed events that were less than beautiful—often because they lacked "fairness," a word with aesthetic as well as moral connotations: Ben Johnson's steroid-laced sprint victory, Diego Maradona's "hand of god" goal, and Sarra Besbes's refusal to raise her foil. Beauty in sport is not just a matter of aesthetic pleasure. As Seneca's account of ancient Roman games and the example of Michael Johnson's duck-like running style show, athletic beauty derives at least partly from a philosophical understanding of sport.

In a sense, all of the values listed above relate to beauty in sport. Sport's beauty derives partly from its autotelicity; like most of the arts and even some sciences like philosophy, it is practiced primarily for its own sake. Part of sport's beauty comes from its framing—from our marking it off from ordinary life and expecting extraordinary, wonderful things to happen within that frame. There is beauty in the freedom experienced as a heightened awareness of possibility, or perhaps through the flow of a perfectly executed movement, such as Nadia Comaneci's "perfect 10" performance on the uneven parallel bars. Fairness can be a synonym of beauty, and it reveals the ethical aspect of aesthetic value; the ancient Greek ideal of *kalokagathia* linked beauty and goodness not just in art but also in athletics and education. Uncertainty gives sport its dramatic beauty, perhaps more authentically than plays or literature since the final outcome is truly unknown. Sport's drama, in turn, is central to our learning; an aesthetic appreciation of virtuous action in sport is important for moral education. Athletic beauty is not merely skin deep but ideally a reflection of the virtues demanded by training and competition. Finally, there is beauty in the athletic community—not least in the image that international sport can give us of a harmonious yet diverse global community.

The philosophical study of sport not only can help us to learn and explain important concepts in metaphysics, ethics, and social-political philosophy but also gives us a better understanding of a significant human activity. People like to say that sport mirrors society, and it is true sport contains myriad reflections of human nature—both good and bad. What we have learned, however, is that sport also has its own nature and logic—one that deserves to be understood, appreciated, and protected so that sport can be not only a significant human activity but a meaningful and valuable one as well.

Appendix

Philosophy of Sport as an Academic Subject

The Olympic revival's effort to blend philosophy and sport (discussed in chapter 2) took place outside of the modern academy. Within the academy, sport and philosophy had their separate places and were rarely if ever seen in a room together. College athletics was regarded as something separate from academics, and philosophers generally shunned sport as a subject unworthy of serious inquiry. It was Johan Huizinga's *Homo Ludens*, a cultural history of play, that planted the academic seeds that would grow into the discipline we now call philosophy of sport.[1] Huizinga's book, first published in 1938 and made widely available in English during the 1950s, claimed that play is prior not just to sport but also to culture and civilization. He further characterized play as not serious, not necessary (i.e., for survival), and separate from ordinary life. Huizinga himself discussed sport only to point out that it was losing its play characteristics in the modern world, but he at least recognized sport as an offspring of play, thereby laying the groundwork for a metaphysical discussion of the nature of sport.

That discussion began in the early 1960s. Sociologist Roger Caillois's book *Man, Play, and Games* applied Huizinga's theory of play to games, including sport, and inspired many others to begin thinking about the metaphysical nature of sport.[2] One of these was John W. Loy Jr., who published "The Nature of Sport: A Definitional Effort" in 1968.[3] Another was the lighthearted logician Bernard Suits, whose 1967 article "What Is a Game?" was published in the journal *Philosophy of Science*.[4] This article foreshadowed what would become one of the most seminal works in philosophy of sport, *The Grasshopper: Games, Life, and Utopia* (discussed in chapter 4).[5] In addition to philosophers, scholars of physical education began to link up theories of play with those of sport. In 1961, Allen V. Sapora and Elmer D. Mitchell published *The Theory of Play and Recreation*, which applied the theory of play to the administration of sports and recreation programs.[6] Meanwhile, Eleanor Metheny began publishing theoretical articles such as "This 'Thing' Called Sport" in physical education journals.[7] In fact, Metheny's work inspired so many others, she might be considered the mother of modern philosophy of sport.

It was also during the 1960s that philosophers began to inquire into the role of sport in human life. In 1964, James W. Keating published "Sportsmanship as a Moral Category" in the philosophy journal *Ethics*, perhaps marking the first time since Plato that mainstream philosophy took sport as a subject for moral speculation.[8] One of Keating's moves was to distinguish "sport" from "athletics" and then to argue for different moral expectations depending on an activity's goals.

The tension between the playful and competitive characteristics of sport continues to have important implications in sports ethics. In 1967, Howard Slusher brought existentialist philosophy and its ethical goal of authenticity to the subject of sport with his book *Man, Sport, and Existence*.[9] Existentialism and phenomenology continue to provide popular modes for the philosophical analysis of sport, not least through Maurice Merleau-Ponty's and Gabriel Marcel's theories of embodiment, Jean-Paul Sartre's discussions of play and freedom, and Simone DeBeauvior's connection between female bodies and female oppression. Among scholars of physical education, Earle F. Zeigler began what would be an exceptionally prolific philosophy of sport publishing career with his 1964 book *Philosophical Foundations for Physical, Health, and Recreation Education*.[10]

Arguably, however, Paul Weiss's 1969 book *Sport: A Philosophic Inquiry* represents the real emergence of sport as a subject within academic philosophy.[11] Weiss's membership in the philosophy department of Yale University and his prominence within the field of metaphysics brought almost instant credibility to the philosophical study of sport. Weiss, neither an expert on nor a practitioner of sport, begins his book with the words "I am not an athlete." Nevertheless, his exceptional research and reasoning skills combined to establish a style for philosophy of sport that reached back to its ancient Greek roots and applied itself directly to modern athletic practices. The book considers not just the metaphysical nature of sport but also "the challenge of the body" and the educational potential of athletics. His chapters on women and amateurism are doubtless out of date and out of touch with modern readers, and in practice his work is infrequently cited in today's sport philosophy literature. Nevertheless, the book marks the beginning of modern philosophy of sport, not least because of Weiss's ancestral role in the forming of the first academic society dedicated to the philosophy of sport.

It is, of course, people rather than books that create an academic field—more specifically, the desire of a group of people to better understand something, in this case, sport. December 28, 1972, is the official birth date of the International Association for the Philosophy of Sport (IAPS), then called the Philosophical Society for the Study of Sport (PSSS). State University of New York (SUNY) at Brockport professor Warren Fraleigh is widely regarded as the father of this organization (and is still active in IAPS today), but he recognizes teachers and scholars from around the world as foundational to the society's development—among them Drew Hyland of Trinity College in Connecticut; Hans Lenk of Karlsruhe University in Germany; Eleanor Metheny and Howard Slusher at the University of Southern California; Ellen Gerber and Harold VanderZwaag from the University of Massachusetts; Shinobu Abe from the Nippon College of Physical Education in Japan; Peter Arnold of Dumfermline College in the United Kingdom; and several of Fraleigh's SUNY colleagues, including Robert Osterhoudt, Klaus Meier, Carolyn Thomas, and R. Scott Kretchmar. [12]

This group was busy throughout the late 1960s and early 1970s teaching courses, organizing conferences, and publishing books and articles on the philosophy of sport. In 1972 alone, academic symposia on the philosophy of sport and on sport and ethics were held at Brockport, and sessions on the philosophy and theology of sport were part of the Pre-Olympic Scientific Congress on Sport held just before the Munich Games. It was at these meetings that plans were made for the inauguration of the Philosophical Society for the Study of Sport, which took place at the Boston Sheraton Hotel in conjunction with the Eastern Division Meeting of the American Philosophical Association. Paul Weiss was elected the first president of the organization, with Warren Fraleigh president-elect, along with a board of directors that represented four different nations. From this point forward, IAPS sponsored annual meetings at various locations in North America and Europe, and sponsored sessions at the quadrennial meetings of the International Congress on Sport Science and Physical Education, as well as the World Congresses of Philosophy, held every five years. Since the year 2000, IAPS has met in Australia, the United States, Britain, the Czech Republic, Canada, Slovenia, Japan, and Italy.

The first issue of the *Journal of the Philosophy of Sport* (*JPS*) appeared in 1974. *JPS* struggled a bit in the early stages, but before the end of the decade it had established itself as the primary source of accomplished scholarship in the field. The journal, like the field in general, is characterized by an inclusive approach toward diverse methodologies and subjects. Early issues focused mostly on aesthetics and metaphysics. R. Scott Kretchmar's 1975 article "From Test to Contest: An Analysis of Two Kinds of Counterpoint in Sport" is frequently cited even today. [13] The 1980s ushered in a new interest in diversity issues with more articles on Eastern martial arts and the role of women in sport. B. C. Postow's "Women and Masculine Sports" was a foundational article in this genre.[14] Ethics was also the subject of much discussion with Craig Lehman's 1981 article "Can Cheaters Play the Game?" posing a foundational question.[15] The ethics of drug use and bans also came in for extensive debate among such scholars as W. Miller Brown, Warren Fraleigh, and Robert Simon.

By the late 1980s, enough articles had been published in *JPS* to establish subfields within the discipline and to populate an anthology suitable for student courses: William J. Morgan and Klaus V. Meier's *Philosophic Inquiry in Sport*. The anthology, originally published in 1988 with a second edition in 1995, complemented the publication of important monographs in the field such as Bernard Suits's *The Grasshopper: Games, Life, and Utopia* (mentioned earlier), Warren Fraleigh's *Right Actions in Sport: Ethics for Contestants*,[16] and William J. Morgan's *Leftist Theories of Sport: A Critique and Reconstruction*.[17] These books represent the three general subfields of sport philosophy that had taken root: metaphysics, ethics, and politics. It is important to note, however, that the emphasis established by IAPS and *JPS* is on interdisciplinary exchange. Although philosophers of sport have diverse interests and academic specialties, the tendency within the field is to be familiar with all its aspects and to welcome discussion from all quarters. Such inclusiveness is certainly among the causes of the field's growth.

After the year 2000, the *Journal of the Philosophy of Sport* went from one to two issues per year. This change was driven by burgeoning interest not just in Britain and North America but also farther afield. In some ways, its growth reflected the growth of sport sciences more generally, but also philosophers of sport were making their field more visible by publishing books for libraries and the classroom as well as articles in traditional philosophy and physical education journals. Drew Hyland's *Philosophy of Sport*, Robert Simon's *Fair Play*, and my book *The Philosophical Athlete* are all monographs suitable for sport-themed undergraduate courses in philosophy.[18] Meanwhile, R. Scott Kretchmar's *Practical Philosophy of Sport*[19] and Sheryle Bergmann Drewe's *Why Sport?*[20] are tailored for physical education and kinesiology students. Sports ethics also became a popular course judging by the variety of anthologies available.[21] In addition, M. Andrew Holowchak's *Philosophy of Sport: Critical Readings, Crucial Issues*, published by the textbook giant Prentice Hall, provides a general anthology of readings suitable for undergraduates.[22] In 1998, Mike McNamee and Jim Parry published *Ethics and Sport* in the United Kingdom. This anthology later spawned Routledge's Ethics and Sport book series, which now includes over twenty volumes.

Although most scholars of sport philosophy came from departments of either philosophy or education, a PhD program combining the history and philosophy of sport was established at Pennsylvania State University in the early 1990s. This program, along with those at Ohio State, Tennessee, and

University of Western Ontario, has produced several philosophers of sport, although the number of scholars trained in traditional departments of philosophy is growing as well. Sessions on the philosophy of sport have been revived at the meetings of the American Philosophical Association and the World Congress of Philosophy. Philosophy's role is growing within the larger field of sports studies as well. Most important, however, is the continued internationalization of the discipline. The Japanese Society for the Philosophy of Sport and Physical Education, active since 1978, was joined in 2002 by the British Philosophy of Sport Association (BPSA), and then the European Association for the Philosophy of Sport (EAPS) in 2009. Even China has shown interest in philosophy of sport. In 2008, they invited me to give a series of lectures at Beijing Sport University in 2008.

The increasing internationalization of the discipline is reflected in its recent publications. A new journal, *Sport, Ethics and Philosophy*, was launched in 2007 partly with the hope, in editor Mike McNamee's words, "the journal may play its part in stimulating areas of philosophical interest that have hitherto been underrepresented."[23] By that he meant not only that the journal will expand its conception of "sport" to include such fields as "physical culture" or "movement culture" but also that it will expand acceptable methodologies beyond the Anglo-American, analytical tradition that had dominated the sport philosophy literature for thirty years. *Sport, Ethics and Philosophy*—publishing three issues a year, including focused special issues, some of which have been reissued as books in the Ethics and Sport series— has been a large success. Further evidence of the journal's international orientation is provided by its inclusion of abstracts in English, Spanish, German, French, and Chinese.

All of this is just a start, of course. Given the international nature of sport and the contemporary phenomena of multiculturalism and globalization, it is inevitable that philosophy of sport must expand its cultural perspectives. Although the subject has a long tradition in Asia—the Japanese Philosophy of Sport Association has for many years boasted more members than its international counterpart—more effort needs to be made to negotiate between the contrasting philosophical traditions of East and West.[24] In addition, voices from more localized philosophical traditions need to contribute their perspectives to the field. This is already happening, with special issues of the *Journal of the Philosophy of Sport* dedicated to neglected national traditions, as well an increasingly diverse group of conference participants and contributors, especially in the journal *Sport, Ethics and Philosophy*. Because modern elite sport is increasingly a global phenomenon and even grassroots sport-for-all programs are addressing universal needs, philosophy of sport simply cannot remain a predominantly Anglo-American discipline. The history of the International Association for the Philosophy of Sport and of the field more generally is one of tolerance and inclusiveness. The future of philosophy of sport, like the future of sport, will be built upon increasing international cooperation.

Notes

INTRODUCTION

1. Plato, *Apology*, trans. G. M. A. Grube (Indianapolis: Hackett, 1980), 36d.

1. THE ANCIENT HELLENIC HERITAGE

1. Pindar, "Pythian 8," in *Olympian Odes, Pythian Odes*, trans. William H. Race, 95–97 (Cambridge, MA: Harvard University Press, 1997).

2. Pindar, "Olympian 8," in *The Complete Odes*, trans. Anthony Verity (Oxford: Oxford University Press, 2007), 1.

3. *The Epic of Gilgamesh*, trans. N. K. Sandars (London: Penguin, 1960), 68.

4. S. K. Kramer, "Hymn of Praise to Shulgi," in *History Begins at Sumer*, 285–88 (Philadelphia: University of Pennsylvania Press, 1981).

5. Donald G. Kyle, *Sport and Spectacle in the Ancient World* (Malden, MA: Blackwell, 2007), 68.

6. According to Ben Brown, "The crisis of social value in the *Iliad* is a crisis within the pre-monetary economy of peer relations. The *Iliad* focuses upon a society composed of many *basileis*, great warriors who find themselves outside of the comfortable hierarchies of home. This world of warrior peers—*homoioi*—is by no means stable. The relations of equality and the claim to deserve recognition must be founded on each man's daily concern for his own time, the complex of his social worth." Ben Brown, "Homer, Funeral Contests and the Origins of the Greek City," in *Sport and Festival in the Ancient Greek World*, ed. David J. Phillips and David Pritchard, 123–62 (Swansea: Classical Press of Wales, 2003), 129.

7. The Greek phrase *aien aristeuein kai upeirochon emmenai allōn* is said twice, at *Iliad* 6.208 and 11.784.

8. For a full exploration of this thesis, see Heather L. Reid, "Sport, Philosophy, and the Quest for Knowledge," *Journal of the Philosophy of Sport* 36, no. 1 (2009): 40–49.

9. Aristotle, "Metaphysics," in *Complete Works*, ed. Jonathan Barnes (Princeton, NJ: Princeton University Press, 1984), 1.2, 982b12–21: "Whoever is puzzled and in a state of wonder believes he is ignorant (this is why the lover of myths is also in a way a philosopher, since myths are made up of wonders). And so, if indeed they pursued philosophy to escape

ignorance, they were obviously pursuing scientific knowledge in order to know and not for the sake of any practical need."

10. Specifically, in the games of the Phaeacians, Odysseus responds to the taunt "You do not look like an athlete" (Homer, *Odyssey*, in *The Iliad and Odyssey*, trans. Robert Fagles [New York: Penguin, 1990], 8.164) by throwing a discus well beyond the marks made by the local boys. And upon his return to Ithaca, he dispatches a lower-class boxer (18.96–7) and defeats the would-be successors to his kingship by besting them in an archery contest (21).

11. For more on the "economics" of ancient Greek religion, see J. Mikalson, *Ancient Greek Religion* (Malden, MA: Blackwell, 2005), 25.

12. Philostratos, "Gymnastics," in Stephen G. Miller, *Arete: Greek Sports from Ancient Sources* (Berkeley: University of California Press, 1991), 38. For a detailed analysis of the passage, see Panos Valavanis, "Thoughts on the Historical Origins of the Olympic Games and the Cult of Pelops in Olympia," *Nikephoros* 19 (2006): 141.

13. For more on the connection between athletic victors and religious sacrifice, see Walter Burkert, *Greek Religion*, trans. John Raffan (Cambridge, MA: Harvard University Press, 1985), 56; and David Sansone, *Greek Athletics and the Genesis of Sport* (Berkeley: University of California Press, 1988).

14. In *Metaphysics* (1000a9–20), Aristotle distinguishes philosophers from theologians by saying that the former offer argument (*apodeixis*) to support their views, while the latter offer only stories or speak *mythikōs*.

15. For a full account of these arguments see Heather L. Reid, "Olympic Sport and Its Lessons for Peace," *Journal of the Philosophy of Sport* 33, no. 2 (2006): 205–13.

16. Pausanias, *Description of Greece*, trans. Peter Levi, 2 vols. (New York: Penguin, 1979), 1:5.21.2–4.

17. See, for example, Stephen G. Miller, "Naked Democracy," in *Polis and Politics*, ed. P. Flensted-Jensen and T. H. Nielsen, 277–96 (Copenhagen: Festschrift, 2000).

18. Nigel James Nicholson, *Aristocracy and Athletics in Archaic and Classical Greece* (Cambridge, UK: Cambridge University Press, 2005), 134.

19. The social class of Olympic victors is a matter of controversy among historians. For a full discussion of the debate, see David Young, *The Olympic Myth of Greek Amateur Athletics* (Chicago: Ares, 1984); and Mark Golden, *Greek Sport and Social Status* (Austin: University of Texas Press, 2008).

20. Aristotle, "Rhetoric," in *Complete Works*, 1.1364a20, 1367b18.

21. For a similar comparison between democracy and sport, especially in relation to education in modern democracies, see Peter Arnold, "Democracy, Education and Sport," *Journal of the Philosophy of Sport* 16 (1989): 100–110.

22. The story is told, in slightly different versions, by Thucydides, *History of the Peloponnesian War*, trans. B. Jowett (Oxford, UK: Clarendon, 1900), 6.56–59, and Aristotle, *The Athenian Constitution*, trans. Sir Frederic G. Kenyon (Washington, DC: Merchant Books, 2009), 18.

23. Miller says, "This equality before absolute standards of distance and speed and strength—as measured by those of the other competitors present—that are subject to the interpretation of no man is basic *isonomia*" ("Naked Democracy," 279).

24. Herodotus, *Histories*, trans. A. D. Godley (Cambridge, MA: Harvard University Press, 1920), 3.80–82.

25. Ian Morris, "Equality and the Origins of Greek Democracy," in *Ancient Greek Democracy*, ed. Eric W. Robinson, 45–73 (Malden, MA: Blackwell, 2004), 63.

26. The term "physical education" is often used by modern translators to render the Greek term *gymnastikē*, which does refer to training exercises not unlike what we now call physical education, but the Greek term does not imply that it is the body rather than the soul, or more accurately, the whole person, that is being educated.

27. See, for example, Aristotle, "De Anima," in *Complete Works*, 415b.

28. For an excellent discussion of these terms and ideas, see Bruno Snell, *The Discovery of the Mind in Greek Philosophy and Literature* (New York: Dover, 1982), 8–22.

29. Plato, *Republic*, trans. G. M. A. Grube (Indianapolis: Hackett, 1992), 410b–411e.

30. Plato sets *Charmides* in the Palaestra of Taureas (153b), in *Euthydemus* we find Socrates with *pankratists* at the Lyceum, and in *Lysis* Socrates is on his way from one gymnasium (the Academy) to another (the Lyceum) when he is pulled aside into a new wrestling school (203–204a). *Theaetetus* is also set in a gymnasium, as indicated by Theaetetus and his friends oiling themselves down before the conversation (144c), and it is likely that *Sophist* and *Politicus* share the same setting—although it's not obvious from the text.

31. Plato, "Euthyphro," in *Complete Works*, ed. John M. Cooper (Indianapolis: Hackett, 1997), 2a. This is the same Lyceum that would become the site of Aristotle's school, but as of the dramatic time (and probably when the dialogue was written), it was simply a gymnasium.

32. Iamblichus, *The Pythagorean Life*, trans. Thomas Taylor (London: Watkins, 1818). 6–7.

33. For a detailed account, see Heather L. Reid, "Wrestling with Socrates," *Sport, Ethics and Philosophy* 4, no. 2 (2010): 157–69. Reprinted in *Athletics and Philosophy in the Ancient World: Contests of Virtue* (London: Routledge, 2011), chap. 4.

34. Plato, *Apology*, trans. G. M. A. Grube (Indianapolis: Hackett, 1980), 19d.

35. See especially, *Protagoras*, *Euthydemus*, and *Gorgias*.

36. Plato, *Apology*, 23b.

37. Plato, *Apology*, 22d–23b.

38. Plato, *Apology*, 36de.

39. Xenophanes, quoted in Athenaeus, "The Deipnosophists," in *The Smell of Sweat: Greek Athletics, Olympics and Culture*, ed. W. B. Tyrell (Wauconda, IL: Bolchazy-Carducci, 2004), 413c–f.

40. Plato, *Apology*, 30b.

41. This understanding of sport is explained by Drew A. Hyland in "Competition and Friendship," *Journal of the Philosophy of Sport* 5 (1978): 27–37.

42. Plato, "Philebus," in *Complete Works*, 14b.

43. For more details, see Heather L. Reid, "Plato's Gymnasium," *Sport, Ethics and Philosophy* 4, no. 2 (2010): 170–82. Reprinted in *Athletics and Philosophy*, chap. 5.

44. See, for example, Nigel Spivey, *The Ancient Olympics: A History* (Oxford: Oxford University Press, 2004).

45. Plato, "Laches," in *Complete Works*, 181b.

46. Alcibiades testifies to Socrates's military valor in Plato, *Symposium*, trans. Alexander Nehamas and Paul Woodruff (Indianapolis: Hackett, 1989), 220de.

47. This is the central argument in Heather L. Reid, "Sport and Moral Education in Plato's Republic," *Journal of the Philosophy of Sport* 34, no. 2 (2007): 160–75.

48. Plato, *Laws*, trans. Trevor Saunders (London: Penguin, 1970), 643e.

49. For more details on this, see Reid, "Plato's Gymnasium" and "Sport and Moral Education."

50. Plato, *Symposium*, 217a.

51. For more on these relationships, see William A. Percy, *Pederasty and Pedagogy in Archaic Greece* (Urbana: University of Illinois Press, 1996).

52. Diogenes Laertius, *Lives of Eminent Philosophers*, trans. R. D. Hicks, vol. 1 (Cambridge, MA: Harvard University Press, 1972), 3.46.

53. For more on Sparta's educational programs, see Nigel M. Kennell, *The Gymnasium of Virtue: Education and Culture in Ancient Sparta* (Chapel Hill: University of North Carolina Press, 1995).

54. For a full analysis, see Nicholas D. Smith, "Plato and Aristotle on the Nature of Women," *Journal of the History of Philosophy* 21, no. 4 (1983): 467–78.

55. Aristotle, "On the Generation of Animals," 737a, and *Politics*, 1260a, both in *Complete Works*.

56. Aristotle, *Nicomachean Ethics*, trans. Terence Irwin, 2nd ed. (Indianapolis: Hackett, 1999), 1103a17–18.

57. Aristotle, *Nicomachean Ethics*, 1114a8–10.

58. Aristotle, *Nicomachean Ethics*, 1120a16–17.

59. Aristotle, *Nicomachean Ethics*, 1099a3–6.

60. Aristotle, *Politics*, trans. C. D. C. Reeve (Indianapolis: Hackett, 1998), 1138b–1139b.

61. Aristotle, *Nicomachean Ethics*, 1106a27–34.

62. This perhaps is why David Young says Aristotle sees physical and mental training as enemies of one another in "Mens Sana in Corpore Sano? Body and Mind in Greek Literature," *Proceedings of the North American Society for Sport History* (1998): 61. Moderate physical activity, however, is not derided as contrary to intellectual development.

63. Aristotle, *Nicomachean Ethics*, 1106b.

64. Aristotle, *Nicomachean Ethics*, 1112b. For a more detailed account of Aristotle's view on sport, see Heather L. Reid, "Aristotle's Pentathlete," *Sport, Ethics and Philosophy* 4, no. 2 (2010): 183–94.

2. THE MODERN OLYMPIC REVIVAL

1. International Olympic Committee, "Fundamental Principles of Olympism," in *The Olympic Charter* (Lausanne, Switzerland: Author, 2010), 11.

2. For a full discussion of Olympism's legitimacy as a philosophy, see Lamartine DaCosta, "A Never-Ending Story: The Philosophical Controversy over Olympism," *Journal of the Philosophy of Sport* 33, no. 2 (2006): 157–73.

3. For a full account see René Descartes, "Discourse on Method," in *The Philosophical Writings of Descartes*, ed. J. Cottingham, R. Stoothoff, and D. Murdoch, 1:111–51 (Cambridge, UK: Cambridge University Press, 1985).

4. In at least one of his early writings, Descartes used the pseudonym "Polybius, citizen of the world." Rene Descartes, "Preliminaries," in *Philosophical Writings of Descartes*, 1:2n1.

5. Descartes, "Discourse on Method," 111.

6. Lao-Tzu, *Tao Te Ching*, trans. S. Addiss and S. Lombardo (Indianapolis: Hackett, 2003), 1.1.

7. The story is related in Marcus Tullius Cicero, *Tusculan Disputations*, trans. J. King (Cambridge, MA: Loeb, 1927), 5.8s.

8. For a more detailed account of Olympism's relationship to Eastern and Western philosophy, see Heather L. Reid, "East to Olympia: Recentering Olympic Philosophy between East and West," *Olympika: The International Journal of Olympic Studies* 19 (2010): 59–79.

9. DaCosta, "A Never-Ending Story," 166.

10. There is, however, a collection of essays by Pierre de Coubertin entitled *Olympism: Selected Writings*, ed. Norbert Müller (Lausanne, Switzerland: International Olympic Committee, 2000); and a collection of philosophical essays about the Olympic Games: Heather L. Reid and Mike W. Austin, eds. *The Olympics and Philosophy* (Lexington: University Press of Kentucky, 2012).

11. Hans Lenk, "Towards a Philosophical Anthropology of the Olympic Athletes and the Achieving Being," in *International Olympic Academy Report*, 163–77 (Ancient Olympia, Greece: 1982).

12. David C. Young, "*Mens Sana in Corpore Sano?* Body and Mind in Greek Literature," *Proceedings of the North American Society for Sport History* (1998): 60–61.

13. International Olympic Committee, "Fundamental Principles," 11.

14. International Olympic Committee, "Fundamental Principles," 11.

15. Immanuel Kant, *Groundwork for the Metaphysic of Morals*, trans. H. J. Paton (New York: Harper and Row, 1948), 96.

16. Lao-Tzu, *Tao Te Ching*, 57; Confucius, *Analects*, trans. E. Slingerland (Indianapolis: Hackett, 2003), 4.11.

17. International Olympic Committee, "Fundamental Principles," 11.

18. For a comparison of Eastern and Western conceptions of virtue applied to sport, see Heather L. Reid, "Athletic Virtue: Between East and West," *Sport Ethics and Philosophy* 4, no. 1 (2010): 16–26.

19. Mike McNamee, "Olympism, Eurocentricity, and Transcultural Virtues," *Journal of the Philosophy of Sport* 33, no. 2 (2006): 174–87.

20. International Olympic Committee, *Olympic Charter*, 31.

21. International Olympic Committee, *Olympic Charter*, 62.

22. International Olympic Committee, *Olympic Charter*, 2007, 98.

23. International Olympic Committee, *Olympic Charter*, 15.

24. International Olympic Committee, *Olympic Charter*, 14.

25. International Olympic Committee, "Fundamental Principles of Olympism," 11.

26. Heather L. Reid, "Olympic Sport and Its Lessons for Peace," *Journal of the Philosophy of Sport* 33, no. 2 (2006): 205–13.

27. Philostratos, "Gymnastics," in *Arete: Greek Sports from Ancient Sources*, ed. Stephen G. Miller (Berkeley: University of California Press, 1991), 38. For a detailed analysis of the passage, see Panos Valavanis, "Thoughts on the Historical Origins of the Olympic Games and the Cult of Pelops in Olympia," *Nikephoros* 19 (2006): 141.

28. Obviously, these are very general observations, and there are exceptions on both the Western and Eastern side. The point is that Olympism needs to account for divergent understandings.

29. This distinction is explained by William J. Morgan, "Cosmopolitanism, Olympism, and Nationalism: A Critical Interpretation of Coubertin's Ideal of International Sporting Life," *Olympika* 4 (1995): 88.

30. International Olympic Committee, *Olympic Charter*, 14.

3. SPORT AND PLAY

1. He repeats the theme in several places, for example, Aristotle, *Politics*, trans. C. D. C. Reeve (Indianapolis: Hackett, 1998), 7.1325b20.

2. Plato, *Laws*, trans. Trevor Saunders (London: Penguin, 1970), 803ad.

3. Johan Huizinga, *Homo Ludens: A Study of the Play Element in Culture* (Boston: Beacon Press, [1944] 1955), 1.

4. Huizinga, *Homo Ludens*, 197.

5. Huizinga, *Homo Ludens*, 13.

6. Huizinga, *Homo Ludens*, 28.

7. Roger Caillois, *Man, Play, and Games*, trans. Meyer Berlash (Urbana: University of Illinois Press, [1958] 2001), 5.

8. Caillois, *Man, Play, and Games*, 9–10.

9. John W. Loy Jr., "The Nature of Sport: A Definitional Effort," *Quest* 10, no. 1 (May 1968): 1–15. Loy accepted Caillois's definition and added such elements as competition and physical skill.

10. David L. Roochnik, "Play and Sport," *Journal of the Philosophy of Sport* 2, no. 1 (1975): 37.

11. Roochnik, "Play and Sport," 39. See also Klaus Meier, "An Affair of Flutes: An Appreciation of Play," *Journal of the Philosophy of Sport* 7, no. 1 (1980): 25.

12. Drew Hyland, "The Stance of Play," *Journal of the Philosophy of Sport* 7, no. 1 (1980): 90.

13. Angela J. Schneider, "Fruits, Apples, and Category Mistakes: On Sport, Games, and Play," *Journal of the Philosophy of Sport* 28, no. 2 (2001): 152.

14. Huizinga, *Homo Ludens*, 7.

15. It figures prominently in Bernard Suits's highly influential definition of games (discussed in chapter 4), and Meier identifies it as one of only two necessary and sufficient conditions for play (the other is autotelicity; "Affair of Flutes," 25).

16. Weiss, *Sport: A Philosophic Inquiry* (Carbondale: Southern Illinois University Press, 1969), 134.

17. Caillois, *Man, Play, and Games*, 3.

18. Huizinga, *Homo Ludens*, 8.

19. Drew A. Hyland, *Philosophy of Sport* (New York: Paragon, 1990), 134.

20. Hyland, "The Stance of Play," 95.

21. Caillois, *Man, Play, and Games*, 8.

22. John Locke, *An Essay concerning Human Understanding* (Oxford, UK: Clarendon, 1975), 238.

23. Albert Camus, *The Myth of Sisyphus and Other Essays*, trans. Justin O'Brien (New York: Random House, 1955), 88–91. For an extended discussion of the arguments made in this paragraph, see Heather L. Reid, *The Philosophical Athlete* (Durham, NC: Carolina Academic Press, 2002), chap. 3.

24. Weiss, *Sport: A Philosophic Inquiry*, 134.

25. Randolph Feezell, *Sport, Play and Ethical Reflection* (Urbana: University of Illinois Press, 2006), 23.

26. Feezell, *Sport, Play*, 25.

27. Drew A. Hyland, *The Question of Play* (Lanham, MD: University Press of America, 1984), 102.

28. This is confirmed by empirical psychology according to Stephen Schmid, "Reconsidering Autotelic Play," *Journal of the Philosophy of Sport* 36, no. 2 (2009): 250.

29. Huizinga, *Homo Ludens*, 8.

30. Meier says, "If play is utilized as a break in routine for the purpose of returning recuperated to work, it is merely another utilitarian link in the chain, serving as a handmaiden to the productive enterprise, and thereby demonstrating essentially a work orientation and structure" ("Affair of Flutes," 28).

31. Weiss, *Sport: A Philosophic Inquiry*, 134.

32. Caillois, *Man, Play, and Games*, 6.

33. Huizinga, *Homo Ludens*, 9.

34. Huizinga, *Homo Ludens*, 19.

35. Roochnik, "Play and Sport," 41.

36. Hyland, "The Stance of Play," 88.

37. Hyland, "The Stance of Play," 89.

38. Roochnik, "Play and Sport," 41.

39. A fact admitted by Huizinga, *Homo Ludens*, 45, and Weiss, *Sport: A Philosophic Inquiry*, 136.

40. Aristotle, *Nicomachean Ethics*, trans. Terence Irwin, 2nd ed. (Indianapolis: Hackett, 1999), 1097b21–2.

41. Huizinga, *Homo Ludens*, 8.

42. Caillois, *Man, Play, and Games*, 5–6.

43. Weiss, *Sport: A Philosophic Inquiry*, 139.

44. Bernard Suits, "The Tricky Triad: Games, Play and Sport," *Journal of the Philosophy of Sport* 15, no. 1 (1988): 9.

45. Suits, "Tricky Triad," 8.

46. Feezell, *Sport, Play*, 26.

47. Suits "Tricky Triad," 9.

48. Schmid, "Reconsidering Autotelic Play," 254.

49. Hyland, *Question of Play*, xv.

50. Roochnik, "Play and Sport," 41.

51. At least Jeremy Bentham's version of utilitarianism.

52. Feezell, *Sport, Play*, 11.

53. Huizinga, *Homo Ludens*, 3.

54. Feezell, *Sport, Play*, 14.

55. Feezell, *Sport, Play*, 14.

56. Schmid, "Reconsidering Autotelic Play," 243.

57. Schmid, "Reconsidering Autotelic Play," 244.

58. Feezell, *Sport, Play*, 23.

59. Hyland, *Philosophy of Sport*, 139.

60. Weiss, *Sport: A Philosophic Inquiry*, 140.

61. Huizinga, *Homo Ludens*, 10.

62. Caillois, *Man, Play, and Games*, 7.

63. Weiss, *Sport: A Philosophic Inquiry*, 137.

64. Spencer K. Wertz, "The Capriciousness of Play: Collingwood's Insight," *Journal of the Philosophy of Sport* 30, no. 1 (2003): 164.

65. Seth Vannata, "A Phenomenology of Sport: Playing and Passive Synthesis," *Journal of the Philosophy of Sport* 35, no. 1 (2008): 63–72.

66. Susan A. Jackson and Mihaly Csikszentmihalyi, *Flow in Sports* (Champaign, IL: Human Kinetics, 1999), 6.

67. Laozi, "Daodejing," in *Readings in Classical Chinese Philosophy*, ed. P. Ivanhoe and B. Van Norden, 161–206, 2nd ed. (Indianapolis: Hackett, 2001), 184.

68. Vannata, "Phenomenology of Sport," 71.

4. SPORT AND GAMES

1. Bernard Suits, *The Grasshopper: Games, Life, and Utopia*, 2nd ed. (Peterborough, Ontario: Broadview, [1978] 2005), 50.

2. Suits, *Grasshopper*, 51.

3. Suits, *Grasshopper*, 39.

4. Suits, *Grasshopper*, 46.

5. Suits, *Grasshopper*, 42.

6. Bernard Suits, "The Tricky Triad: Games, Play and Sport," *Journal of the Philosophy of Sport* 15, no. 1 (1988): 7.

7. Suits, "Tricky Triad," 5.

8. Suits "Tricky Triad," 8.

9. Suits, *Grasshopper*, 37.

10. Suits, *Grasshopper*, 42.

11. Suits, *Grasshopper*, 52.

12. Suits, *Grasshopper*, 54–55.

13. Bernard Suits, "The Elements of Sport," in *Philosophic Inquiry in Sport*, ed. W. J. Morgan and Klaus V. Meier, 39–48 (Champaign, IL: Human Kinetics, 1988), 43.

14. The diagram also implies that not all games are play, not all sports are play, and the reverse of these statements, a position Suits reaffirms in "Venn and the Art of Category Maintenance," *Journal of the Philosophy of Sport* 31, no. 1 (2004): 6.

15. Suits, "Tricky Triad," 2.

16. Suits, "Tricky Triad," 3.

17. International Olympic Committee, *Factsheet on the Olympic Programme* (Lausanne, Switzerland: Author, 2007), 5.

18. This is Klaus V. Meier's interpretation of one of Suits's requirements (which he goes on to reject), "Triad Trickery: Playing with Sport and Games," *Journal of the Philosophy of Sport* 15, no. 1 (1988): 16.

19. Thomas P. Curtis, "Amusing Then Amazing: American Wins 1896 Discus," *Technology Review*, July 24, 1924, reprinted in *MIT News*, July 18, 1996, http://web.mit.edu/.

20. Concludes Meier in "Triad Trickery," "Any recourse to institutionalization, as an integral, necessary component of the essential nature of sport, is arbitrary, as well as erroneous and counterproductive; consequently, it should be actively rejected" (17).

21. Suits, "Tricky Triad," 5–6.

22. William J. Morgan, "The Logical Incompatibility Thesis and Rules: A Reconsideration of Formalism as an Account of Games," *Journal of the Philosophy of Sport* 14, no. 1 (1987): 3.

23. Warren P. Fraleigh, *Right Actions in Sport: Ethics for Contestants* (Champaign, IL: Human Kinetics, 1984), 69.

24. Suits, "Tricky Triad," 5–6.

25. Meier, "Triad Trickery," 19.

26. Meier, "Triad Trickery," 13.

27. Meier, "Triad Trickery," 21.

28. R. Scott Kretchmar, "Beautiful Games," *Journal of the Philosophy of Sport* 16, no. 1 (1989): 42.

29. Meier, "Triad Trickery," 24.
30. Morgan, "Logical Incompatibility," 1.
31. Graham McFee, *Sports, Rules and Values: Philosophical Investigations into the Nature of Sport* (London: Routledge, 2004), 43.
32. Fred D'Agostino, "The Ethos of Games," in *Philosophic Inquiry in Sport*, ed. W. J. Moran and K. V. Meier, 48–49, 2nd ed. (Champaign, IL: Human Kinetics, 1995).
33. Morgan, "Logical Incompatibility," 16.
34. Morgan, "Logical Incompatibility," 16.
35. Morgan, "Logical Incompatibility," 8.
36. Fraleigh, *Right Actions*, 69.
37. Fraleigh, *Right Actions*, 70.
38. Morgan, "Logical Incompatibility," 8.
39. Fraleigh, *Right Actions*, 71.
40. McFee, *Sports, Rules and Values*, 69.

5. SPORT AND SOCIAL PRACTICES

1. Graham McFee, *Sports, Rules and Values: Philosophical Investigations into the Nature of Sport* (London: Routledge, 2004), 74.
2. On sport as a social contract, see Heather L. Reid, *The Philosophical Athlete* (Durham, NC: Carolina Academic Press, 2002), 218–23; and Simon Eassom, "Games, Rules, and Contracts," in *Ethics and Sport*, ed. Mike McNamee and Jim Parry, 57–78 (London: E & FN Spon, 1998).
3. John Rawls, *A Theory of Justice* (Cambridge, MA: Harvard University Press, 1971).
4. Robert Simon, *Fair Play: Sports, Values, and Society* (Boulder, CO: Westview, 1991), 23.
5. Alasdair MacIntyre, *After Virtue* (Notre Dame, IN: University of Notre Dame Press, 1981), 175.
6. MacIntyre, *After Virtue*, 184.
7. Says MacIntyre, "We call them internal [goods] for two reasons: first . . . because we can only specify them in terms of chess or some other game of that specific kind and by means of examples from such games . . . and secondly because they can only be identified and recognized by the experience of participating in the practice in question. Those who lack the relevant experience are incompetent thereby as judges of internal goods" (*After Virtue*, 177).
8. MacIntyre, *After Virtue*, 178.
9. For more on this paradox of competition, see Drew A. Hyland, "Competition and Friendship," *Journal of the Philosophy of Sport* 5, no. 1 (1978): 27–37; and Heather L. Reid, "Wrestling with Socrates," *Sport, Ethics and Philosophy* 4, no. 2 (2010): 157–69.
10. MacIntyre explains, "The kind of cooperation, the kind of recognition of authority and of achievement, the kind of respect for standards and the kind of risk-taking which are characteristically involved in practices demand for example fairness in judging oneself and others . . . and willingness to trust the judgments of those whose achievement in the practice give them an authority to judge which presupposes fairness and truthfulness in those judgments, and from time to time the taking of self-endangering, reputation-endangering and even achievement-endangering risks" (*After Virtue*, 180).
11. MacIntyre, *After Virtue*, 178.
12. MacIntyre, *After Virtue*, 180.
13. Angela Schneider and Robert Butcher, "Why Olympic Athletes Should Avoid the Use and Seek the Elimination of Performance-Enhancing Substances and Practices from the Olympic Games," *Journal of the Philosophy of Sport* 20–21 (1993–1994): 71.
14. Schneider and Butcher, "Why Olympic Athletes," 71.
15. Reid, *Philosophical Athlete*, 150–51.
16. Schneider and Butcher show that the competitive advantages gained by doping depend on others' compliance with a ban ("Why Olympic Athletes," 73).

17. W. M. Brown, "Practices and Prudence," *Journal of the Philosophy of Sport* 17, no. 1 (1990): 77.

18. Brown, "Practices and Prudence," 76.

19. Brown, "Practices and Prudence," 74.

20. McFee, *Sports, Rules and Values*, 76.

21. Mike McNamee, "Sporting Practices, Institutions and Virtues: A Critique and Restatement," *Journal of the Philosophy of Sport* 22, no. 1 (1995): 75.

22. According to IOC president Jacques Rogge, "The IOC's statistics and those in countries where the authorities perform tests at competitions or during training show that top level athletes, whether amateur or professional, dope less than the mainly amateur athletes at ordinary national level" ("An Apologia for Professionalism," *Olympic Review* 26, no. 4 [1995]: 52).

23. MacIntyre, *After Virtue*, 183.

24. MacIntyre, *After Virtue*, 181.

25. MacIntyre, *After Virtue*, 183.

26. MacIntyre, *After Virtue*, 191.

27. MacIntyre, *After Virtue*, 180.

28. William J. Morgan, *Leftist Theories of Sport: A Critique and Reconstruction* (Chicago: University of Illinois Press, 1994), 130.

29. Bernard Suits, *The Grasshopper: Games, Life, and Utopia*, 2nd ed. (Peterborough, Ontario: Broadview, [1978] 2005), 55.

30. MacIntyre, *After Virtue*, 181.

31. MacIntyre, *After Virtue*, 179.

32. Peter J. Arnold, "Sport and Moral Education," *Journal of Moral Education* 23, no. 1 (1994): 84.

33. MacIntyre, *After Virtue*, 240.

34. Brown, "Practices and Prudence," 82.

35. MacIntyre brings this up in his description of the goods internal to painting. He says, "It is the painter's living out a greater or lesser part of his or her life as a painter that is the second kind of good internal to painting" (*After Virtue*, 177).

36. Emma Gates, quoted in *Hoop Dreams*, dir. Steve James, Kartemquin Films, 1994.

37. MacIntyre, *After Virtue*, 174.

38. MacIntyre, *After Virtue*, 189.

39. MacIntyre, *After Virtue*, 189.

40. MacIntyre encourages an aesthetic conception of this life: "The contrast, indeed the opposition between art and life, which is often in fact the premise rather than the conclusion of such theorists, provides a way of exempting art—including narrative—from its moral tasks . . . to think of a human life as a narrative unity is to think in a way alien to the dominant individualist and bureaucratic models of modern culture" (*After Virtue*, 211).

41. McFee, *Sports, Rules and Values*, 81.

42. McFee, *Sports, Rules and Values*, 81.

6. SPORT AND ART

1. Friedrich von Schiller, "Letter XV," in *Essays and Letters*, trans. A. Lodge, E. B. Eastwick, and A. J. W. Morrison, vol. 8 (London: Anthological Society, 1882). Reprinted in Ellen Gerber, ed., *Sport and the Body: A Philosophical Symposium* (Philadelphia: Lea & Febiger, 1974), 299.

2. Schiller, "Letter XV," 299.

3. Schiller, "Letter XV," 300.

4. Joseph Kupfer, "Sport: The Body Electric," in *Philosophic Inquiry in Sport*, ed. W. Morgan and K. Meier, 390–406, 2nd ed. (Champaign, IL: Human Kinetics, 1995), 391.

5. Karl Groos, "Play from the Aesthetic Standpoint," in *The Play of Man* (New York: D. Appleton, 1901). Reprinted in Gerber, *Sport and the Body*, 304.

6. According to Robert Stecker, the aesthetic conception defines art neatly as something made to create significant aesthetic value (or a significant aesthetic experience) *Aesthetics and the Philosophy of Art* (Lanham, MD: Rowman & Littlefield, 2005), 6.

7. Stecker, *Aesthetics*, 9.

8. Groos, "Play from the Aesthetic Standpoint," 303.

9. Christopher Cordner, "Differences between Sport and Art," in Morgan and Meier, *Philosophic Inquiry*, 427.

10. Aristotle, *Poetics*, trans. Malcom Heath (London: Penguin, 1997), 1450b.

11. Friedrich Nietzsche, *The Birth of Tragedy*, trans. Shaun Whiteside (London: Penguin, 1994).

12. Marjorie Fisher, "Sport as an Aesthetic Experience," in Gerber, *Sport and the Body*, 318.

13. Arthur Danto, "The Artworld," *Journal of Philosophy* 61 (1964): 580.

14. Drew A. Hyland, *Philosophy of Sport* (New York: Paragon, 1990), 121.

15. Jean-Paul Sartre, *Being and Nothingness*, trans. Hazel E. Barnes (New York: Philosophical Library, 1956), 580.

16. Elizabeth A. Hanley, "A Perennial Dilemma: Artistic Sports in the Olympic Games" (unpublished manuscript, 2000), 5.

17. As Spencer K. Wertz points out, "The artistic merit or value of a particular sporting event is measured by whether that given game equals its moment, that is, whether or not it has lived up to its historical antecedents—its tradition" ("Representation and Expression in Sport and Art," *Journal of the Philosophy of Sport* 12 [1985]: 13).

18. Lesley Wright, "Aesthetic Implicitness in Sport and the Role of Aesthetic Concepts," *Journal of the Philosophy of Sport* 30, no. 1 (2003): 91.

19. Groos, "Play from the Aesthetic Standpoint," 302.

20. Stecker, *Aesthetics*, 4.

21. David Best, "The Aesthetic in Sport," in Morgan and Meier, *Philosophic Inquiry*, 379.

22. Best, "Aesthetic in Sport," 380.

23. Best, "Aesthetic in Sport," 381.

24. Terence J. Roberts, "Sport, Art, and Particularity: The Best Equivocation," in Morgan and Meier, *Philosophic Inquiry*, 418.

25. Roberts, "Sport, Art, and Particularity," 422.

26. Roberts, "Sport, Art, and Particularity," 419.

27. Cordner, "Differences between Sport and Art," 427.

28. Bill Bradley, *Values of the Game* (New York: Broadway Books, 1998), 5.

29. Stephen Mumford, *Watching Sport: Aesthetics, Ethics, and Emotion* (Abingdon, UK: Routledge, 2011), chap. 8.

30. Plato, *Two Comic Dialogues: Ion and Hippias Major*, trans. Paul Woodruff (Indianapolis: Hackett, 1983), 297bc.

31. For more on Plato's theory of athletics in education, see Heather L. Reid, "Sport and Moral Education in Plato's *Republic*," *Journal of the Philosophy of Sport* 34, no. 2 (2007): 160–75; and Heather L. Reid, "Plato's Gymnasium," *Sport, Ethics and Philosophy* 4, no. 2 (2010): 170–82.

32. Cordner, "Differences between Sport and Art," 434.

33. Best, "Aesthetic in Sport," 385.

34. I do remember figure skater Katarina Witt explaining the music and choreography of her long program as a critique of the Balkan wars—but this is at best an exception that proves the general rule.

35. Heather L. Reid, *Athletics and Philosophy in the Ancient World: Contests of Virtue* (London: Routledge, 2011), 11–12.

36. Cordner, "Differences between Sport and Art," 429, 434.

37. Cordner, "Differences between Sport and Art," 427.

38. For a philosophical account of the significance of Boulmerka's performance, see William J. Morgan, "Multinational Sport and Literary Practices and Their Communities: The Moral Salience of Cultural Narratives," in *Ethics and Sport*, ed. Mike McNamee and Jim Parry, 184–204 (London: E & FN Spon, 1998).

39. Drew Hyland suggests that athletes and artists both share the stance of play, that is, the stance of responsive openness: "What is a poet, if not one more open to the possibilities of words, of language, and more responsive to them? A painter's openness and responsiveness to light and to color astonishes us, as does the potter's to clay and form, the musician's to sound and rhythm, the dancer's to space, time, and the movement of the human body" (*Philosophy of Sport*, 118).

40. Aristophanes, "Clouds," in *The Comedies of Aristophanes*, trans. William James Hickie (London: Bohn, 1853), lines 1011–15.

41. Fisher, "Sport as an Aesthetic Experience," 320.

42. C. D. Cordner, "Grace and Functionality," in Morgan and Meier, *Philosophic Inquiry*, 412–13.

7. MIND AND BODY

1. Plato mentions Ikkos at *Protagoras*, 316d, and *Laws*, 839e.

2. Plato, *Republic*, trans. G. M. A. Grube (Indianapolis: Hackett, 1992), 410bc.

3. Plato, *Republic*, 620b.

4. Aristotle more or less concurred with Plato's view, not because he endorsed the theory of the forms, but rather because the mind/soul was an organ—unlike the eye or ear—that could perceive any kind of material or immaterial object. Aristotle, "De Anima," in *Complete Works*, ed. Jonathan Barnes, 2 vols. (Princeton, NJ: Princeton University Press, 1984), 429ab.

5. Plato, *Phaedo*, 78b–84b.

6. René Descartes, "Second Meditation," in *The Philosophical Writings of Descartes*, ed. J. Cottingham, R. Stoothoff, and D. Murdoch, 2:17–25 (Cambridge, UK: Cambridge University Press, 1985). Note that "I think therefore I exist" is a paraphrase of Descartes's main point in the Second Meditation; it is not an exact quotation. He uses the exact phrase in French, in *Discourse on Method*, chap. 4, and in Latin, in *Principles of Philosophy*, part 1, art. 7.

7. See David Young, "Mens Sana in Corpore Sano? Body and Mind in Greek Literature," *Proceedings of the North American Society for Sport History* (1998): 60–61.

8. Paul Weiss, *Sport: A Philosophic Inquiry* (Carbondale: Southern Illinois University Press, 1969), 37.

9. Weiss, *Sport*, 37.

10. Weiss, *Sport*, 38.

11. Weiss, *Sport*, 39.

12. Weiss, *Sport*, 41.

13. Weiss, *Sport*, 216–17.

14. Daniel Dombrowski, *Contemporary Athletics and Ancient Greek Ideals* (Chicago: University of Chicago Press, 2009), 57–60.

15. Weiss, *Sport*, 99.

16. Dombrowski, *Contemporary Athletics*, 43.

17. Dombrowski, *Contemporary Athletics*, 126–31.

18. George Berkeley, *A Treatise Concerning the Principles of Human Knowledge* (Stilwell, KS: Digireads, [1734] 2006), §45.

19. David Hume, *A Treatise of Human Nature*, ed. L. A. Selby-Bigge, 2nd ed. (Oxford, UK: Clarendon, 1978), 253.

20. Friedrich Nietzsche, "Thus Spoke Zarathustra," in *The Portable Nietzsche*, ed. Walter Kaufmann, 146–47 (New York: Viking, 1982), 146.

21. John Hoberman, *Mortal Engines: The Science of Performance and the Dehumanization of Sport* (New York: Free Press, 1992), 62–69.

22. R. Scott Kretchmar, *Practical Philosophy of Sport* (Champaign, IL: Human Kinetics, 1994), 74–77.

23. Maxine Sheets-Johnstone, "Rationality and Caring: An Ontogenetic and Phylogenetic Perspective," *Journal of the Philosophy of Sport* 29, no. 2 (2002): 136.

24. Sheets-Johnstone, "Rationality and Caring," 138.

25. Sheets-Johnstone, "Rationality and Caring," 144.

26. Sheets-Johnstone, "Rationality and Caring," 145.

27. My comments about "Eastern philosophy" are, for the purpose of this book, discursive and generalized. I do not purport to take full account of this very rich and varied philosophical tradition. Rather, my aim is to provide an illuminating contrast to the Western ways of thinking with which most readers of this book are more likely to be familiar.

28. Zhuangzi, quoted in Arthur Waley, *Three Ways of Thought in Ancient China* (Stanford, CA: Stanford University Press, 2002), 9.

29. Thomas P. Kasulis, introduction, in *The Body: Toward an Eastern Mind-Body Theory*, by Yasuo Yuasa (Albany: State University of New York Press, 1987), 2.

30. Chung-Ying Cheng, "On the Metaphysical Significance of *ti* (Body-Embodiment) in Chinese Philosophy: *benti* (Origin-Substance) and *ti-yong* (Substance and Function)," *Journal of Chinese Philosophy* 29, no. 2 (2002): 145.

31. Akio Inoue, "Critique of Modern Olympism: A Voice from the East," in *Sports: The East and the West*, ed. G. Pfister and L. Yueye, 163–67 (Sant Agustin, Germany: Academia Verlag, 1999), 165.

32. Waley, *Three Ways of Thought*, 44.

33. Cheng, "On the Metaphysical," 147.

34. Susan Brownell, *Training the Body for China* (Chicago: University of Chicago Press, 1995), 125.

35. Carl B. Becker, "Philosophical Perspectives on the Martial Arts in America," *Journal of the Philosophy of Sport* 19, no. 1 (1982): 19.

36. Yasuo Yuasa, *The Body, Self-Cultivation and Ki-Energy* (Albany: State University of New York Press, 1993), 32.

37. Drew A. Hyland, *Philosophy of Sport* (New York: Paragon, 1990), 96.

38. Phil Jackson, *Sacred Hoops: Spiritual Lessons of a Hardwood Warrior* (New York: Hyperion, 1995), 115.

39. Maurice Merleau-Ponty, *The Phenomenology of Perception*, trans. Colin Smith (London: Routledge and Kegan Paul, 1962), 198–99.

40. Hyland, *Philosophy of Sport*, 97.

41. Yuasa, *The Body*, 26.

42. Yuasa, *The Body*, 8.

43. Yuasa, *The Body*, 26.

8. CONSEQUENTIALISM AND PLAY

1. John Stuart Mill, *On Liberty* (Indianapolis, IN: Hackett, 1978), 56.

2. Mill, *On Liberty*, 16.

3. W. M. Brown, "Paternalism, Drugs, and the Nature of Sports," *Journal of the Philosophy of Sport* 11, no. 1 (1985): 14–22.

4. Mill, *On Liberty*, 9.

5. Brown, "Paternalism," 21.

6. Drew A. Hyland, *Philosophy of Sport* (New York: Paragon, 1990), 121.

7. Eleanor Metheny, "The Symbolic Power of Sport," presented to the Eastern District Association for Health, Physical Education and Recreation in Washington, DC, April 26, 1968. Reprinted in *Sport and the Body: A Philosophical Symposium*, ed. E. Gerber and W. J. Morgan, 231–36 (Philadelphia: Lea & Febiger, 1979), 235.

8. Warren P. Fraleigh, "Performance-Enhancing Drugs in Sport: The Ethical Issue," *Journal of the Philosophy of Sport* 11, no. 1 (1985): 26.

9. M. Andrew Holowchak, "'Aretism' and Pharmacological Ergogenic Aids in Sport: Taking a Shot at the Use of Steroids," *Journal of the Philosophy of Sport* 27, no. 1 (2000): 39.

10. Robert Simon, "Good Competition and Drug-Enhanced Performance," *Journal of the Philosophy of Sport* 11, no. 1 (1985): 9.

11. Anonymous cyclist, quoted in Verner Moller, "The Athlete's Viewpoint," in *The Ethics of Sports: A Reader*, ed. Mike McNamee, 160–68 (London: Routledge, 2010), 162.

12. Robert Voy, *Drugs, Sport, and Politics* (Champaign, IL: Human Kinetics, 1991), xv.

13. Hamilton, quoted in Tom Goldman, "Athlete's 'Nope to Dope' Became 'No to Sports,'" National Public Radio, 2011, http://www.npr.org/.

14. Paul Weiss, *Sport: A Philosophic Inquiry* (Carbondale: Southern Illinois University Press, 1969), 134.

15. Weiss, *Sport*, 140.

16. Randolph Feezell, *Sport, Play and Ethical Reflection* (Urbana: University of Illinois Press, 2006), 13.

17. The character Lord Andrew Lindsay is fictional but based on Lord David Burghley, the sixth marquess of Exeter, who won the 400-meter hurdle race at the 1928 Olympic Games.

18. David C. Young, *A Brief History of the Olympic Games* (Malden, MA: Blackwell, 2004), 93–94. For a full account of Olympic amateurism, see David C. Young, *The Olympic Myth of Greek Amateur Athletics* (Chicago: Ares, 1984).

19. Taylor Branch, "The Shame of College Sports," *Atlantic Monthly*, October, 2011, http://www.theatlantic.com/.

20. Voy, *Drugs, Sport, and Politics*, 101.

21. Jacques Rogge, "An Apologia for Professionalism," *Olympic Review* 26, no. 4 (1995): 52.

22. David L. Roochnik, "Play and Sport," *Journal of the Philosophy of Sport* 2, no. 1 (1975): 41.

23. Brown, "Paternalism," 8.

24. Robert Simon, *Fair Play: The Ethics of Sport*, 2nd ed. (Boulder, CO: Westview, 2004), 77.

25. Roochnik, "Play and Sport," 41.

26. Feezell, *Sport, Play and Ethical Reflection*, 25.

27. Klaus V. Meier, "An Affair of Flutes: An Appreciation of Play," *Journal of the Philosophy of Sport* 7, no. 1 (1980): 27.

28. Sigmund Loland, "The Ethics of Performance-Enhancing Technology in Sport," *Journal of the Philosophy of Sport* 36, no. 1 (2009): 156.

29. Loland, "Ethics of Performance," 157.

30. However, some take issue with the idea that drug-assisted sports performance is indeed the performance of "persons" to be tested in conventional models of sport. See Simon, "Good Competition," 9.

31. Loland, "Ethics of Performance," 158.

32. Drew A. Hyland, "The Stance of Play," *Journal of the Philosophy of Sport* 7, no. 1 (1980): 98.

33. Roochnik, "Play and Sport," 41.

34. Susan A. Jackson and Mihaly Csikszentmihalyi, *Flow in Sports* (Champaign, IL: Human Kinetics, 1999), 6.

9. DEONTOLOGY AND FAIRNESS

1. The incident was reported in several Italian newspapers, including Marco Ansaldo, "Immobile in pedana, tunisina boicatta Israele ai Mondiali," *La Stampa*, October 11, 2011, http://www3.lastampa.it/.

2. Ansaldo, "Immobile in pedana."

3. Besbes, quoted in Aymen Wafi, "Sarra Besbes: « je m'en fiche . . . j'ai fait mon devoir," Koora.com, October 19, 2011, http://www.koora.com/.

4. Immanuel Kant, *Groundwork for the Metaphysic of Morals*, trans. H. J. Paton (New York: Harper and Row, 1948), 70.

5. Kant, *Groundwork*, 96.

6. Warren P. Fraleigh, "The Ends of the Sports Contest," in *The Ethics of Sports: A Reader*, ed. Mike McNamee (London: Routledge, 2010), 107.

7. Nicholas Dixon, "On Winning and Athletic Superiority," *Journal of the Philosophy of Sport* 26, no. 1 (1999): 10.

8. Edwin J. Delattre, "Some Reflections on Success and Failure in Competitive Athletics," *Journal of the Philosophy of Sport* 2, no. 1 (1975): 138.

9. David Carr, "Where's the Merit If the Best Man Wins?" *Journal of the Philosophy of Sport* 26, no. 1 (1999): 2.

10. Dean Hood, quoted in Ryan Alves, "Real Life Lessons from the Gridiron," *Eastern Progress*, October 12, 2011, http://www.easternprogress.com/.

11. Lombardi, quoted in Gary M. Walton, *Beyond Winning: The Timeless Wisdom of Great Philosopher Coaches* (Champaign, IL: Leisure Press, 1992), xi.

12. British Broadcasting Service, "FINA Extends Swimsuit Regulations," *BBC Mobile Sport*, March 19, 2009, http://news.bbc.co.uk/.

13. Michael Phelps, quoted in Associated Press, "FINA Moves Up Bodysuit Ban," *ESPN Olympic Sports*, July 31, 2009, accessed October 20, 2011, http://sports.espn.go.com/.

14. Sigmund Loland, "Fairness in Sport: An Ideal and Its Consequences," in McNamee, *Ethics of Sports*, 117.

15. Associated Press, "FINA Moves Up Bodysuit Ban."

16. Bernard Suits, *The Grasshopper: Games, Life, and Utopia*, 2nd ed. (Peterborough, Ontario: Broadview, [1978] 2005), 54–55.

17. Loland, "Fairness in Sport," 118.

18. Loland, "Fairness in Sport," 121.

19. J. S. Russell, "Are Rules All an Umpire Has to Work With?" *Journal of the Philosophy of Sport* 25, no. 1 (1999): 39.

20. Martin Luther King Jr., *I Have a Dream: Writings and Speeches that Changed the World* (New York: Harper Collins, 1992), 90.

21. Robert Simon, *Fair Play: The Ethics of Sport*, 2nd ed. (Boulder, CO: Westview, 2004), 48.

22. Lao-Tzu, *Tao Te Ching*, trans. S. Addiss and S. Lombardo (Indianapolis: Hackett, 2003), 57.

23. Thierry Henry, quoted in Peter Singer, "Is It Okay to Cheat in Football?" Project Syndicate, June 26, 2010, accessed April 10, 2011, http://www.project-syndicate.org/.

24. Russell, "Are Rules All?" 30.

25. Russell, "Are Rules All?" 35–36.

26. Graham McFee, *Sports, Rules and Values: Philosophical Investigations into the Nature of Sport* (London: Routledge, 2004), 69.

27. Rick Weinberg, "Pine Tar Nullifies Home Run, So Brett Goes Ballistic," *ESPN*, 2009, accessed October 20, 2011, http://sports.espn.go.com/.

28. Singer, "Is It Okay?"

29. Suits, *Grasshopper*, 50.

30. Suits, *Grasshopper*, 17.

31. Robert Butcher and Angela Schneider, "Fair Play as Respect for the Game," *Journal of the Philosophy of Sport* 25, no. 1 (1998): 15.

32. Graham McFee, "Spoiling: An Indirect Reflection of Sport's Moral Imperative?" in McNamee, *Ethics of Sports*, 146.

33. Claudia Pawlenka, "The Idea of Fairness: A General Ethical Concept or One Particular to Sports Ethics?" *Journal of the Philosophy of Sport* 32, no. 1 (2005): 57.

10. VIRTUES AND VICES

1. Naoto Kan, quoted in Cable News Network, "Sumo 'Fixing' Scandal Rocks Japan," CNN International Edition, February 4, 2011, accessed October 21, 2011, http://edition.cnn.com/.

2. Allan Bäck, "The *Way* to Virtue in Sport," *Journal of the Philosophy of Sport* 36 (2009): 217.

3. Bäck, "The *Way*," 217. The empirical studies cited by Bäck are called into question by Mike McNamee, *Sports, Virtues and Vices: Morality Plays* (London: Routledge, 2008), chap. 4, for their methodologies and theoretical assumptions about the nature of morality.

4. Justin McCurry, "Sumo Threatened by Scandal and Crime," *Guardian*, July 4, 2010, accessed October 21, 2011, http://www.guardian.co.uk/.

5. A martial art, says Bäck, is a "method for enlightenment on the human condition through the ritualized practice of techniques designed to neutralize violence" ("The *Way*," 217).

6. Zhao, quoted in Gene Ching and Gigi Oh, "Where Wushu Went Wrong," *Kungfu Magazine*, November 3, 2006, accessed October 21, 2011, http://ezine.kungfumagazine.com/.

7. Anthony Kuhn, "Chinese Martial Art Form Sports Less Threatening Moves," *Los Angeles Times*, October 16, 1988, accessed October 21, 2011, http://articles.latimes.com/.

8. Heather L. Reid argues that the concepts of virtue in ancient Greek and Chinese philosophy, *aretē* and *de*, respectively, are both understood as forms of psychic power cultivated through training. "Athletic Virtue: Between East and West," *Sport, Ethics and Philosophy* 4, no. 1 (2010): 19.

9. Aristotle, *Nicomachean Ethics*, trans. Terence Irwin, 2nd ed. (Indianapolis: Hackett, 1999), 1103a15–18.

10. Confucius, *Analects*, trans. E. Slingerland (Indianapolis: Hackett, 2003), 1.12, 2.3, 9.10.

11. Alasdair MacIntyre, *After Virtue* (Notre Dame, IN: University of Notre Dame Press, 1981), 175.

12. MacIntyre, *After Virtue*, 180.

13. Aristotle, *Nicomachean Ethics*, 1097b9–1.

14. Aristotle, *Politics*, trans. C. D. C. Reeve (Indianapolis: Hackett, 1998), 1281a2–3.

15. MacIntyre, *After Virtue*, 181; McNamee, *Sports, Virtues*, 18.

16. Bäck, "The *Way*," 225.

17. Confucius, *Analects*, 17.6; Mengzi, *Mencius*, trans. Irene Bloom (New York: Columbia University Press, 2009), 4B18. The honesty I have in mind here is not the Western idea of being forthright and telling the truth unbidden; that idea runs up against concern with "saving face" in Chinese culture. Rather, I am thinking about accurate self-assessment—much like Aristotelian *apseudeia*.

18. Aristotle, *Nicomachean Ethics*, 4.7.

19. MacIntyre, *After Virtue*, 191.

20. Eugen Herrigel, *Zen in the Art of Archery*, trans. R. F. C. Hull (New York: Vintage, 1999), 50–52.

21. Bäck, "The *Way*," 218. The case, of course, is different with martial arts sports, which generally employ referees as well as multiple judges.

22. Jay Busbee, "Davis Calls Penalty on Himself, Gives Up Shot at First PGA Win," Yahoo Sports, April 18, 2010, accessed October 21, 2011, http://sports.yahoo.com/. It is worth noting that Davis did win over half that amount for coming second.

23. Sun Tzu, *The Art of War*, trans. Lionel Giles (Hong Kong: Forgotten Books, 2007), 1.18.

24. Plato, *Hippias Minor*, in *Complete Works*, ed. John M. Cooper (Indianapolis: Hackett, 1997), 364c–370e.

25. M. Andrew Holowchak and Heather L. Reid, *Aretism: An Ancient Sports Philosophy for the Modern Sports World* (Lanham, MD: Lexington Books, 2011), 176.

26. Plato, *Republic*, trans. G. M. A. Grube (Indianapolis: Hackett, 1992), 338c.

27. He had such a hard time explaining exactly what justice is, however, that he devoted a separate book to the subject. Alasdair MacIntyre, *Whose Justice? Which Rationality?* (Notre Dame, IN: University of Notre Dame Press, 1989).

28. Aristotle, *Nicomachean Ethics*, 1130a8–10, V.3 1131a10–25.

29. Says Confucius, "The Master said, Gentlemen never compete. You will say that in archery they do so. But even then they bow and make way for one another when they are going up to the archery-ground, when they are coming down and at the subsequent drinking-bout.

Thus even when competing, they still remain gentlemen." *The Analects of Confucius*, trans. Arthur Waley (New York: Vintage, 1989), 3.7.

30. Bäck, "The *Way*," 223.

31. Coach Bill Easton in *Running Brave*, dir. D. S. Everett and Donald Shebib, Englander Productions, 1984.

32. Nicholas Dixon, "Why Losing by a Wide Margin Is Not in Itself a Disgrace," *Journal of the Philosophy of Sport* 25, no. 1 (1998): 67.

33. Mike McNamee, "Hubris, Humility, and Humiliation: Vice and Virtue in Sporting Communities," *Journal of the Philosophy of Sport* 29, no. 1 (2002): 38.

34. This is the theory expounded in Heather L. Reid, "Sport, Philosophy, and the Quest for Knowledge," *Journal of the Philosophy of Sport* 36, no. 1 (2009): 40–49.

35. Mike McNamee, *Sports, Virtues*, 159.

36. Susan A. Jackson and Mihaly Csikszentmihalyi, *Flow in Sports* (Champaign, IL: Human Kinetics, 1999), 6.

37. Bäck, "The *Way*," 234 n.1.

38. It is hard for me to believe that even traditional martial artists, when faced with a fight, never hope for a moment that the ground will give way under their opponent's feet. In fact, the serious stakes involved in martial arts fighting seem more conducive to the idea of survival by any means necessary than the "playful" context of Western sports.

39. Truth be told, nor do most modern martial artists. In fact, Western risk sports like mountain climbing and scuba diving seem to present more danger than their Eastern counterparts these days. I am grateful to Jesús Ilundáin for this comment.

40. Bäck, "The *Way*," 230.

41. Bäck, "The *Way*," 230.

42. MacIntyre, *After Virtue*, 191.

43. Aristotle, *Nicomachean Ethics*, 3.6. Fearing appropriate things, furthermore, excludes irrational fears of benign things like mice.

44. Aristotle, *Nicomachean Ethics*, 1107a.

45. Plato, "Laches," in *Complete Works*, 196d and 192e ff.

46. Plato, *Republic*, 430b, 442c.

47. Winston King, *Zen and the Way of the Sword* (New York: Oxford University Press, 1993), 177.

48. John Russell, "The Value of Dangerous Sports," *Journal of the Philosophy of Sport* 32, no. 1 (2005): 1–19. Norman Fischer, "Competitive Sport's Imitation of War: Imaging the Completeness of Virtue," *Journal of the Philosophy of Sport* 29, no. 1 (2002): 16–37.

49. Paul Davis, "Ethical Issues in Boxing," *Journal of the Philosophy of Sport* 20–21 (1993–1994), 56.

50. A prime example is Oedipus's killing of his father (whom he did not know) in a dispute over right of way at a road crossing.

51. Plato, *Apology*, trans. G. M. A. Grube (Indianapolis: Hackett, 1980), 22e; and Laozi, "Daodejing," in *Readings in Classical Chinese Philosophy*, ed. P. Ivanhoe and B. Van Norden, 161–206, 2nd ed. (Indianapolis: Hackett, 2001), 179, chap. 34.

52. Russell, "The Value of Dangerous Sports," 1.

53. McNamee, "Hubris, Humility, and Humiliation," 38–53.

54. MacIntyre, *After Virtue*, 191.

55. Bäck, "The *Way*," 218.

56. Bäck, "The *Way*," 221.

57. Bäck, "The *Way*," 222.

58. MacIntyre, *After Virtue*, 174.

59. MacIntyre, *After Virtue*, 189.

60. Aristotle, *Nicomachean Ethics*, 1094a, 1097b.

61. Aristotle, *Nicomachean Ethics*, 10.7.1.

62. Albert Camus, *The Myth of Sisyphus and Other Essays*, trans. Justin O'Brien (New York: Random House, 1955).

63. Bäck, "The *Way*," 228.

64. Holowchak and Reid, *Aretism*, 168–69.

65. Reid, "Athletic Virtue," 25.
66. MacIntyre, *After Virtue*, 181.

11. ETHICAL SPECTACLE

1. Corpus Inscriptionum Latinarum 4.4418, quoted in Allison Futrell, ed., *The Roman Games* (Malden, MA: Blackwell, 2006), 240n55.

2. Lucius Annaeus Seneca, *Letters from a Stoic (Epistulae Morales ad Lucilium)*, trans. R. Campbell (London: Penguin, 1969), 7.2–3.

3. Seneca, *Letters*, 7.5.

4. This point is argued in detail in Heather L. Reid, "Seneca's Gladiators," in *Athletics and Philosophy in the Ancient World: Contests of Virtue*, 90–98 (London: Routledge, 2011).

5. Seneca, "On Providence," 3.4, in Futrell, *Roman Games*, 95.

6. Seneca, "Letters," 70.20–27, in Futrell, *Roman Games*, 148.

7. Christopher Lasch, "The Degradation of Sport," *New York Review of Books* 24, no. 7 (1977), reprinted in *The Ethics of Sports: A Reader*, ed. Mike McNamee, 369–81 (London: Routledge, 2010).

8. William Morgan, *Why Sports Morally Matter* (Abingdon, UK: Routledge, 2006), 26.

9. Mike McNamee, *Sports, Virtues and Vices: Morality Plays* (London: Routledge, 2008), introduction.

10. Graham McFee, *Sports, Rules and Values: Philosophical Investigations into the Nature of Sport* (London: Routledge, 2004), chap. 8.

11. Stephen Mumford, *Watching Sport: Aesthetics, Ethics, and Emotion* (Abingdon, UK: Routledge, 2011), chap. 10.

12. Lasch, "Degradation of Sport," 369.

13. Excellence is meant here in its connection to the ancient Greek idea of virtue (*aretē*) discussed in chapter 10. A term that even better connects excellence in performance with virtue would be "virtuosity," but the term "virtuoso" is rarely applied in sport, and we are looking for a quality that is relatively common.

14. Drew Hyland suggests that athletes and artists both share the stance of play, that is, the stance of responsive openness. "What is a poet, if not one more open to the possibilities of words, of language, and more responsive to them? A painter's openness and responsiveness to light and to color astonishes us, as does the potter's to clay and form, the musician's to sound and rhythm, the dancer's to space, time, and the movement of the human body" (*Philosophy of Sport* [New York: Paragon, 1990], 118).

15. Teresa Lacerda and Stephen Mumford, "The Genius in Art and in Sport: A Contribution to the Investigation of Aesthetics of Sport," *Journal of the Philosophy of Sport* 37, no. 2 (2010): 182.

16. Bernard Suits, *The Grasshopper: Games, Life, and Utopia*, 2nd ed. (Peterborough, Ontario: Broadview, [1978] 2005), 55.

17. Lacerda and Mumford, "Genius in Art," 187.

18. Marcia Muelder Eaton claims that aesthetic appeal is generally tied up with cultural values and traditions. *Merit, Aesthetic and Ethical* (New York: Oxford University Press, 2001), 13.

19. Lasch, "Degradation of Sport," 380.

20. Morgan, *Why Sports*, 30.

21. Lasch, "Degradation of Sport," 381.

22. This is too simplistic an explanation, in my view; for a more detailed account, see Heather L. Reid, "Was the Roman Gladiator an Athlete?" *Journal of the Philosophy of Sport* 33, no. 1 (2006): 37–49; and "The Epicurean Spectator," *Sport, Ethics and Philosophy* 4, no. 2 (2010): 195–203, reprinted in *Athletics and Philosophy*, 81–89.

23. Plato, *Republic*, trans. G. M. A. Grube (Indianapolis: Hackett, 1992), 569b–608e.

24. Heather L. Reid, "Olympia: Running towards Truth," *Sport, Ethics and Philosophy* 4, no. 2 (2010): 136–45.

25. According to Cesar Torres, aesthetic values in sport are properly derived from its internal goods. Cesar Torres, "Furthering Interpretivism's Integrity: Bringing Together Ethics and Aesthetics," presidential address to the International Association for the Philosophy of Sport, Rochester, New York, September 2011, 21.

26. Morgan, *Why Sports*, 26.

27. Aristotle, *Nicomachean Ethics*, trans. Terence Irwin, 2nd ed. (Indianapolis: Hackett, 1999), 1120a24.

28. David Best, "The Aesthetic in Sport," in *Philosophic Inquiry in Sport*, ed. W. Morgan and K. Meier, 377–89, 2nd ed. (Champaign, IL: Human Kinetics, 1995), 379.

29. Torres, "Furthering Interpretivism's Integrity," 9–10.

30. Torres, "Furthering Interpretivism's Integrity," 20.

31. Lasch, "Degradation of Sport," 380.

32. Morgan, *Why Sports*, 25.

33. Víctor Durà-Vilà, "Why Playing Beautifully Is Morally Better," in *Soccer and Philosophy: Beautiful Thoughts on the Beautiful Game*, ed. T. Richards, 141–48 (Chicago: Open Court, 2010), 146.

34. Morgan, *Why Sports*, 31.

35. Morgan, *Why Sports*, 25.

36. Eaton, *Merit*, 57.

37. Torres, "Furthering Interpretivism's Integrity," 10.

38. Mumford, *Watching Sport*, 61.

39. Mumford, *Watching Sport*, 66–67. I might add that, if the doping accusations surrounding Armstrong turn out to be true, they will then detract from the beauty of these very same victories.

40. The Phelps and Woods examples should be distinguished from the Maradona and Johnson examples in that the relevant ethical breaches were external to sport.

41. Aristotle, *Nicomachean Ethics*, 1120a.

42. Morgan, *Why Sports*, 32.

43. Christopher Cordner, "Differences between Sport and Art," in Morgan and Meier, *Philosophic Inquiry in Sport*, 429, 434.

44. Jeffry Dean, "Aesthetics and Ethics: The State of the Art," *Aesthetics Online*, 2002, accessed November 1, 2011, http://aesthetics-online.org/.

45. Mumford, *Watching Sport*, 81–82.

46. McFee, *Sports, Rules*, 137.

47. Plato, *Two Comic Dialogues: Ion and Hippias Major*, trans. Paul Woodruff (Indianapolis: Hackett, 1983), 297bc.

12. SPORT AND EDUCATION

1. The story is recounted in Iamblichus, *The Pythagorean Life*, trans. Thomas Taylor (London: Watkins, 1818), chap. 5.

2. Strabo, *The Geography of Strabo*, ed. H. L. Jones (Cambridge, MA: Harvard University Press, 1924), 6.1.12.

3. Stephen G. Miller calculates that 28 percent of the Olympic victors in the gymnic (i.e., nonequestrian) events between 588 and 488 bce were from Kroton. Milo won six Olympic wrestling titles between 540 and 520 bce; Pythagoras arrived in Kroton around 530 bce. *Ancient Greek Athletics* (New Haven, CT: Yale University Press, 2004), 217.

4. The story of Plato's visits to Italy is recounted in *Letters III* and *VII*.

5. Plato, *Republic*, trans. G. M. A. Grube (Indianapolis: Hackett, 1992), 410bc.

6. Plato, *Laws*, trans. Trevor Saunders (London: Penguin, 1970), 805cd, 833cd.

7. Heather L. Reid, "Wrestling with Socrates," *Sport, Ethics and Philosophy* 4, no. 2 (2010): 157–69.

8. Heather L. Reid, "Aristotle's Pentathlete," *Sport, Ethics and Philosophy* 4, no. 2 (2010): 183–94.

9. Plato, *Republic*, 424e.

10. For example, Plato, *Republic*, 502d–503e. For a full account, see Heather L. Reid, "Sport and Moral Education in Plato's *Republic*," *Journal of the Philosophy of Sport* 34, no. 2 (2007): 166–69.

11. When sports humanities courses are part of these programs, furthermore, they are often taught by retired coaches or administrators with little training or interest in the subject.

12. Paul Weiss, *Sport: A Philosophic Inquiry* (Carbondale: Southern Illinois University Press, 1969), 41.

13. Jim Parry, "Sport, Ethos and Education," in *The Ethics of Sports: A Reader*, ed. Mike McNamee, 316–26 (London: Routledge, 2010), 319.

14. Pierre de Coubertin, "The Olympic Games of 1896," in *The Olympic Idea: Pierre de Coubertin—Discourses and Essays*, ed. Carl-Diem Institut, 10–14 (Stuttgart, Germany: Olympisher Sportverlag, 1966).

15. Chung-Ying Cheng, "On the Metaphysical Significance of *ti* (Body-Embodiment) in Chinese Philosophy: *benti* (Origin-Substance) and *ti-yong* (Substance and Function)," *Journal of Chinese Philosophy* 29, no. 2 (2002): 147.

16. Albert Camus, "The Wager of Our Generation," in *Resistance, Rebellion, and Death*, trans. Justin O'Brien (New York: Vintage, 1960), 242.

17. In reviewing over forty years of social scientific research on the subject, Jennifer Beller and Sharon Stoll say that "a constant was found: Sport does not appear to develop character no matter how defined." Sharon K. Stoll and Jennifer M. Beller, "Do Sports Build Character?" in *Sports in School: The Future of an Institution*, ed. John Gerdy, 18–30 (New York: Columbia University Press, 2000), 20.

18. David Carr, "What Moral Educational Significance Has Physical Education?" in McNamee, *Ethics of Sports*, 308.

19. Plato, *Republic*, 502d–503a.

20. Graham McFee, *Sports, Rules and Values: Philosophical Investigations into the Nature of Sport* (London: Routledge, 2004), 142.

21. Carwyn Jones, "Character, Virtue, and Physical Education," *European Physical Education Review* 11, no. 2 (2005): 140–42; Robert Simon, "Does Athletics Undermine Academics? Examining Some Issues," *Journal of Intercollegiate Sport* 1, no. 1 (2008): 48.

22. McFee, *Sports, Rules*, 140.

23. McFee, *Sports, Rules*, 142.

24. McFee, *Sports, Rules*, 145.

25. Carr, "What Moral?" 313.

26. Parry, "Sport, Ethos and Education," 324.

27. McFee, *Sports, Rules*, 140.

28. Robert Simon, *Fair Play: The Ethics of Sport*, 2nd ed. (Boulder, CO: Westview, 2004), 157.

29. Drew A. Hyland, "Paidia and Paideia: The Educational Power of Athletics," *Journal of Intercollegiate Sport* 1, no. 1 (2008): 67.

30. Hyland, "Paidia and Paideia," 70.

31. This idea is endorsed by both Hyland and Simon. Hyland, "Paidia and Paideia," 71; Simon, *Fair Play*, 162.

32. Myles Brand, "The Role and Value of Intercollegiate Athletics in Universities," *Journal of the Philosophy of Sport* 33, no. 1 (2006): 20.

33. Foreign language is in fact declining in popularity as a graduation requirement and more generally as a subject on American campuses; the need for constant practice for success might be one reason for this.

34. Derek Bok, "Can Higher Education Foster Higher Morals?" in *Social and Personal Ethics*, ed. W. H. Shaw, 493–503 (Belmont, CA: Wadsworth, 1996), 501.

35. The question of whether collegiate athletes are financially exploited is currently making its way through the courts; for an analysis of the question, see Taylor Branch, "The Shame of College Sports," *Atlantic Monthly*, October 2011, http://www.theatlantic.com/.

36. Simon, *Fair Play*, 167.

37. Hyland, "Paidia and Paideia," 67.

13. SPORT AND SOCIAL CATEGORIES

1. Sigmund Loland, *Fair Play in Sport: A Moral Norm System* (New York: Routledge, 2001), 60.

2. For a full treatment, see David Young, *The Olympic Myth of Greek Amateur Athletics* (Chicago: Ares, 1984).

3. Heather L. Reid, "Athletic Heroes," *Sport, Ethics and Philosophy* 4, no. 2 (2010): 125–35.

4. The accounts are in Xenophon, *Agesilaus* 9.6, and Plutarch, *Ages* 20.1, both in *Arete: Greek Sports from Ancient Sources*, ed. Stephen G. Miller (Berkeley: University of California Press, 1991). The motivations and extent of female exclusion at the ancient Olympic Games is the subject of scholarly debate; for a good overview, see John Mouratidis, "Heracles at Olympia and the Exclusion of Women from the Ancient Olympic Games," *Journal of Sport History* 11, no. 3 (1984): 41–55; and Thomas F. Scanlon, *Eros and Greek Athletics* (New York: Oxford University Press, 2002), esp. chaps. 4–7.

5. These arguments are made in detail in Heather L. Reid, *Athletics and Philosophy in the Ancient World: Contests of Virtue* (London: Routledge, 2011), chaps. 1–3. The democracy thesis was originally proposed by Stephen G. Miller, "Naked Democracy," in *Polis and Politics*, ed. P. Flensted-Jensen and T. H. Nielsen, 277–96 (Copenhagen: Festschrift, 2000).

6. Heather L. Reid, "Olympia: Running towards Truth," *Sport, Ethics and Philosophy* 4, no. 2 (2010): 136–45.

7. Heather L. Reid, "Was the Roman Gladiator an Athlete?" *Journal of the Philosophy of Sport* 33, no. 1 (2006): 43.

8. International Olympic Committee, "Olympic Solidarity Commission," Olympic.org, accessed November 28, 2011, http://www.olympic.org/.

9. National Collegiate Athletic Association, "Estimated Probability of Competing in Athletics beyond the High School Interscholastic Level," NCAA.com, 2011, accessed November 21, 2011, http://www.ncaa.org/.

10. The issue is still a matter of debate; for a recent treatment, see Koffi N. Maglo, "The Case against Biological Realism about Race: From Darwin to the Post-Genomic Era," *Perspectives on Science* 19, no. 4 (2011): 361–90.

11. National Collegiate Athletic Association, *2009–2010 Student Athlete Ethnicity Report* (Indianapolis: Author, 2010); Richard Lapchick, *2010 Racial and Gender Report Card* (Chicago: Institute for Diversity and Ethics in Sport, 2010).

12. For example, Jim Litke, "Black Athletes Eased Obama's Presidential Path," *NBC Sports*, November 5, 2008, accessed November 21, 2011, http://nbcsports.msnbc.com/.

13. Drew Hyland, "Paidia and Paideia: The Educational Power of Athletics," *Journal of Intercollegiate Sport* 1, no. 1 (2008): 69.

14. John Hoberman, *Darwin's Athletes: How Sport Has Damaged Black America and Preserved the Myth of Race* (Boston: Houghton Mifflin, 1997), 146.

15. Hoberman, *Darwin's Athletes*, 99–114.

16. Bill Russell, *Second Wind: The Memoirs of an Opinionated Man* (New York: Random House, 1979), 188.

17. Ato Boldon, quoted in Christopher Clarey, "A French Revolution in the Fast Lanes," *International Herald Tribune*, November 18, 2011, Kindle edition.

18. Christophe Lemaitre, quoted in Clarey, "A French Revolution."

19. Angela J. Schneider, "On the Definition of 'Woman' in the Sport Context," in *Values in Sport*, ed. T. Tännsjö and C. Tamburrini, 123–38 (London: Routledge, 2000), 132.

20. Eileen L. McDonagh and Laura Pappano, *Playing with the Boys: Why Separate Is Not Equal in Sports* (New York: Oxford University Press, 2008), 33.

21. Donald F. Sabo et. al. "High School Athletic Participation, Sexual Behavior and Adolescent Pregnancy: A Regional Study," *Journal of Adolescent Health* 25, no. 3 (1999): 207–16.

22. For a recent report on the subject, see Gretchen Livingston and D'Vera Cohn, "Childlessness Up among All Women, Down among Women with Advanced Degrees," Pew Research Center, June 25, 2010, accessed November 21, 2011, http://www.pewsocialtrends.org/.

23. The comparison is made in detail in Heather L. Reid, "Aristotle's Pentathlete," *Sport, Ethics and Philosophy* 4, no. 2 (2010): 191–92.

24. Torbjörn Tännsjö, "Against Sexual Discrimination in Sports," in Tännsjö and Tamburrini, *Values in Sport*, 103.

25. Heather L. Reid, *The Philosophical Athlete* (Durham, NC: Carolina Academic Press, 2002), 260–64.

26. John Gleaves, "Too Fit to Fly: How Female Nordic Ski Jumping Challenges the IOC's Approach to Gender Equality," in *Rethinking Matters Olympic: Investigations into the Socio-Cultural Study of the Modern Olympic Movement*, ed. International Center for Olympic Studies, 278–88 (London: University of Western Ontario, 2010).

27. Jamie Northrup, quoted in Barbara Pinto and Olivia Katrandjian, "Wrestler Joel Northup Forfeits to Female Opponent in Iowa State Championships," *ABC News*, February 18, 2011, accessed November 21, 2011, http://abcnews.go.com/.

28. Robert Simon, *Fair Play: The Ethics of Sport* (Boulder, CO: Westview, 2004), 136.

29. Simon, *Fair Play*, 118.

30. Schneider, "On the Definition of 'Woman,'" 137.

31. B. C. Postow, "Masculine Sports Revisited," *Journal of the Philosophy of Sport* 8, no. 1 (1981): 60.

32. M. Andrew Holowchak and Heather L. Reid, *Aretism: An Ancient Sports Philosophy for the Modern Sports World* (Lanham, MD: Lexington Books, 2011), 59.

33. Tännsjö, "Against Sexual Discrimination," 111.

34. For example, Jane English, "Sex Equality in Sports," *Philosophy and Public Affairs* 7 (1978): 269–77.

35. I am grateful to John Gleaves for this example.

36. Reid, *Philosophical Athlete*, 253.

37. For an overview of this issue, see Carwyn Jones and P. David Howe, "The Conceptual Boundaries of Sport for the Disabled: Classification and Athletic Performance," *Journal of the Philosophy of Sport* 32, no. 2 (2005): 133–46.

38. Stanislav Pinter, Tjasa Filipcic, Ales Solar, and Maja Smrdu, "Integrating Children with Physical Impairments into Sports Activities: A 'Golden Sun' for All Children?" *Journal of the Philosophy of Sport* 32, no. 2 (2005): 147.

39. Ivo van Hilvoorde and Laurens Landerweerd, "Disability or Extraordinary Talent?" in *The Ethics of Sports*, ed. Mike McNamee, 231–41 (London: Routledge, 2010), 232.

40. Murphy, quoted in Steven Schnee and Astrid Rodrigues, "The Amputee Wrestler: Rohan Murphy Can Take You Down," *ABC Sports*, December 9, 2010, accessed November 21, 2011, http://abcnews.go.com/.

41. At the beginning of the current millennium, Paralympians held outright powerlifting world records in four weight classes. For example, while the able-bodied, 60-kilogram-weight-class world record holder lifts 190 kilograms, Paralympic athlete Mathana Metwaly Ibrahim from Egypt holds the world record at 202.50 kilograms in the same weight class. International Paralympic Committee, "Powerlifting on an Upswing," Paralympian Online, 2000, accessed November 21, 2011, http://www.paralympic.org/.

42. David Epstein, "Double Amputee Pistorius Keeping Olympic Sprinting Dreams Alive," SI.com, June 11, 2011, accessed November 22, 2011, http://sportsillustrated.cnn.com/.

43. Hilvoorde and Landerweerd, "Disability or Extraordinary Talent?" 238.

14. SPORT AND POLITICAL IDEALS

1. International Olympic Committee, "The New Exhibition at the Olympic Museum on the Theme of Hope," Olympic.org, March 28, 2011, accessed November 25, 2011, http://www.olympic.org/.

2. International Olympic Committee members swear to keep themselves free from political influence; national Olympic committees are commanded to keep themselves free from political pressures; and political demonstrations or speeches by politicians are forbidden in Olympic

venues according to the *Olympic Charter* (Lausanne, Switzerland: International Olympic Committee, 2010), 31, 62, 98, 103.

3. Brundage, quoted in Richard Mandell, *The Nazi Olympics* (Champaign: University of Illinois Press, 1987), 289.

4. Heather L. Reid, "Athletic Heroes," *Sport, Ethics and Philosophy* 4, no. 2 (2010): 125.

5. Heather L. Reid, "The Epicurean Spectator," *Sport, Ethics and Philosophy* 4, no. 2 (2010): 196.

6. The Roman writer Cassiodorus compares the Circus Maximus as a whole to a model of the universe. The twelve gates represent the signs of the zodiac, two-horse chariots are imitations of the moon, and four-horse chariots the sun. The attendants who announce the heats play the role of the morning star, forerunner of the sun. The race's even goals stand in for the days of the week, and the twenty-four heats represent the hours in a day. The turning posts signify the limits of east and west being orbited by the planetlike racing chariots. The dolphin sculpture at the center of the track represents the sea, while the Egyptian obelisks that mark the turns honor the sun and moon. "Variae," 3.51, in *The Roman Games*, ed. Alison Futrell (Malden, MA: Blackwell, 2006), 74.

7. Mandell, *Nazi Olympics*, 205.

8. Mandell, *Nazi Olympics*, xvii.

9. Stephen G. Miller, *Ancient Greek Athletics* (New Haven, CT: Yale University Press, 2004), 233.

10. Heather L. Reid, "Boxing with Tyrants," *Sport, Ethics and Philosophy* 4, no. 2 (2010): 146.

11. Peter J. Arnold, "Democracy, Education and Sport," *Journal of the Philosophy of Sport* 16 (1989): 100–110.

12. Miller, *Ancient Greek Athletics*, 233.

13. Donald G. Kyle, *Spectacles of Death in Ancient Rome* (New York: Routledge, 1998), 87.

14. Arnold, "Democracy, Education and Sport," 107.

15. Arnold, "Democracy, Education and Sport," 107.

16. Reid, "Boxing with Tyrants," 149.

17. Stephen G. Miller, "Naked Democracy," in *Polis and Politics*, ed. P. Flensted-Jensen and T. H. Nielsen, 277–96 (Copenhagen: Festschrift, 2000), 279.

18. Pericles, quoted in Thucydides, *History of the Peloponnesian War*, trans. B. Jowett (Oxford, UK: Clarendon, 1900), 2.37.1.

19. Arnold, "Democracy, Education and Sport," 101.

20. Miller, "Naked Democracy," 283.

21. Arnold, "Democracy, Education and Sport," 107.

22. Torbjörn Tännsjö, "Is Our Admiration of Sports Heroes Fascistoid?" *Journal of the Philosophy of Sport* 25, no. 1 (1998): 23.

23. Tännsjö, "Admiration of Sports Heroes," 23.

24. American Israeli Cooperative Enterprise, "The Nazi Olympics," Jewish Virtual Library, 2001, accessed November 25, 2011, http://www.jewishvirtuallibrary.org/.

25. Alfred Erich Senn, *Power, Politics and the Olympic Games* (Champaign, IL: Human Kinetics, 1999), 20.

26. The main Nazi newspaper, *Volkischer Beobachter*, quoted in Hugh Murray, "Review of Hoberman's *The Olympic Crisis*," *Journal of Sport History* 16, no. 1 (1989): 106.

27. Tännsjö, "Admiration of Sports Heroes," 25.

28. Tännsjö, "Admiration of Sports Heroes," 25.

29. International Olympic Committee, *Olympic Charter*, 19.

30. Tännsjö, "Admiration of Sports Heroes," 26.

31. Tännsjö, "Admiration of Sports Heroes," 28.

32. Claudio Tamburrini, "Sport, Fascism and the Market," *Journal of the Philosophy of Sport* 25, no. 1 (1998): 37.

33. Tamburrini, "Sport, Fascism and the Market," 39.

34. Tamburrini, "Sport, Fascism and the Market," 43.

35. M. Andrew Holowchak, "Fascistoid Heroism Revisited: A Deontological Twist in a Recent Debate," *Journal of the Philosophy of Sport* 32, no. 2 (2005): 104.

36. Holowchak, "Fascistoid Heroism Revisited," 102.

37. James Riordan, *Sport, Politics, and Communism* (Manchester, UK: Manchester University Press, 1991), 25.

38. Vladimir Lenin, quoted in Riordan, *Sport, Politics, and Communism*, 25.

39. Romanov, quoted in Robert Edelman, *Serious Fun: A History of Spectator Sports in the USSR* (New York: Oxford University Press, 1993), 122.

40. Susan Brownell, *Training the Body for China* (Chicago: University of Chicago Press, 1995), 26.

41. Lenin, quoted in Riordan, *Sport, Politics, and Communism*, 26.

42. Riordan, *Sport, Politics, and Communism*, 3.

43. W. Franke and B. Berendonk, "Hormonal Doping and Androgenization of Athletes: A Secret Program of the German Democratic Republic Government," *Clinical Chemistry* 43, no. 7 (1997): 1262–79. The story is also told in Steven Ungerleider, *Faust's Gold* (New York: St. Martin's, 2001).

44. Ann E. Cudd, "Sporting Metaphors: Competition and the Ethos of Capitalism," *Journal of the Philosophy of Sport* 34, no. 1 (2007): 52.

45. Cudd, "Sporting Metaphors," 56.

46. Cudd, "Sporting Metaphors," 58.

47. Cudd, "Sporting Metaphors," 60.

48. Robert Simon, *Fair Play: Sports, Values, and Society* (Boulder, CO: Westview, 1991), 23.

49. Cudd, "Sporting Metaphors," 62.

50. Cudd, "Sporting Metaphors," 62.

51. Cudd, "Sporting Metaphors," 66.

52. M. Andrew Holowchak and Heather L. Reid, *Aretism: An Ancient Sports Philosophy for the Modern Sports World* (Lanham, MD: Lexington Books, 2011), 193.

53. William J. Morgan, *Leftist Theories of Sport: A Critique and Reconstruction* (Champaign: University of Illinois Press, 1994), 29.

54. William J. Morgan, *Why Sports Morally Matter* (Abingdon, UK: Routledge, 2006), 7.

55. Morgan, *Why Sports Morally Matter*, 26.

56. Morgan, *Why Sports Morally Matter*, 107.

57. Morgan, *Leftist Theories of Sport*, 45.

58. Morgan, *Leftist Theories of Sport*, 130.

59. Morgan, *Leftist Theories of Sport*, 204.

60. Morgan, *Leftist Theories of Sport*, 234.

15. SPORT AND GLOBALIZATION

1. John Ian Wing, "Letter Saved the Games," National Library of Australia, Papers of Sir Wilfred Kent Hughes, NS 4856/series 19, accessed December 5, 2011, http://www.johnwing.co.uk/.

2. William Scheuerman, "Globalization," in *The Stanford Encyclopedia of Philosophy*, ed. Edward N. Zalta, Summer 2010 ed., accessed December 5, 2011, http://plato.stanford.edu/.

3. Heather L. Reid, "Sport, Philosophy, and the Quest for Knowledge," *Journal of the Philosophy of Sport* 36, no. 1 (2009): 42.

4. Baron Pierre de Coubertin, quoted in Foundation for the Hellenic World, "The Revival of the Ancient Olympic Games," From Ancient Olympia to Athens of 1896, accessed December 12, 2011, http://www.fhw.gr/.

5. Nielsen Company, "Beijing Olympics Draw Largest Ever Global Television Audience," Nielsenwire, September 8, 2008, accessed April 10, 2012, http://blog.nielsen.com/.

6. Martin Heidegger, *Poetry, Language, Thought* (New York: Harper & Row, 1971), 166.

7. International Olympic Committee, *The Olympic Charter* (Lausanne, Switzerland: Author, 2010), 11.

8. A key example is Kant's categorical imperative; for a detailed argument, see Heather L. Reid, "East to Olympia: Recentering Olympic Philosophy between East and West," *Olympika: The International Journal of Olympic Studies* 19 (2010): 59–79.

9. Reid, "East to Olympia," 61.

10. Jim Parry, "Sport and Olympism: Universals and Multiculturalism," *Journal of the Philosophy of Sport* 33, no. 2 (2006): 194.

11. Scheuerman, "Globalization."

12. Parry, "Sport and Olympism," 197.

13. International Olympic Committee, "Olympic Solidarity Commission," Olympic.org, 2011, accessed November 28, 2011, http://www.olympic.org/.

14. Andrew B. Bernard and Meghan R. Busse, "Who Wins the Olympic Games: Economic Resources and Medal Totals," *Review of Economics and Statistics* 86, no. 1 (2004): 413–17.

15. Thomas Erdbrink, "FIFA Bans Headscarves for Iranian Women's Soccer Team," *Washington Post*, June 6, 2011, http://www.washingtonpost.com/.

16. Parry, "Sport and Olympism," 191.

17. Parry, "Sport and Olympism," 202.

18. Nigel Crowther, "The Ancient Olympics and Their Ideals," in *Athletika: Studies on the Olympic Games and Greek Athletics*, ed. W. Decker and I. Weiler, 1–11 (Hildesheim, Germany: Weidemann, 2004), 11.

19. For more on this aspect of the ancient Olympic Games, see Heather L. Reid, "The Political Heritage of the Olympic Games: Relevance, Risks, and Possible Rewards," *Sport, Ethics and Philosophy: Special Issue on the Olympic Games* 6, no. 2 (2012): 108–20.

20. World Commission on Environment and Development, *Our Common Future* (Oxford: Oxford University Press, 1987), 8.

21. Scheuerman, "Globalization."

22. Scheuerman, "Globalization."

23. International Olympic Committee, "The Sport and Environment Commission," Olympic.org, 2009, accessed December 5, 2011, http://www.olympic.org/.

24. Sigmund Loland, "Record Sports: An Ecological Critique and a Reconstruction," *Journal of the Philosophy of Sport* 27, no. 2 (2001): 130.

25. Loland, "Record Sports," 138.

26. International Olympic Committee (IOC), *Olympic Movement's Agenda 21: Sport for Sustainable Development* (Lausanne, Switzerland: Author, 1999). http://www.olympic.org/.

27. IOC, *Agenda 21*, 23–24.

28. IOC, *Agenda 21*, 26–27.

29. Heather L. Reid, "Olympic Sport and Its Lessons for Peace," *Journal of the Philosophy of Sport* 33, no. 2 (2006): 205–13.

30. Bruce Kidd, "Taking the Rhetoric Seriously: Proposals for Olympic Education," *Quest* 48 (1996): 85.

31. Glen Levy, "British Athletes Told to Avoid Shaking Hands at the Olympics," *Time* Newsfeed, March 6, 2012, accessed March 7, 2012, http://newsfeed.time.com/.

32. Kidd, "Taking the Rhetoric Seriously," 86.

33. Kidd, "Taking the Rhetoric Seriously," 89.

APPENDIX

1. Johan Huizinga, *Homo Ludens: A Study of the Play Element in Culture* (Boston: Beacon Press, [1944] 1955).

2. Roger Caillois, *Man, Play, and Games*, trans. Meyer Berlash (Urbana: University of Illinois Press, [1958] 2001).

3. John W. Loy Jr., "The Nature of Sport: A Definitional Effort," *Quest* 10, no. 1 (May 1968): 1–15.

4. Bernard Suits, "What Is A Game?" *Philosophy of Science* 34, no. 1 (June 1967), 148–56.

5. Bernard Suits, *The Grasshopper: Games, Life, and Utopia*, 2nd ed. (Peterborough, Ontario: Broadview, [1978] 2005).

6. Allen V. Sapora and Elmer D. Mitchell, *The Theory of Play and Recreation* (New York: Ronald Press, 1961).

7. Eleanor Metheny, "This 'Thing' Called Sport," *Journal of Health, Physical Education, and Recreation* 40 (March 1969): 59–60.

8. James W. Keating, "Sportsmanship as a Moral Category," *Ethics* 75 (October 1964): 25–35.

9. Howard S. Slusher, *Man, Sport, and Existence* (Philadelphia: Lea & Febiger, 1967).

10. Earle F. Zeigler, *Philosophical Foundations for Physical, Health, and Recreation Education* (Englewood Cliffs, NJ: Prentice Hall, 1964).

11. Paul Weiss, *Sport: A Philosophic Inquiry* (Carbondale: Southern Illinois University Press, 1969).

12. Warren P. Fraleigh, "The Philosophic Society for the Study of Sport, 1972–1983," *Journal of the Philosophy of Sport* 10 (1984): 3–7.

13. R. Scott Kretchmar, "From Test to Contest: An Analysis of Two Kinds of Counterpoint in Sport," *Journal of the Philosophy of Sport* 1 (1975): 23–30.

14. B. C. Postow, "Women and Masculine Sports," *Journal of the Philosophy of Sport* 7 (1980): 51–58.

15. Craig Lehman, "Can Cheaters Play the Game?" *Journal of the Philosophy of Sport* 8 (1981): 41–46.

16. Warren P. Fraleigh, *Right Actions in Sport: Ethics for Contestants* (Champaign, IL: Human Kinetics, 1984).

17. William J. Morgan, *Leftist Theories of Sport: A Critique and Reconstruction* (Chicago: University of Illinois Press, 1994).

18. Drew A. Hyland, *Philosophy of Sport* (New York: Paragon, 1990); Robert Simon, *Fair Play: Sports, Values, and Society* (Boulder, CO: Westview, 1991); Heather L. Reid, *The Philosophical Athlete* (Durham, NC: Carolina Academic Press, 2002).

19. R. Scott Kretchmar, *Practical Philosophy of Sport* (Champaign, IL: Human Kinetics, 1994).

20. Sheryle Bergmann Drewe, *Why Sport?* (Toronto: Thompson, 2003).

21. William J. Morgan, Klaus V. Meier, and Angela J. Schneider, eds., *Ethics in Sport* (Champaign, IL: Human Kinetics, 2001), with a second edition in 2007; Jan Boxill, ed., *Sports Ethics* (Malden, MA: Blackwell, 2003); Mike McNamee, ed., *The Ethics of Sports: A Reader* (London: Routledge, 2010).

22. M. Andrew Holowchak, ed., *Philosophy of Sport: Critical Readings, Crucial Issues* (Upper Saddle River, NJ: Prentice Hall, 2002).

23. Mike McNamee, "*Sport, Ethics and Philosophy*: Context, History and Prospects," *Sport, Ethics and Philosophy* 1, no. 1 (2007): 5.

24. An attempt at comparative Eastern and Western philosophy applied to sport is Heather L. Reid, "Athletic Virtue: Between East and West," *Sport, Ethics and Philosophy* 4, no. 1 (2010): 16–26.

Glossary

amateurism. The belief that activities like sport should be performed out of love for the game rather than any external reward, especially money.

aretē. Greek word for excellence, both mental and physical, often translated as virtue.

aristeia. Heroic idea of "being the best and outdoing all others," often cited in Homer.

autotelic. Quality of being an end in itself; needing no external purpose or justification. Contrast **instrumentalism**.

consequentialist. Category of ethical theories, such as utilitarianism, that focus on the consequences of actions rather than principles or virtues. Contrast **virtue ethics**; **deontological**.

constitutive rules. Rules thought to define a game and distinguish it from other games.

cosmopolitanism. Theory that people should consider themselves citizens of a world community, in addition to their particular nations or states.

deontological. Category of ethical theories, such as that of Immanuel Kant, which focus on moral laws or principles rather than virtues or consequences. Contrast **virtue ethics**; **consequentialist**.

dualism. Theory that minds and bodies are metaphysically distinct. Usually the body is thought to be material, while the mind is immaterial.

ekecheiria. The ancient Greek ban on attacking travelers to the Olympic Games, which sometimes extended to a suspension of military hostilities known as the Olympic Truce.

empiricism. Theory that knowledge is acquired primarily through the senses. Contrast **rationalism**.

ethics. Branch of philosophy that examines theories of right and wrong, also known as moral philosophy.

ethos. The social expectations and conventions within sport, as opposed to its formal rules.

eudaimonia. Aristotle's term for an ethical person's final good or end, a happiness or thriving that can only be understood in terms of a complete lifetime.

external goods. Goods, like wealth or fame, that are not specific to a particular practice but can be achieved through a variety of activities. Contrast **internal goods**.

flow. A feeling of perfect control and effortlessness; also described as being "in the zone."

formalism. The understanding of sports as games defined exclusively in terms of their formal rules.

globalization. The process of change in travel and communication technology that increases contact between people despite geographical and cultural distance.

golden mean. The middle state between excess and deficiency that represents virtue in Aristotle's ethics, for example, courage is the golden mean between foolhardiness and cowardice.

gymnastikē. Greek word for athletic training and exercise associated with the gymnasium.

hegemony. The imposition of a more powerful class's values and worldview upon others as a societal norm.

holism. A metaphysical approach that focuses on the connections between things rather than their distinctions. Contrast **dualism**.

hylomorphism. Metaphysical theory of persons based on the Greek *hyle* (matter) and *morphē* (the form or structure given to matter by the mind) that understands sport in terms of the mind reshaping the body to achieve excellence (*aretē*).

idealism. Metaphysical theory that affirms only the existence of ideas, denying that of matter.

instrumentalism. The belief that games should be used to achieve external goods, such as prizes and salaries. Contrast **autotelic**.

internal goods. Goods experienced through achievements according to the standards of excellence within a particular social practice. Contrast **external goods**.

internal logic of sport. The characteristic of setting up unnecessary or gratuitous obstacles for the sake of creating games—as in soccer's prohibition on handling the ball.

isēgoria. Greek word for equal opportunity, a concept shared by sport and democracy.

isonomia. Greek word for equality before the law, a concept shared by sport and democracy.

kalokagathia. Educational ideal of ancient Greek gymnasia that combines beauty and goodness.

logical incompatibility thesis. The claim that one cannot intentionally break a rule and play a game at the same time. Since games are just sets of rules, according to formalism, intentionally violating a rule amounts to intentionally failing to play the game.

lusory attitude. In Bernard Suits's account of games, the attitude exhibited by players that enables them to adopt less efficient instead of more efficient means of achieving the game's goal.

lusory goal. In Bernard Suits's account of games, the state of affairs that constitutes winning a game.

metaphysics. Branch of philosophy that examines the fundamental nature of things.

moral relativism. Belief that there are no universal truths in ethics but rather that moral principles are relative to particular communities, or perhaps individual opinion.

multiculturalism. Belief that diversity should be valued and preserved despite the homogenizing forces of globalization.

Olympism. Set of philosophical principles behind the modern Olympic Games.

ontological. Of or relating to the nature or being of a thing.

paternalism. The restriction of persons's liberty against their will, especially for their own protection.

phenomenology. Philosophical approach focused on the structure of human experience.

philosophical anthropology. Philosophy concerned with the nature and status of humanity.

physicalism. Theory of mind and body that asserts both to be nothing more than matter.

Platonic love. Intense affection that excludes sexual intercourse and focuses instead on education and *aretē*.

politics. Branch of philosophy that deals with social and community issues and organization.

postmodernism. Philosophical approach that is skeptical of objective explanations claiming to be valid for everyone.

psychē. Greek word for the soul; encompasses the ideas of life, mind, spirit, and emotion.

rationalism. Theory that knowledge is based primarily upon internal reasoning. Contrast **empiricism**.

segregation. The practice of separating athletes into different classes based on social categories such as sex or race. Desegregation is the removal of such classes.

social practice theory. An understanding of sports (and other activities) as communities based on the shared pursuit of excellence within a mutually valued practice.

sōma. Greek word for the physical body, conceived as lifeless matter in the absence of *psychē*.

sustainability. The ability to meet our present needs without compromising the ability of future generations to meet their own needs.

technē. Greek word for a practical skill or art, to be contrasted with moral qualities like *aretē*.

telos. Greek word for the end or goal that characterizes the motivation and purpose for an activity.

utilitarianism. A moral philosophy that focuses on consequences, striving to achieve the greatest good for the greatest number affected by any action.

virtue ethics. Moral philosophy that focuses on the character of the agent (i.e., the person who acts) rather than principles or consequences.

wide theory. Understanding of sport as having social, cultural, and moral value beyond mere internal concerns such as victory and performance.

wu-wei. Eastern philosophical term that expresses the strength of nonaction or effortlessness.

yin-yang. Eastern philosophical symbol of harmony among complementary opposites.

Bibliography

Alves, Ryan. "Real Life Lessons from the Gridiron." *Eastern Progress*, October 12, 2011. Accessed October 20, 2011. http://www.easternprogress.com/.

American Israeli Cooperative Enterprise. "The Nazi Olympics." Jewish Virtual Library, 2001. Accessed November 25, 2011. http://www.jewishvirtuallibrary.org/.

Ansaldo, Marco. "Immobile in pedana, tunisina boicatta Israele ai Mondiali." *La Stampa*, October 11, 2011. http://www3.lastampa.it/.

Aristophanes. "Clouds." In *The Comedies of Aristophanes*, translated by William James Hickie. London: Bohn, 1853.

Aristotle. *The Athenian Constitution*. Translated by Sir Frederic G. Kenyon. Washington, DC: Merchant Books, 2009.

———.*Complete Works*. Edited by Jonathan Barnes. 2 vols. Princeton, NJ: Princeton University Press, 1984.

———. *Nicomachean Ethics*. Translated by Terence Irwin. 2nd ed. Indianapolis: Hackett, 1999.

———. *Poetics*. Translated by Malcom Heath. London: Penguin, 1997.

———. *Politics*. Translated by C. D. C. Reeve. Indianapolis: Hackett, 1998.

Arnold, Peter J. "Democracy, Education and Sport." *Journal of the Philosophy of Sport* 16 (1989): 100–110.

———. "Sport and Moral Education." *Journal of Moral Education* 23, no. 1 (1994): 75–90.

Associated Press. "FINA Moves Up Bodysuit Ban." *ESPN Olympic Sports*, July 31, 2009. Accessed October 20, 2011. http://sports.espn.go.com/.

Athenaeus. "The Deipnosophists." In *The Smell of Sweat: Greek Athletics, Olympics and Culture*, edited by W. B. Tyrell. Wauconda, IL: Bolchazy-Carducci, 2004.

Bäck, Allan. "The *Way* to Virtue in Sport." *Journal of the Philosophy of Sport* 36 (2009): 217–37.

Becker, Carl B. "Philosophical Perspectives on the Martial Arts in America." *Journal of the Philosophy of Sport* 19, no. 1 (1982): 19–29.

Berkeley, George. *A Treatise Concerning the Principles of Human Knowledge*. Stilwell, KS: Digireads, [1734] 2006.

Bernard, Andrew B., and Meghan R. Busse. "Who Wins the Olympic Games: Economic Resources and Medal Totals." *Review of Economics and Statistics* 86, no. 1 (2004): 413–17.

Best, David. "The Aesthetic in Sport." In *Philosophic Inquiry in Sport*, edited by W. Morgan and K. Meier, 377–89. 2nd ed. Champaign, IL: Human Kinetics, 1995.

Bok, Derek. "Can Higher Education Foster Higher Morals?" In *Social and Personal Ethics*, edited by W. H. Shaw, 494–503. Belmont, CA: Wadsworth, 1996.

Boxill, Jan, ed. *Sports Ethics*. Malden, MA: Blackwell, 2003.

Bradley, Bill. *Values of the Game*. New York: Broadway Books, 1998.
Branch, Taylor. "The Shame of College Sports." *Atlantic Monthly*, October 2011. http://www.theatlantic.com/.
Brand, Myles. "The Role and Value of Intercollegiate Athletics in Universities." *Journal of the Philosophy of Sport* 33, no. 1 (2006): 9–20.
British Broadcasting Service. "FINA Extends Swimsuit Regulations." *BBC Mobile Sport*, March 19, 2009. Accessed October 20, 2011. http://news.bbc.co.uk/.
Brown, Ben. "Homer, Funeral Contests and the Origins of the Greek City." In *Sport and Festival in the Ancient Greek World*, edited by David J. Phillips and David Pritchard, 123–62. Swansea: Classical Press of Wales, 2003.
Brown, W. M. "Paternalism, Drugs, and the Nature of Sports." *Journal of the Philosophy of Sport* 11, no. 1 (1985): 14–22.
———. "Practices and Prudence." *Journal of the Philosophy of Sport* 17, no. 1 (1990): 71–84.
Brownell, Susan. *Training the Body for China*. Chicago: University of Chicago Press, 1995.
Burkert, Walter. *Greek Religion*. Translated by J. Raffan. Cambridge, MA: Harvard University Press, 1985.
Busbee, Jay. "Davis Calls Penalty on Himself, Gives Up Shot at First PGA Win." Yahoo Sports, April 18, 2010. Accessed October 21, 2011. http://sports.yahoo.com/.
Butcher, Robert, and Angela Schneider. "Fair Play as Respect for the Game." *Journal of the Philosophy of Sport* 25, no. 1 (1998): 1–22.
Cable News Network. "Sumo 'Fixing' Scandal Rocks Japan." CNN International Edition, February 4, 2011. Accessed October 21, 2011. http://edition.cnn.com/.
Caillois, Roger. *Man, Play, and Games*. Translated by Meyer Berlash. Urbana: University of Illinois Press, [1958] 2001.
Camus, Albert. *The Myth of Sisyphus and Other Essays*. Translated by Justin O'Brien. New York: Random House, 1955.
———. "The Wager of Our Generation." In *Resistance, Rebellion, and Death*, translated by Justin O'Brien. New York: Vintage, 1960.
Carr, David. "What Moral Educational Significance Has Physical Education?" In *The Ethics of Sports: A Reader*, edited by Mike McNamee, 306–15. London: Routledge, 2010.
———. "Where's the Merit If the Best Man Wins?" *Journal of the Philosophy of Sport* 26, no. 1 (1999): 1–9.
Cassiodorus. "Variae." In *The Roman Games*, edited by Alison Futrell, 74. Malden, MA: Blackwell, 2006.
Cheng, Chung-Ying. "On the Metaphysical Significance of *ti* (Body-Embodiment) in Chinese Philosophy: *benti* (Origin-Substance) and *ti-yong* (Substance and Function)." *Journal of Chinese Philosophy* 29, no. 2 (2002): 145–61.
Ching, Gene, and Gigi Oh. "Where Wushu Went Wrong." *Kungfu Magazine*, November 3, 2006. Accessed October 21, 2011. http://ezine.kungfumagazine.com/.
Cicero, Marcus Tullius. *Tusculan Disputations*. Translated by J. King. Cambridge, MA: Loeb, 1927.
Clarey, Christopher. "A French Revolution in the Fast Lanes." *International Herald Tribune*, November 18, 2011. Kindle edition.
Confucius. *Analects*. Translated by E. Slingerland. Indianapolis: Hackett, 2003.
———. *The Analects of Confucius*. Translated by Arthur Waley. New York: Vintage, 1989.
Cordner, Christopher. "Differences between Sport and Art." In *Philosophic Inquiry in Sport*, edited by W. Morgan and K. Meier, 424–36. 2nd ed. Champaign, IL: Human Kinetics, 1995.
Cordner, C. D. "Grace and Functionality." In *Philosophic Inquiry in Sport*, edited by W. Morgan and K. Meier, 407–14. 2nd ed. Champaign, IL: Human Kinetics, 1995.
Coubertin, Pierre de. *Olympism: Selected Writings*. Edited by Norbert Müller. Lausanne, Switzerland: International Olympic Committee, 2000.
———. "The Olympic Games of 1896." In *The Olympic Idea: Pierre de Coubertin—Discourses and Essays*, edited by Carl-Diem Institut, 10–14. Stuttgart, Germany: Olympisher Sportverlag, 1966.

Crowther, Nigel. "The Ancient Olympics and Their Ideals." In *Athletika: Studies on the Olympic Games and Greek Athletics*, edited by W. Decker and I. Weiler, 1–11. Hildesheim, Germany: Weidemann, 2004.

Cudd, Ann E. "Sporting Metaphors: Competition and the Ethos of Capitalism." *Journal of the Philosophy of Sport* 34, no. 1 (2007): 52–67.

Curtis, Thomas P. "Amusing Then Amazing: American Wins 1896 Discus." *Technology Review*, July 24, 1924. Reprinted in *MIT News*, July 18, 1996. http://web.mit.edu/.

DaCosta, Lamartine. "A Never-Ending Story: The Philosophical Controversy over Olympism." *Journal of the Philosophy of Sport* 33, no. 2 (2006): 157–73.

D'Agostino, Fred. "The Ethos of Games." In *Philosophic Inquiry in Sport*, edited by W. Morgan and K. Meier, 48–49. 2nd ed. Champaign, IL: Human Kinetics, 1995.

Danto, Arthur. "The Artworld." *Journal of Philosophy* 61 (1964): 571–84.

Davis, Paul. "Ethical Issues in Boxing." *Journal of the Philosophy of Sport* 20–21 (1993–1994): 48–63.

Dean, Jeffry. "Aesthetics and Ethics: The State of the Art." *Aesthetics Online*, 2002. Accessed November 1, 2011. http://aesthetics-online.org/.

Delattre, Edwin J. "Some Reflections on Success and Failure in Competitive Athletics." *Journal of the Philosophy of Sport* 2, no. 1 (1975): 133–39.

Descartes, René. *The Philosophical Writings of Descartes*. Edited by J. Cottingham, R. Stoothoff, and D. Murdoch. 2 vols. Cambridge, UK: Cambridge University Press, 1985.

Diogenes Laertius. *Lives of Eminent Philosophers*. Translated by R. D. Hicks. Vol. 1. Cambridge, MA: Harvard University Press, 1972.

Dixon, Nicholas. "On Sportsmanship and Running Up the Score." *Journal of the Philosophy of Sport* 19 (1992): 1–13.

———. "On Winning and Athletic Superiority." *Journal of the Philosophy of Sport* 26, no. 1 (1999): 10–26.

———. "Why Losing by a Wide Margin Is Not in Itself a Disgrace." *Journal of the Philosophy of Sport* 25, no. 1 (1998): 61–79.

Dombrowski, Daniel. *Contemporary Athletics and Ancient Greek Ideals*. Chicago: University of Chicago Press, 2009.

Drewe, Sheryle Bergmann. *Why Sport?* Toronto: Thompson, 2003.

Durà-Vilà, Víctor. "Why Playing Beautifully Is Morally Better." In *Soccer and Philosophy: Beautiful Thoughts on the Beautiful Game*, edited by T. Richards, 141–48. Chicago: Open Court, 2010.

Eassom, Simon. "Games, Rules, and Contracts." In *Ethics and Sport*, edited by Mike McNamee and Jim Parry, 57–78. London: E & FN Spon, 1998.

Eaton, Marcia Muelder. *Merit, Aesthetic and Ethical*. New York: Oxford University Press, 2001.

Edelman, Robert. *Serious Fun: A History of Spectator Sports in the USSR*. New York: Oxford University Press, 1993.

English, Jane. "Sex Equality in Sports." *Philosophy and Public Affairs* 7 (1978): 269–77.

The Epic of Gilgamesh. Translated by N. K. Sandars. London: Penguin, 1960.

Epstein, David. "Double Amputee Pistorius Keeping Olympic Sprinting Dreams Alive." SI.com, June 11, 2011. Accessed November 22, 2011. http://sportsillustrated.cnn.com/.

Erdbrink, Thomas. "FIFA Bans Headscarves for Iranian Women's Soccer Team." *Washington Post*, June 6, 2011. http://www.washingtonpost.com/.

Evangeliou, C. *Hellenic Philosophy: Origin and Character*. Burlington, VT: Ashgate, 2006.

Feezell, Randolph. *Sport, Play and Ethical Reflection*. Urbana: University of Illinois Press, 2006.

Fischer, Norman. "Competitive Sport's Imitation of War: Imaging the Completeness of Virtue." *Journal of the Philosophy of Sport* 29, no. 1 (2002): 16–37.

Fisher, Marjorie. "Sport as an Aesthetic Experience." In *Sport and the Body: A Philosophical Symposium*, edited by Ellen Gerber, 315–21. Philadelphia: Lea & Febiger, 1974.

Foundation for the Hellenic World. "The Revival of the Ancient Olympic Games." From *Ancient Olympia to Athens of 1896*. Accessed December 12, 2011. http://www.fhw.gr.

Fraleigh, Warren P. "The Ends of the Sports Contest." In *The Ethics of Sports: A Reader*, edited by Mike McNamee, 106–15. London: Routledge, 2010.

———. "Performance-Enhancing Drugs in Sport: The Ethical Issue." *Journal of the Philosophy of Sport* 11, no. 1 (1985): 23–29.

———. "The Philosophic Society for the Study of Sport, 1972–1983." *Journal of the Philosophy of Sport* 10 (1984): 3–7.

———. *Right Actions in Sport: Ethics for Contestants*. Champaign, IL: Human Kinetics, 1984.

Franke, W., and B. Berendonk. "Hormonal Doping and Androgenization of Athletes: A Secret Program of the German Democratic Republic Government." *Clinical Chemistry* 43, no. 7 (1997): 1262–79.

Futrell, Alison, ed. *The Roman Games*. Malden, MA: Blackwell, 2006.

Gerber, Ellen, ed. *Sport and the Body: A Philosophical Symposium*. Philadelphia: Lea & Febiger, 1974.

Gleaves, John. "Too Fit to Fly: How Female Nordic Ski Jumping Challenges the IOC's Approach to Gender Equality." In *Rethinking Matters Olympic: Investigations into the Socio-Cultural Study of the Modern Olympic Movement*, edited by International Center for Olympic Studies, 278–88. London: University of Western Ontario, 2010.

Golden, Mark. *Greek Sport and Social Status*. Austin: University of Texas Press, 2008.

———. *Sport and Society in Ancient Greece*. Cambridge, UK: Cambridge University Press, 1998.

———. *Sport in the Ancient World from A to Z*. New York: Routledge, 2004.

Goldman, Tom. "Athlete's 'Nope to Dope' Became 'No to Sports.'" National Public Radio, 2011. http://www.npr.org/.

Groos, Karl. "Play from the Aesthetic Standpoint." In *The Play of Man*. New York: D. Appleton, 1901. Reprinted in Gerber, *Sport and the Body*, 302–4.

Hanley, Elizabeth A. "A Perennial Dilemma: Artistic Sports in the Olympic Games." Unpublished manuscript, 2000.

Hardman, Alun, Luanne Fox, Doug McLaughlin, and Kurt Zimmerman. "On Sportsmanship and Running Up the Score: Issues of Incompetence and Humiliation." *Journal of the Philosophy of Sport* 23: (1996): 58–69.

Heidegger, Martin. *Poetry, Language, Thought*. New York: Harper & Row, 1971.

Herodotus. *Histories*. Translated by A. D. Godley. Cambridge, MA: Harvard University Press, 1920.

Herrigel, Eugen. *Zen in the Art of Archery*. Translated by R. F. C. Hull. New York: Vintage, 1999.

Hoberman, John. *Darwin's Athletes: How Sport Has Damaged Black America and Preserved the Myth of Race*. Boston: Houghton Mifflin, 1997.

———. *Mortal Engines: The Science of Performance and the Dehumanization of Sport*. New York: Free Press, 1992.

Holowchak, M. Andrew. "'Aretism' and Pharmacological Ergogenic Aids in Sport: Taking a Shot at the Use of Steroids." *Journal of the Philosophy of Sport* 27, no. 1 (2000): 35–50.

———. "Fascistoid Heroism Revisited: A Deontological Twist in a Recent Debate." *Journal of the Philosophy of Sport* 32, no. 2 (2005): 96–104.

———, ed. *Philosophy of Sport: Critical Readings, Crucial Issues*. Upper Saddle River, NJ: Prentice Hall, 2002.

Holowchak, M. Andrew, and Heather L. Reid. *Aretism: An Ancient Sports Philosophy for the Modern Sports World*. Lanham, MD: Lexington Books, 2011.

Homer. *The Iliad and Odyssey*. Translated by Robert Fagles. New York: Penguin, 1990.

Huizinga, Johan. *Homo Ludens: A Study of the Play Element in Culture*. Boston: Beacon Press, [1944] 1955.

Hume, David. *A Treatise of Human Nature*. Edited by L. A. Selby-Bigge. 2nd ed. Oxford, UK: Clarendon, 1978.

Hyland, Drew A. 1978. "Competition and Friendship." *Journal of the Philosophy of Sport* 5, no. 1 (1978): 27–37.

———. "Paidia and Paideia: The Educational Power of Athletics." *Journal of Intercollegiate Sport* 1, no. 1 (2008): 66–71.

————. *Philosophy of Sport*. New York: Paragon, 1990.

————. *The Question of Play*. Lanham, MD: University Press of America, 1984.

————. "The Stance of Play." *Journal of the Philosophy of Sport* 7, no. 1 (1980): 87–99.

Iamblichus. *The Pythagorean Life*. Translated by Thomas Taylor. London: Watkins, 1818.

Inoue, Akio. "Critique of Modern Olympism: A Voice from the East." In *Sports: The East and the West*, edited by G. Pfister and L. Yueye, 163–67. Sant Agustin, Germany: Academia Verlag, 1999.

International Olympic Committee. *Factsheet on the Olympic Programme*. Lausanne, Switzerland: Author, 2007.

————. "The New Exhibition at the Olympic Museum on the Theme of Hope." Olympic.org, March 28, 2011. Accessed November 25, 2011. http://www.olympic.org/.

————. *The Olympic Charter*. Lausanne, Switzerland: Author, 2010.

————. *Olympic Movement's Agenda 21: Sport for Sustainable Development*. Lausanne, Switzerland: Author, 1999. http://www.olympic.org/.

————. "Olympic Solidarity Commission." Olympic.org, 2011. Accessed November 28, 2011. http://www.olympic.org/.

————. "The Sport and Environment Commission." Olympic.org, 2009. Accessed December 5, 2011. http://www.olympic.org/.

International Paralympic Committee. "Powerlifting on an Upswing." Paralympian Online, 2000. Accessed November 21, 2011. http://www.paralympic.org/.

Jackson, Phil. *Sacred Hoops: Spiritual Lessons of a Hardwood Warrior*. New York: Hyperion, 1995.

Jackson, Susan A., and Mihaly Csikszentmihalyi. *Flow in Sports*. Champaign, IL: Human Kinetics, 1999.

Jones, Carwyn. "Character, Virtue, and Physical Education." *European Physical Education Review* 11, no. 2 (2005): 140–42.

Jones, Carwyn, and P. David Howe. "The Conceptual Boundaries of Sport for the Disabled: Classification and Athletic Performance." *Journal of the Philosophy of Sport* 32, no. 2 (2005): 133–46.

Kant, Immanuel. *Groundwork for the Metaphysic of Morals*. Translated by H. J. Paton. New York: Harper and Row, 1948.

Keating, James W. "Sportsmanship as a Moral Category." *Ethics* 75 (October 1964): 25–35.

Kennell, Nigel M. *The Gymnasium of Virtue: Education and Culture in Ancient Sparta*. Chapel Hill: University of North Carolina Press, 1995.

Kidd, Bruce. "Taking the Rhetoric Seriously: Proposals for Olympic Education." *Quest* 48 (1996): 82–92.

King, Martin Luther, Jr. *I Have a Dream: Writings and Speeches that Changed the World*. New York: Harper Collins, 1992.

King, Winston. *Zen and the Way of the Sword*. New York: Oxford University Press, 1993.

Kramer, S. K. "Hymn of Praise to Shulgi." In *History Begins at Sumer*, 285–88. Philadelphia: University of Pennsylvania Press, 1981.

Kretchmar, R. Scott. "Beautiful Games." *Journal of the Philosophy of Sport* 16, no. 1 (1989): 34–43.

————. "Ethics and Sport: An Overview." *Journal of the Philosophy of Sport* 10, no. 1 (1984): 21–32.

————. "From Test to Contest: An Analysis of Two Kinds of Counterpoint in Sport." *Journal of the Philosophy of Sport* 1 (1975): 23–30.

————. *Practical Philosophy of Sport*. Champaign, IL: Human Kinetics, 1994.

Kuhn, Anthony. "Chinese Martial Art Form Sports Less Threatening Moves." *Los Angeles Times*, October 16, 1988. Accessed October 21, 2011. http://articles.latimes.com/.

Kupfer, Joseph. "Sport: The Body Electric." In *Philosophic Inquiry in Sport*, edited by W. Morgan and K. Meier, 390–406. 2nd ed. Champaign, IL: Human Kinetics, 1995.

Kyle, Donald G. *Spectacles of Death in Ancient Rome*. New York: Routledge, 1998.

————. *Sport and Spectacle in the Ancient World*. Malden, MA: Blackwell, 2007.

Lacerda, Teresa, and Stephen Mumford. "The Genius in Art and in Sport: A Contribution to the Investigation of Aesthetics of Sport." *Journal of the Philosophy of Sport* 37, no. 2 (2010). 182–93.

Lao-Tzu. *Tao Te Ching*. Translated by S. Addiss and S. Lombardo. Indianapolis: Hackett, 2003.

Laozi. "Daodejing." In *Readings in Classical Chinese Philosophy*, edited by P. Ivanhoe and B. Van Norden, 161–206. 2nd ed. Indianapolis: Hackett, 2001.

Lapchick, Richard. *2010 Racial and Gender Report Card*. Chicago: Institute for Diversity and Ethics in Sport, 2010.

Lasch, Christopher. "The Degradation of Sport." *New York Review of Books* 24, no. 7 (1977). Reprinted in *The Ethics of Sports: A Reader*, edited by Mike McNamee, 369–81. London: Routledge, 2010.

Lehman, Craig. "Can Cheaters Play the Game?" *Journal of the Philosophy of Sport* 8 (1981): 41–46.

Lenk, Hans. "Towards a Philosophical Anthropology of the Olympic Athletes and the Achieving Being." In *International Olympic Academy Report*, 163–77 (Ancient Olympia, Greece: 1982).

Levy, Glen. "British Athletes Told to Avoid Shaking Hands at the Olympics." *Time* Newsfeed. March 6, 2012. Accessed March 7, 2012. http://newsfeed.time.com/.

Litke, Jim. "Black Athletes Eased Obama's Presidential Path." *NBC Sports*, November 5, 2008. Accessed November 21, 2011. http://nbcsports.msnbc.com/.

Livingston, Gretchen, and D'Vera Cohn. "Childlessness Up among All Women, Down among Women with Advanced Degrees." Pew Research Center, June 25, 2010. Accessed November 21, 2011. http://www.pewsocialtrends.org/.

Locke, John. *An Essay Concerning Human Understanding*. Oxford, UK: Clarendon, 1975.

Loland, Sigmund. "The Ethics of Performance-Enhancing Technology in Sport." *Journal of the Philosophy of Sport* 36, no. 1 (2009): 152–61.

———. "Fairness in Sport: An Ideal and Its Consequences." In *The Ethics of Sports: A Reader*, edited by Mike McNamee, 116–24. London: Routledge, 2010.

———. *Fair Play in Sport: A Moral Norm System*. New York: Routledge, 2001.

———. "Record Sports: An Ecological Critique and a Reconstruction." *Journal of the Philosophy of Sport* 27, no. 2 (2001): 127–39.

Loy, John W., Jr. "The Nature of Sport: A Definitional Effort." *Quest* 10, no. 1 (May 1968): 1–15. Reprinted in Holowchak, *Philosophy of Sport*, 16–28.

MacIntyre, Alasdair. *After Virtue*. Notre Dame, IN: University of Notre Dame Press, 1981.

———. *Whose Justice? Which Rationality?* Notre Dame, IN: University of Notre Dame Press, 1989.

Maglo, Koffi N. "The Case against Biological Realism about Race: From Darwin to the Post-Genomic Era." *Perspectives on Science* 19, no. 4 (2011): 361–90.

Mandell, Richard. *The Nazi Olympics*. Champaign: University of Illinois Press, 1987.

McBride, Frank. "Toward a Non-Definition of Sport." *Journal of the Philosophy of Sport* 2 (1975): 4–11.

McCurry, Justin. "Sumo Threatened by Scandal and Crime." *Guardian*, July 4, 2010. Accessed October 21, 2011. http://www.guardian.co.uk/.

McDonagh, Eileen L., and Laura Pappano. *Playing with the Boys: Why Separate Is Not Equal in Sports*. New York: Oxford University Press, 2008.

McFee, Graham. "Spoiling: An Indirect Reflection of Sport's Moral Imperative?" In *The Ethics of Sports: A Reader*, edited by Mike McNamee, 145–52. London: Routledge, 2010.

———. *Sports, Rules and Values: Philosophical Investigations into the Nature of Sport*. London: Routledge, 2004.

McNamee, Mike, ed. *The Ethics of Sports: A Reader*. London: Routledge, 2010.

———. "Hubris, Humility, and Humiliation: Vice and Virtue in Sporting Communities." *Journal of the Philosophy of Sport* 29, no. 1 (2002): 38–53.

———. "Olympism, Eurocentricity, and Transcultural Virtues." *Journal of the Philosophy of Sport* 33, no. 2 (2006): 174–87.

———. "*Schadenfreude* in Sport: Envy, Justice, and Self-esteem." *Journal of the Philosophy of Sport* 30, no. 1 (2003): 1–16.

———. "*Sport, Ethics and Philosophy*: Context, History and Prospects." *Sport, Ethics and Philosophy* 1, no. 1 (2007): 1–6.

———. "Sporting Practices, Institutions and Virtues: A Critique and Restatement." *Journal of the Philosophy of Sport* 22, no. 1 (1995): 61–82.

———. *Sports, Virtues and Vices: Morality Plays*. London: Routledge, 2008.

Meier, Klaus V. "An Affair of Flutes: An Appreciation of Play." *Journal of the Philosophy of Sport* 7, no. 1 (1980): 24–45.

———. "Triad Trickery: Playing with Sport and Games." *Journal of the Philosophy of Sport* 15, no. 1 (1988): 11–30.

Mengzi. *Mencius*. Translated by Irene Bloom. New York: Columbia University Press, 2009.

Merleau-Ponty, Maurice. *The Phenomenology of Perception*. Translated by Colin Smith. London: Routledge and Kegan Paul, 1962.

Metheny, Eleanor. "The Symbolic Power of Sport." Presented to the Eastern District Association for Health, Physical Education and Recreation in Washington, DC, April 26, 1968. Reprinted in *Sport and the Body: A Philosophical Symposium*, edited by E. Gerber and W. J. Morgan, 231–36. Philadelphia: Lea & Febiger, 1979.

———. "This 'Thing' Called Sport." *Journal of Health, Physical Education, and Recreation* 40 (March 1969): 59–60.

Mikalson, J. *Ancient Greek Religion*. Malden, MA: Blackwell, 2005.

Mill, John Stuart. *On Liberty*. Indianapolis, IN: Hackett, 1978.

Miller, Stephen G. *Ancient Greek Athletics*. New Haven, CT: Yale University Press, 2004.

———, ed. *Arete: Greek Sports from Ancient Sources*. Berkeley: University of California Press, 1991.

———. "Naked Democracy." In *Polis and Politics*, edited by P. Flensted-Jensen and T. H. Nielsen, 277–96. Copenhagen: Festschrift, 2000.

Moller, Verner. "The Athlete's Viewpoint." In *The Ethics of Sports: A Reader*, edited by Mike McNamee, 160–68. London: Routledge, 2010.

Morgan, William J. "Cosmopolitanism, Olympism, and Nationalism: A Critical Interpretation of Coubertin's Ideal of International Sporting Life." *Olympika* 4 (1995): 79–91.

———. *Leftist Theories of Sport: A Critique and Reconstruction*. Chicago: University of Illinois Press, 1994.

———. "The Logical Incompatability Thesis and Rules: A Reconsideration of Formalism as an Account of Games." *Journal of the Philosophy of Sport* 14, no. 1 (1987): 1–20.

———. "Multinational Sport and Literary Practices and Their Communities: The Moral Salience of Cultural Narratives." In *Ethics and Sport*, edited by Mike McNamee and Jim Parry, 184–204. London: E & FN Spon, 1998.

———. *Why Sports Morally Matter*. Abingdon, UK: Routledge, 2006.

Morgan, William J., Klaus V. Meier, and Angela, J. Schneider, eds. *Ethics in Sport*. Champaign, IL: Human Kinetics, 2001. 2nd ed., 2007.

Morris, Ian. "Equality and the Origins of Greek Democracy." In *Ancient Greek Democracy*, edited by Eric W. Robinson, 45–73. Malden, MA: Blackwell, 2004.

Mouratidis, John. "Heracles at Olympia and the Exclusion of Women from the Ancient Olympic Games." *Journal of Sport History* 11, no. 3 (1984): 41–55.

Mumford, Stephen. *Watching Sport: Aesthetics, Ethics, and Emotion*. Abingdon, UK: Routledge, 2011.

Murray, Hugh. "Review of Hoberman's *The Olympic Crisis*." *Journal of Sport History* 16, no. 1 (1989): 104–8.

National Collegiate Athletic Association. "Estimated Probability of Competing in Athletics beyond the High School Interscholastic Level." NCAA.com, 2011. Accessed November 21, 2011. http://www.ncaa.org/.

———. *2009–2010 Student Athlete Ethnicity Report*. Indianapolis: Author, 2010.

Nicholson, Nigel James. *Aristocracy and Athletics in Archaic and Classical Greece*. Cambridge, UK: Cambridge University Press, 2005.

Nielsen Company. "Beijing Olympics Draw Largest Ever Global Television Audience." Niel-schwire, September 8, 2008. Accessed April 10, 2012. http://blog.nielsen.com/.

Nietzsche, Friedrich. *The Birth of Tragedy*. Translated by Shaun Whiteside. London: Penguin, 1994.

———. "Thus Spoke Zarathustra." In *The Portable Nietzsche*, edited by Walter Kaufmann, 146–47. New York: Viking, 1982.

Osterhoudt, R. G. "The Term 'Sport': Some Thoughts on a Proper Name." *International Journal of Physical Education* 14, no. 2 (1977): 11–16.

Parry, Jim. "Sport and Olympism: Universals and Multiculturalism." *Journal of the Philosophy of Sport* 33, no. 2 (2006): 188–204.

———. "Sport, Ethos and Education." In *The Ethics of Sports: A Reader*, edited by Mike McNamee, 316–26. London: Routledge, 2010.

Pausanias. *Description of Greece*. Translated by Peter Levi. 2 vols. New York: Penguin, 1979.

Pawlenka, Claudia. "The Idea of Fairness: A General Ethical Concept or One Particular to Sports Ethics." *Journal of the Philosophy of Sport* 32, no. 1 (2005): 49–64.

Percy, William A. *Pederasty and Pedagogy in Archaic Greece*. Urbana: University of Illinois Press, 1996.

Pindar. *The Complete Odes*. Translated by Anthony Verity. Oxford: Oxford University Press, 2007.

———. *Olympian Odes, Pythian Odes*. Translated by William H. Race. Cambridge, MA: Harvard University Press, 1997.

Pinter, Stanislav, Tjasa Filipcic, Ales Solar, and Maja Smrdu. "Integrating Children with Physical Impairments into Sports Activities: A 'Golden Sun' for All Children?" *Journal of the Philosophy of Sport* 32, no. 2 (2005): 147–54.

Pinto, Barbara, and Olivia Katrandjian. "Wrestler Joel Northup Forfeits to Female Opponent in Iowa State Championships." *ABC News*, February 18, 2011. Accessed November 21, 2011. http://abcnews.go.com/.

Plato. *Apology*. Translated by G. M. A. Grube. Indianapolis: Hackett, 1980.

———. *Complete Works*. Edited by John M. Cooper. Indianapolis: Hackett, 1997.

———. *Laws*. Translated by Trevor Saunders. London: Penguin, 1970.

———. *Republic*. Translated by G. M. A. Grube. Indianapolis: Hackett, 1992.

———. *Symposium*. Translated by Alexander Nehamas and Paul Woodruff. Indianapolis: Hackett, 1989.

———. *Two Comic Dialogues: Ion and Hippias Major*. Translated by Paul Woodruff. Indianapolis: Hackett, 1983.

Postow, B. C. "Masculine Sports Revisited." *Journal of the Philosophy of Sport* 8, no. 1 (1981): 60–63.

———. "Women and Masculine Sports." *Journal of the Philosophy of Sport* 7 (1980): 51–58.

Rawls, John. *A Theory of Justice*. Cambridge, MA: Harvard University Press, 1971.

Reid, Heather L. "Aristotle's Pentathlete." *Sport, Ethics and Philosophy* 4, no. 2 (2010): 183–94.

———. "Athletic Heroes." *Sport, Ethics and Philosophy* 4, no. 2 (2010): 125–35.

———. *Athletics and Philosophy in the Ancient World: Contests of Virtue*. London: Routledge, 2011.

———. "Athletic Virtue: Between East and West." *Sport, Ethics and Philosophy* 4, no. 1 (2010): 16–26. Reprinted in McNamee, *Ethics of Sports*, 340–47.

———. "Boxing with Tyrants." *Sport, Ethics and Philosophy* 4, no. 2 (2010): 146–56.

———. "East to Olympia: Recentering Olympic Philosophy between East and West." *Olympika: The International Journal of Olympic Studies* 19 (2010): 59–79.

———. "The Epicurean Spectator." *Sport, Ethics and Philosophy* 4, no. 2 (2010): 195–203. Reprinted in *Athletics and Philosophy in the Ancient World: Contests of Virtue*, 81–89. London: Routledge, 2011.

———. "Of Sport, Service, and Sacrifice: Rethinking the Religious Heritage of the Olympic Games." In *Cultural Imperialism in Action: Critiques in the Global Olympic Trust*, edited by N. Crowther, R. Barney, and M. Heine, 32–40. London, Ontario: International Centre for Olympic Studies, 2006.

———. "Olympia: Running towards Truth." *Sport, Ethics and Philosophy* 4, no. 2 (2010): 136–45.

———. "Olympic Sport and Its Lessons for Peace." *Journal of the Philosophy of Sport* 33, no. 2 (2006): 205–13. Reprinted with revisions in *Olympic Truce: Sport as a Platform for Peace*, edited by K. Georgiadis and A. Syrigos, 25–35. Athens: International Olympic Truce Center, 2009.

———. *The Philosophical Athlete*. Durham, NC: Carolina Academic Press, 2002.

———. "Plato's Gymnasium." *Sport, Ethics and Philosophy* 4, no. 2 (2010): 170–82.

———. "The Political Heritage of the Olympic Games: Relevance, Risks, and Possible Rewards." *Sport, Ethics and Philosophy: Special Issue on the Olympic Games* 6, no. 2 (2012): 108–20.

———. "Sport and Moral Education in Plato's *Republic*." *Journal of the Philosophy of Sport* 34, no. 2 (2007): 160–75.

———. "Sport, Philosophy, and the Quest for Knowledge." *Journal of the Philosophy of Sport* 36, no. 1 (2009): 40–49.

———. "Was the Roman Gladiator an Athlete?" *Journal of the Philosophy of Sport* 33, no. 1 (2006): 37–49.

———. "Wrestling with Socrates." *Sport, Ethics and Philosophy* 4, no. 2 (2010): 157–69.

Reid, Heather L., and Mike W. Austin, eds. *The Olympics and Philosophy*. Lexington: University Press of Kentucky, 2012.

Riordan, James. *Sport, Politics, and Communism*. Manchester, UK: Manchester University Press, 1991.

Roberts, Terence J. "Sport, Art, and Particularity: The Best Equivocation." In *Philosophic Inquiry in Sport*, edited by W. Morgan and K. Meier, 415–525. 2nd ed. Champaign, IL: Human Kinetics, 1995.

Rogge, Jacques. "An Apologia for Professionalism." *Olympic Review* 26, no. 4 (1995): 52.

Roochnik, David L. "Play and Sport." *Journal of the Philosophy of Sport* 2, no. 1 (1975): 36–44.

Russell, Bill. *Second Wind: The Memoirs of an Opinionated Man*. New York: Random House, 1979.

Russell, J. S. "Are Rules All an Umpire Has to Work With?" *Journal of the Philosophy of Sport* 25, no. 1 (1999): 27–40.

Russell, John. "The Value of Dangerous Sports." *Journal of the Philosophy of Sport* 32, no. 1 (2005): 1–19.

Sabo, Donald F., et al. "High School Athletic Participation, Sexual Behavior and Adolescent Pregnancy: A Regional Study." *Journal of Adolescent Health* 25, no. 3 (1999): 207–16.

Sansone, David. *Greek Athletics and the Genesis of Sport*. Berkeley: University of California Press, 1988.

Sapora, Allen V., and Elmer D. Mitchell. *The Theory of Play and Recreation*. New York: Ronald Press, 1961.

Sartre, Jean-Paul. *Being and Nothingness*. Translated by Hazel E. Barnes. New York: Philosophical Library, 1956.

Scanlon, Thomas F. *Eros and Greek Athletics*. New York: Oxford University Press, 2002.

Scheuerman, William. "Globalization." In *The Stanford Encyclopedia of Philosophy*, edited by Edward N. Zalta. Summer 2010 ed. Accessed December 5, 2011. http://plato.stanford.edu/.

Schmid, Stephen. "Reconsidering Autotelic Play." *Journal of the Philosophy of Sport* 36, no. 2 (2009): 238–57.

Schnee, Steven, and Astrid Rodrigues. "The Amputee Wrestler: Rohan Murphy Can Take You Down." *ABC Sports*, December 9, 2010. Accessed November 21, 2011. http://abcnews.go.com/.

Schneider, Angela J. "Fruits, Apples, and Category Mistakes: On Sport, Games, and Play." *Journal of the Philosophy of Sport* 28, no. 2 (2001): 151–59.

———. "On the Definition of 'Woman' in the Sport Context." In *Values in Sport*, edited by T. Tännsjö and C. Tamburrini, 123–38. London: Routledge, 2000.

Schneider, Angela, and Robert Butcher. "Why Olympic Athletes Should Avoid the Use and Seek the Elimination of Performance-Enhancing Substances and Practices from the Olympic Games." *Journal of the Philosophy of Sport* 20–21 (1993–1994): 64–81.

Seneca, Lucius Annaeus. *Letters from a Stoic (Epistulae Morales ad Lucilium).* Translated by R. Campbell. London: Penguin, 1969.

Senn, Alfred Erich. *Power, Politics and the Olympic Games.* Champaign, IL: Human Kinetics, 1999.

Sheets-Johnstone, Maxine. "Rationality and Caring: An Ontogenetic and Phylogenetic Perspective." *Journal of the Philosophy of Sport* 29, no. 2 (2002): 136–48.

Simon, Robert. "Does Athletics Undermine Academics? Examining Some Issues." *Journal of Intercollegiate Sport* 1, no. 1 (2008): 40–58.

———. *Fair Play: Sports, Values, and Society.* Boulder, CO: Westview, 1991. 2nd ed., *Fair Play: The Ethics of Sport*, 2004.

———. "Good Competition and Drug-Enhanced Performance." *Journal of the Philosophy of Sport* 11, no. 1 (1985): 6–13.

Singer, Peter. "Is It Okay to Cheat in Football?" Project Syndicate, June 26, 2010. Accessed April 10, 2011. http://www.project-syndicate.org/.

Slusher, Howard S. *Man, Sport, and Existence.* Philadelphia: Lea & Febiger, 1967.

Smith, Nicholas D. "Plato and Aristotle on the Nature of Women." *Journal of the History of Philosophy* 21, no. 4 (1983): 467–78.

Snell, Bruno. *The Discovery of the Mind in Greek Philosophy and Literature.* New York: Dover, 1982.

Spivey, Nigel. *The Ancient Olympics: A History.* Oxford: Oxford University Press, 2004.

Stecker, Robert. *Aesthetics and the Philosophy of Art.* Lanham, MD: Rowman & Littlefield, 2005.

Stoll, Sharon K., and Jennifer M. Beller. "Do Sports Build Character?" In *Sports in School: The Future of an Institution*, edited by John Gerdy, 18–30. New York: Columbia University Press, 2000.

Strabo. *The Geography of Strabo.* Edited by H. L. Jones. Cambridge, MA: Harvard University Press, 1924.

Suits, Bernard. "The Elements of Sport." In *Philosophic Inquiry in Sport*, edited by W. J. Morgan and Klaus V. Meier, 39–48. Champaign, IL: Human Kinetics, 1988.

———. *The Grasshopper: Games, Life, and Utopia.* 2nd ed. Peterborough, Ontario: Broadview, [1978] 2005.

———. "The Tricky Triad: Games, Play and Sport." *Journal of the Philosophy of Sport* 15, no. 1 (1988): 1–9.

———. "Venn and the Art of Category Maintenance." *Journal of the Philosophy of Sport* 31, no. 1 (2004): 1–14.

———. "What Is a Game?" *Philosophy of Science* 34, no. 1 (June 1967): 148–56.

Sun Tzu. *The Art of War.* Translated by Lionel Giles. Hong Kong: Forgotten Books, 2007.

Tamburrini, Claudio. "Sport, Fascism and the Market." *Journal of the Philosophy of Sport* 25, no. 1 (1998): 35–47.

Tännsjö, Torbjörn. "Against Sexual Discrimination in Sports." In *Values in Sport*, edited by T. Tännsjö and C. Tamburrini, 101–15. London: Routledge, 2000.

———. "Is Our Admiration of Sports Heroes Fascistoid?" *Journal of the Philosophy of Sport* 25, no. 1 (1998): 23–34.

Thucydides. *History of the Peloponnesian War.* Translated by B. Jowett. Oxford, UK: Clarendon, 1900.

Torres, Cesar. "Furthering Interpretivism's Integrity: Bringing Together Ethics and Aesthetics." Presidential address to the International Association for the Philosophy of Sport, Rochester, New York, September 2011.

Ungerleider, Steven. *Faust's Gold.* New York: St. Martin's, 2001.

Valavanis, Panos. "Thoughts on the Historical Origins of the Olympic Games and the Cult of Pelops in Olympia." *Nikephoros* 19 (2006): 137–52.

Van Hilvoorde, Ivo, and Laurens Landerweerd. "Disability or Extraordinary Talent?" In *The Ethics of Sports*, edited by Mike McNamee, 231–41. London: Routledge, 2010.

Vannata, Seth. "A Phenomenology of Sport: Playing and Passive Synthesis." *Journal of the Philosophy of Sport* 35, no. 1 (2008): 63–72.

Von Schiller, Friedrich. "Letter XV." In *Essays and Letters*, translated by A. Lodge, E. B. Eastwick, and A. J. W. Morrison. Vol. 8. London: Anthological Society, 1882. Reprinted in Gerber, *Sport and the Body*, 299–301.

Voy, Robert. *Drugs, Sport, and Politics*. Champaign, IL: Human Kinetics, 1991.

Wafi, Aymen. "Sarra Besbes: je m'en fiche . . . j'ai fait mon devoir." Koora.com, October 19, 2011. Accessed October 20, 2011. http://www.koora.com/.

Waley, Arthur. *Three Ways of Thought in Ancient China*. Stanford, CA: Stanford University Press, 2002.

Walton, Gary M. *Beyond Winning: The Timeless Wisdom of Great Philosopher Coaches*. Champaign, IL: Leisure Press, 1992.

Weinberg, Rick. "Pine Tar Nullifies Home Run, So Brett Goes Ballistic." *ESPN*, 2009. Accessed October 20, 2011. http://sports.espn.go.com/.

Weiss, Paul. *Sport: A Philosophic Inquiry*. Carbondale: Southern Illinois University Press, 1969.

Wertz, Spencer K. "The Capriciousness of Play: Collingwood's Insight." *Journal of the Philosophy of Sport* 30, no. 1 (2003): 159–65.

———. "Is Sport Unique? A Question of Definability." *Journal of the Philosophy of Sport* 22, no. 1 (1995): 83–93.

———. "Representation and Expression in Sport and Art." *Journal of the Philosophy of Sport* 12 (1985): 8–25.

Wing, John Ian. "Letter Saved the Games." National Library of Australia, Papers of Sir Wilfrid Kent Hughes, NS 4856/series 19. Accessed December 5, 2011. http://www.johnwing.co.uk/.

World Commission on Environment and Development. *Our Common Future*. Oxford: Oxford University Press, 1987.

Wright, Lesley. "Aesthetic Implicitness in Sport and the Role of Aesthetic Concepts." *Journal of the Philosophy of Sport* 30, no. 1 (2003): 83–92.

Young, David C. *A Brief History of the Olympic Games*. Malden, MA: Blackwell, 2004.

———. "Mens Sana in Corpore Sano? Body and Mind in Greek Literature." *Proceedings of the North American Society for Sport History* (1998): 60–61.

———. *The Olympic Myth of Greek Amateur Athletics*. Chicago: Ares, 1984.

Yuasa, Yasuo. *The Body, Self-Cultivation and Ki Energy*. Albany: State University of New York Press, 1993.

———. *The Body: Toward an Eastern Mind-Body Theory*. Edited by Thomas P. Kasulis. Albany: State University of New York Press, 1987.

Zeigler, Earle F. *Philosophical Foundations for Physical, Health, and Recreation Education*. Englewood Cliffs, NJ: Prentice Hall, 1964.

Index

About the Author

Heather L. Reid is professor and chair of philosophy at Morningside College in Sioux City, Iowa. A competitive cyclist in her youth, she won a national intercollegiate championship and qualified for the final Olympic trials in 1984 and 1988. As a scholar she has published numerous books and articles in ancient philosophy, philosophy of sport, and Olympic studies, including *The Philosophical Athlete* (2002), *Athletics and Philosophy in the Ancient World: Contests of Virtue* (2011), and *Aretism: An Ancient Sports Philosophy for the Modern Sports World* (with M. A. Holowchak, 2011). She has also been invited to lecture on these topics in Beijing, London, Rome, and at the International Olympic Academy in Olympia, Greece. She serves on the boards of the *Journal of the Philosophy of Sport* and *Sport, Ethics and Philosophy* and is coeditor of the Ethics and Sport book series. A longtime member of the International Association of the Philosophy of Sport, she served as president from 2005 to 2007 and received its Distinguished Service Award in 2009. She remains an active cyclist, leading tours through Italy, where she is also developing a study abroad program that uses sport as a medium for intercultural communication.